FAMILIES IN TROUBLED TIMES

SOCIAL INSTITUTIONS AND SOCIAL CHANGE

An Aldine de Gruyter Series of Texts and Monographs

EDITED BY

Michael Useem • James D. Wright

FAMILIES IN TROUBLED TIMES
Adapting to Change in Rural America

Rand D. Conger and Glen H. Elder, Jr.

In collaboration with

Frederick O. Lorenz, Ronald L. Simons,
and Les B. Whitbeck

ALDINE DE GRUYTER

New York

About the Authors

Rand D. Conger is a Professor of Sociology at Iowa State University and Director of the NIMH-funded Center for Family Research in Rural Mental Health.

Glen H. Elder, Jr. is the Howard W. Odum Distinguished Professor of Sociology and Research Professor of Psychology at the University of North Carolina, Chapel Hill.

Frederick O. Lorenz is an Associate Professor of Sociology and Statistics at Iowa State University.

Ronald L. Simons is a Professor of Sociology and Associate Director for the Center for Family Research in Rural Mental Health at Iowa State University.

Les B. Whitbeck is an Associate Professor of Sociology at Iowa State University.

ALDINE DE GRUYTER
A division of Walter de Gruyter, Inc.
200 Saw Mill River Road
Hawthorne, New York 10532

This publication is printed on acid-free paper ∞

Library of Congress Cataloging-in-Publication Data
Conger, Rand.
  Families in troubled times : adapting to change in rural America /
Rand D. Conger and Glen H. Elder, Jr., in collaboration with
Frederick O. Lorenz, Ronald L. Simons, Les B. Whitbeck.
    p.   cm. — (Social institutions & social change)
  Includes bibliographical references and index.
  ISBN 0-202-30487-6 (alk. paper : cloth). — ISBN 0-202-30488-4
(alk. paper : pbk.)
  1. Rural families—Iowa—Economic conditions.   2. Rural families—
Iowa—Social conditions.   3. Family—Iowa—Psychological aspects.
4. Stress (Psychology)   5. Social change—Iowa.   I. Elder, Glen H.
II. Title.   III. Series: Social institutions and social change.
HQ555.I8C66   1994
306.85'09777—dc20   93-38397
                                                                    CIP

Manufactured in the United States of America

10 9 8 7 6 5 4 3 2 1

*This book is dedicated to
the hundreds of families who shared their
stories with us and to our families,
who unselfishly gave us the time and support
to pursue this work.*

Contents

PART III. HUSBANDS AND WIVES

PART IV. ADOLESCENT DEVELOPMENT

PART V. REVIEWING THE EVIDENCE

Preface

The turbulent decade of the 1980s began with financial calamity in several sectors of the U.S. economy from automaking to agriculture (Dooley & Catalano, 1988; Voydanoff, 1990). News stories featured the plight of families leaving the Rust Belt of the Midwest for an uncertain economic future in the southern or coastal states. Images still remain of network television interviews of farmers expressing their concern that high debt and decreasing land values, coupled with low commodity prices, would drive them from their land.

In Iowa we remember too well pictures of white crosses around courthouse steps as the land and equipment of bankrupt farmers were auctioned off to the highest bidders. In her award-winning novel *A Thousand Acres,* Jane Smiley (1992) captures the drama of the times. Her fictional Iowa family reflects the experience of too many rural people, both farmers and residents of small towns, who were caught in a massive economic restructuring that left many of them demoralized and with diminished economic prospects for the future.

Smiley's novel also illustrates the fact that significant economic and social changes occur within the context of people's everyday lives and relationships. In a very real sense, economic stress most affects individuals through the reactions of those around them. In the report that follows, we build on this proposition in an investigation involving several hundred Iowa families who lived through the "farm crisis" years of the 1980s. These rural families include farmers, people from small towns, and those who lost farms and other businesses as a result of the decade's rural economic depression.

The impetus for the study, known as the Iowa Youth and Families Project, came during the mid-1980s, when faculty members from several departments at Iowa State University came together to discuss the state's economic troubles and how they were affecting rural people and their families. We were especially concerned that the experiences of these families be documented in a fashion that might help families of the future cope more successfully with economic reversals. We also hoped that the stories these families would tell could be used to fashion more effective social policies designed to reduce the adverse impact of economic decline on individual lives.

Fortunately, the Iowa State University administrative team, from the president to college deans to department chairs, was highly supportive of an initiative to investigate the consequences of the economic crisis in rural Iowa. They provided funds to obtain assistance from several renowned scientists who served as consultants in the design of the research. They also contributed to the development of the research infrastructure necessary to conduct the inquiry, including the establishment of a research center within the College of Agriculture to study rural health issues. This significant university support led to the submission of the research grant proposals that produced the funding for the work reported here. This university interest also led to a proposal for the Center for Family Research in Rural Mental Health, which has been funded by the National Institute of Mental Health to build upon and extend the research reported here.

Several consulting scientists helped in the development of our ideas regarding the design and execution of this study. During the early planning stage, Delbert Elliott, Marion Forgatch, John Gottman, Ron Kessler, Gerald Patterson, and Jon Rolf visited with us, responded to our proposed plans, and offered important guidance in the development of the work. Irving Tallman and Joseph Veroff, members of a National Institute of Mental Health site visit team, led us to new insights regarding the research through their thoughtful questions and concerns. Glen Elder began as a consultant, but his ideas became so central in the formulation of the study that he was invited to become an investigator on the project. He graciously accepted the invitation.

As we consider the final form of the research effort reflected in this volume, it is difficult to untangle exactly who is responsible for which theoretical insights or research strategies. We hope we have fairly reflected the important advice we have obtained in the process of developing the study, but we also take full responsibility for the limitations in the work.

In many ways this report represents an interesting hybrid that reflects the research team approach we have taken in conducting a complex and ambitious inquiry. This book both is and is not an edited volume. We recognize the complementary contributions of the separate investigators on the Iowa Youth and Families Project (Conger, Elder, Lorenz, Simons, and Whitbeck) by utilizing separate authorships for the individual chapters. At the same time we have organized the book around a specific theory of family economic stress and each chapter empirically evaluates different dimensions of that theory. The end result, we hope, is a coherent research monograph that clearly reflects the breadth and depth of the inquiry.

Literally hundreds of people have contributed to the conduct of this study. We are indebted to the many interviewers who have visited with the families, the observers who have scored the videotapes of family interaction, and the research associates and assistants who have analyzed data and helped in the preparation of research reports. Many of these individuals appear as coauthors throughout this volume.

We also wish to thank the clerical and support staff who keep us going on a day-to-day basis: especially Jan Peterson, who handled the word processing for this volume; Sue Proescholdt, whose watchful budgeting assured that we did not go bankrupt before the research was completed; and Anne Eagle, who provided valuable editorial review. Of course, we are especially indebted to the hundreds of families who shared their most intimate thoughts and feelings with us to help us understand the consequences of the rural crisis.

A large-scale, labor-intensive study such as this one cannot succeed without significant research support. We have been fortunate to receive funding from several sources including the National Institute of Mental Health (MH43270, MH48165, MH00567), the National Institute on Drug Abuse (DA05347), the Bureau of Maternal and Child Health (MCJ109572), the John D. and Catherine T. MacArthur Foundation Program for Successful Adolescent Development among Youth in High-Risk Settings, the Iowa Methodist Health Systems, and the Iowa Agriculture and Home Economics Experiment Station (Project No. 2931).

Program and review staff in the federal agencies that fund this study have been a constant source of support and guidance in our conduct of the research. We are especially indebted to Ms. Joy Schulterbrandt (retired) and Ms. Sheila O'Malley at the National Institute of Mental Health, who helped us better understand the review and funding process in our initial attempts to secure research support. We also owe special thanks to Dr. William Bukoski at the National Institute on Drug Abuse, who alerted us to the need to study the link between economic stress and problems of substance abuse.

Finally, we are indebted to Dr. Peggy Barlett, who kindly took the time to review several chapters of the manuscript. Her questions and comments proved most helpful in the final revisions.

PART I

Families and Hardship

Chapter 1

Families in Troubled Times:
The Iowa Youth and
Families Project

Rand D. Conger and Glen H. Elder, Jr.

It is possible that farm families were pioneers in learning to face, with lowered expectations, a future of declining living standards and limited business growth. More and more Americans may have to learn the same hard lesson in the next decade.
　　—M. Friedberger, *Farm Families and Change in 20th Century America*

Economic cycles of boom and bust have left their indelible mark on American families, altering the lifeways of successive generations. Most notably, the Great Depression brought unparalleled hardship to all regions of the country, placing whole communities at risk. Half a century later, hard times returned once again with a severity resembling the 1930s, taking the form of an agricultural crisis, particularly in the midwestern states (Murdock & Leistritz, 1988). In the premier farm state of Iowa, dreams of prosperity were suddenly crushed and replaced by economic nightmares as plummeting land values generated economic decline and dislocation in communities and individual lives. This book examines the experience of over 400 Iowa families, parents and children who lived through the Great Farm Crisis of the 1980s and now face an uncertain future.

These families are members of the Iowa Youth and Families Project (IYFP), which was launched in 1989 at Iowa State University. They live on farms or in small rural communities that are financially dependent on what has recently been a highly volatile agricultural economy (Friedberger, 1989). The rural character of these families may have a significant influence on their interpretation of and response to socioeconomic change, but the Iowa study contains a more general message regarding

3

the role of economic hardship in family life, that of a generality beyond our time and place.

Indeed, as subsequent chapters demonstrate, the experiences of these families substantially replicate and extend results from studies of urban families and children conducted both during the Great Depression (Elder, 1974; Liker & Elder, 1983) and during the past decade (McLoyd, 1989, 1990; Voydanoff, 1990). In addition, the data presented here may well anticipate the fate of many American families, rural and urban, minority and majority, who are entering the economically troubled times of the 1990s.

At the beginning of this chapter, Friedberger's (1989) reference to farm families as pioneers in a new world of scarcity expresses our view, as well as the view of many other investigators (e.g., McLoyd, 1989; Voydanoff, 1990), that the American economy will continue to undergo dramatic structural changes over the foreseeable future and will not soon return to the relatively unbridled prosperity of previous decades. The globalization of world markets has contributed to a decrease in the material well-being of the average American family. The impact of such change has tended to affect specific segments of the economy at different times. During the 1980s, for instance, agriculture and related manufacturing were especially hard hit, and more recently we see major recessions in the high-technology industry of the Northeast and in California's military-driven economy.

The message seems clear. As a citizenry, we will need to become more capable of adapting successfully to economic uncertainty and change. In some cases, negative economic events may reflect rapid decline followed by a fairly immediate recovery. This scenario reflects the experience of many urban centers in rural states during the 1980s (Davidson, 1990). Even more destructive of personal well-being, however, are circumstances in which economic decline produces chronic poverty or disadvantage, social conditions increasingly characteristic of both inner-city urban (Wilson, 1987) and rural areas (Davidson, 1990). For many of the families in this study, the 1980s set in motion a trend toward increasing and continuing economic disadvantage. The information they provide can assist us in the future in helping those families that are likely to experience similar difficulties as a result of economic fluctuations and misfortune.

RURAL IOWA FAMILIES AND ECONOMIC DECLINE

In April of 1992, an editorial in the *Times Citizen*, a local newspaper in Iowa Falls, noted that "rural Iowa has been damaged the most by the changing economic winds. While not broken, the rural fiber has been stretched until vacant store fronts, lost jobs, dwindling population, and decaying small towns dot the rural scene." This quote helps to illustrate the changing world experienced by the Iowa families in this study who witnessed a dramatic reversal from the prosperous times of the 1970s to economic disadvantage and uncertainty by the 1990s.

A few simple statistics starkly illustrate the economic crisis in Iowa, a state with a population about the size of Chicago's, approximately 2.78 million people each in 1990 (U.S. Bureau of the Census, 1991). During the decade of the 1980s, the state saw approximately 20% of Iowa farmers lose their operations, 75 banks and savings and loans close their doors, 41% of rural gas stations go out of business, the loss of 260 automobile dealerships and almost 500 grocery stores, and a staggering 46% increase in bankruptcies in 1985 alone (*Des Moines Register*, November, 1989; Davidson, 1990). Construction sales declined by more than 40% during the decade, and in 1989 economic activity in the state had still not returned to the levels achieved during the 1970s (Friedberger, 1989). Many families in this study felt the pain of these events directly through the loss of a farm, a job, or decreased wages. Others maintained their level of living, but saw friends and family financially decimated by the economic depression.

As one middle-aged farmer told us during an interview, his best friend since childhood, who lived on a nearby farm, had recently committed suicide when it became clear that he would lose his operation, his way of life, and had no viable economic options for the future. This experience not only caused him great sadness and sense of personal loss, but also permanently alienated him from an economic and political system that seemed to have so little regard for rural people. Thus, even for those in our study who maintained their financial well-being, the economic crisis of the 1980s brought much distress through the difficulties of those around them.

When we first interviewed these rural families during the winter of 1989, their experiences during the past several years created at least four different economic scenarios: (1) those who had experienced financial difficulties during the early and mid-1980s and had not yet recovered, (2) families that had largely rebounded economically after a period of decline, (3) those who had not suffered financial losses and had maintained a satisfactory level of living throughout the 1980s, and (4) families that entered the decade with low incomes and either maintained or improved that status. The important point here is that, for these families, current economic circumstances may reflect several different, earlier financial trajectories. In the following analyses, we examine the consequences of these different trajectories by investigating financial circumstances at a single point in time, 1989. This research strategy provides an assessment of economic status and its consequences after a lengthy period of economic crisis in the rural heartland.

The chapters that follow provide more detail regarding the recruitment and characteristics of these Iowa families. Briefly, we interviewed four members in each of 451 rural families. The families lived on farms or in small towns in eight counties in north-central Iowa that were hard hit by the 1980s financial crisis. The families shared a North European ethnic heritage; almost 80% had a German ancestral history.

All of the families in the study included a seventh-grade adolescent when they were interviewed in 1989. In addition to this target adolescent, both parents of the seventh-grader and a sibling within four years of age participated in the study. This family configuration allowed us to study the influence of economic hardship on the behaviors, emotions, and sense-of-self of adults, children, and adolescents. It also provided the information needed to assess the impact of disadvantage on the several dimensions of nuclear family relationships: marital, parent-child, and sibling. The following review of our theoretical perspective indicates the importance of investigating all of these variations in family process and individual development.

A THEORETICAL PERSPECTIVE ON FAMILY STRESS

This research draws upon an evolving *Family Stress Model* that we have developed to guide our analyses of family stress processes in general and family economic hardship in particular (Conger, Burgess, & Barrett, 1979; Conger, McCarthy, Yang, Lahey, & Kropp, 1984; Conger et al., 1990, 1992; Conger, Conger, et al., 1993; Conger, Lorenz, Elder, Simons, & Ge, 1993). This theoretical perspective draws from several sources including (1) early research on families during the depression years of the 1930s, (2) contemporary studies of economic stress, including the integration of life course distinctions with more traditional stress research (Elder, 1985; George, 1993), and (3) current conceptualizations of the social epidemiology of emotional distress (Mirowsky & Ross, 1989).

Gore and Colten (1991) suggest that research within the life course or developmental tradition too often assumes a benign social environment, which equally affects adaptation by most individuals. Life stress research, on the other hand, typically does not consider the timing of stressful events in individual lives nor the contribution of earlier life experiences to the generation of later stresses, strains, or coping resources. In the present study we combine the stress and life course perspectives by evaluating the impact of economic difficulties on individuals at varying life stages (parents and adolescents) and by considering stress-mediating factors appropriate to the different developmental levels of adults and youth.

By joining life course and social stress insights, our Family Stress Model illuminates the socially interdependent nature of stressful life experiences, consistent with a life course paradigm (Elder, 1994). In their important review of theory and research on stress processes, Coyne and Downey (1991) note that chronic and acute stresses or strains, including financial difficulties, often have their greatest impact on individual well-being through the troubles they create in one's closest social ties, such as those found in the family. Indeed, the conflict and withdrawal in family relations that sometimes result from economic problems may become the most significant stressors in family life, continuing in time even when the original external precipitant, e.g., unemployment for the family breadwinner, no longer exists (Conger et al., 1984; Liker & Elder, 1983).

Our conceptual framework rests on this central idea: For parents and children living together, both the long- and short-term effects of economic hardship, as well as other family stresses and strains, are strongly influenced by the interdependent emotions and behaviors of family members. Within the family, the dynamic of interdependent lives connects broad socioeconomic changes to the experiences and well-being of individual family members (Elder, 1992).

Families of the Great Depression

Studies of families in the Great Depression of the 1930s frequently reported that the way in which family members responded to one another was a major determinant of their eventual adaptation to severe hardship. Angell (1965), Cavan and Ranck (1938), Komarovsky (1940), and others provide rich descriptions of adaptive, mutually supportive families coming together in the face of adversity while less cohesive families became mired in conflict, tensions, and mutual avoidance. These processes have been most systematically documented by Elder and his colleagues, who have studied the records of families living in Oakland and Berkeley, California, prior to, during, and following the decade of the 1930s.

According to project reports (e.g., Elder, 1974; Elder & Caspi, 1988; Elder, Caspi, & Downey, 1986; Elder, Liker, & Cross, 1984; Elder, Nguyen, & Caspi, 1985; Liker & Elder, 1983), income loss in families accentuated the explosiveness and irritability of fathers, particularly those who tended to be more emotionally unstable prior to the onset of financial crises. In these analyses, the father's behavior appeared to set the stage for the family's adaptive trajectory in response to economic stress. When fathers reacted to economic crises by becoming more hostile and irritable, they oftentimes set in motion a sequence of events that led to increased risk for conflicts in the marriage, disruptions in effective parenting, and—through these mediating processes—developmental difficulties for children and adolescents.

An especially important dimension of this research is the finding that the emotions and behaviors of parents largely determined how their children were affected by financial difficulties. When parents, and especially fathers, maintained their emotional equilibrium in the face of hardship, the destructive chain of events just described was much less likely to occur.

Taken together, the cumulative findings from this program of work suggest that mounting economic pressures alter relationships by changing individual behavior, and they also change individual behavior by changing family relationships. These pressures modify and accentuate the dynamics and substantive content of these interdependencies. In *Children of the Great Depression* (Elder, 1974), for example, the analysis traces the effect of drastic income loss on children through three types of microprocesses: (1) the family economy, which became more labor intensive and assigned children important roles to perform; (2) family relationships, in which affection and authority roles shifted to mothers; and (3) patterns of family discord and disorganization. Each of these processes involves stress-initiated change in the chemistry and matrix of family-based interdependent lives.

Three linking mechanisms identified in this depression-era research (Elder, 1992) played an especially important role in the formulation of the theoretical model for the present study. According to *the life stage principle*, the influence of a social change on life experience depends on the life stage at which individuals experience the change. People of different ages are influenced differentially by the same transition or change event. This is so because they bring differing experiences, skills, and options to the change. With this perspective in mind, we should find that the impact of economic misfortune among Iowa families has different implications for parents and children, even within the same household.

Second, economic misfortune entails some loss of control over outcomes and consequently prompts efforts to regain control, as through efforts to curtail consumption expenditures and the entry of other family members into the labor market. This *dynamic in control cycles* includes family survival strategies among the Iowa families, as in cutting back on expenditures, which represent an effort to restore family and individual control. Finally, economic misfortune places families in a new situation of scarcity with its behavioral requirements and options. We refer to the demands of the new situation as *situational imperatives*. When families became more labor-intensive under conditions of hardship during the Great Depression, the new imperatives called for greater contributions from older children and they responded accordingly (Elder, 1974). The austere imperatives of hard times among Iowa families may have similar effects on the responsibilities of children.

Economic Hardship and Economic Pressure

Depression-era research, and particularly the work by Elder and his colleagues, provides the initial point of departure for the present study. The following discussion presents our Family Stress Model, which we apply to the family's experience of economic problems. More generally, our theoretical framework for understanding family stress proposes that stressful events or conditions create strains or pressures in daily living. These strains affect the moods and behaviors of individual family members and, in this fashion, the developmental trajectories of parents and children.

The investigation of hard-pressed families during the 1930s primarily focused on two dimensions of economic stress: income loss (e.g., Elder, 1974) and the status of being unemployed (e.g., Komarovsky, 1940). As shown in Figure 1.1, our theoretical model includes these dimensions—unstable work and income loss—as two of the exogenous variables indicative of economic hardship. This is where our study begins, the degree of hardship experienced by these Iowa families in 1989.

In addition to these two measures of financial stress from the Depression-era studies, from the tradition of poverty research (Duncan, 1984) we selected income level as another construct in a set of four designed to assess the current economic state of the family. Families with the lowest incomes should experience the most severe economic problems. More recently, rural social scientists have found that the ratio of family debts to assets increases family economic stress (Murdock and Leistritz, 1988) and we include it as the final construct describing the degree of family economic hardship (Figure 1.1).

The model in Figure 1.1 includes another important extension of the family research of the 1930s. Based on findings from contemporary studies of individuals and families reported by ourselves and others (e.g., Conger et al., 1990, 1992; Elder, Conger, Foster, & Ardelt, 1992; Kessler, Turner, & House, 1988; Voydanoff & Donnelly, 1988), as well as on current thinking in the field of stress research (Pearlin, 1989), we expected that hardship conditions would affect the lives of family members primarily through the degree of economic pressure they produced in

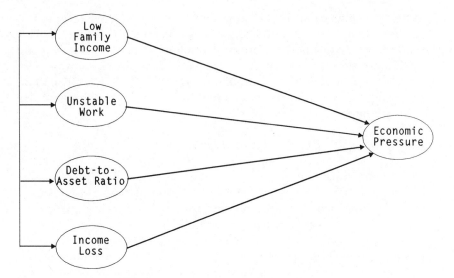

Figure 1.1.   Relating dimensions of economic hardship to the experience of
    economic pressure.

everyday living. We proposed that financial stresses, operationalized
as low income, unstable work, a high debt load, and declining income,
would increase financial pressure such as the inability to pay bills, purchase life's necessities, or avoid painful cutbacks in expenditures.

The construct *economic pressure* in Figure 1.1 reflects these daily financial
difficulties associated with stressful economic conditions. These hardship-
related strains were expected to be pivotal in translating objective economic circumstances into daily experiences that could demoralize family members and disrupt family interaction processes. Chapter 4 provides specific
details regarding our approach to assessing family economic life.

From Hardship to Parents' Moods and Behaviors

Just as recent research on social epidemiology has provided advances
in the measurement of economic conditions and strains since the seminal
studies of the 1930s, other work since that time on the measurement of
emotions, behaviors, and social process also allows us to extend those
early investigations. Two areas of progress in measurement are particularly important for the present analyses.

First, research during the past 50 years has substantially increased the
availability of standardized, carefully developed research instruments for
assessing psychological well-being or disorder, family functioning, the

quality of interpersonal relationships, and behavioral interaction among intimates. A number of measurement scales now exist that (1) deal with these phenomena, (2) have sound psychometric properties, and (3) can be used to evaluate the influence of hardship on family life. These new measurement tools have both methodological and theoretical significance.

For example, the report by Liker and Elder (1983) demonstrated that father's emotional instability was the central mediator between economic hardship and disrupted marital relations. The only measure of instability available to these investigators, however, involved tense, irritable, and explosive behavior; dispositions that may be more characteristic of a male than female response to stress (Conger, Conger, et al., 1993). We suspect that a measure of emotion more prevalent among women, e.g., dysphoric mood, might bring them more directly into the process of family response to economic stress. This hypothesis is tested in later analyses.

A second important advance in measurement involves the growing recognition that the study of families, social stress, and psychological functioning may produce significant confounds in the estimation of relationships among theoretical constructs if only one source of information is employed in the analyses (Bank, Dishion, Skinner, & Patterson, 1990; Lorenz, Conger, Simons, Whitbeck, & Elder, 1991). For example, family members who report higher levels of depressive symptoms will typically attribute more hostility to other family members than individuals who report little or no dysphoric mood. With only one reporter, we do not know whether family hostility leads to the reporter's depression or whether a depressed state exaggerates perceived hostility, reflecting simply a predisposition to see self and others in a negative light (Bank et al., 1990). Thus, information from other agents is needed to validate the reports from a single respondent.

This finding has led to the development of measures based on reports involving multiple informants (e.g., mothers and fathers) and multiple methodologies (e.g., self-reports and observer ratings). These evolving measurement strategies are employed to evaluate the next step in our theoretical framework, shown in Figure 1.2. They are described in greater detail in Chapter Two of this volume.

In Figure 1.2 we draw on earlier research (e.g., Conger et al., 1990, 1992; Elder et al., 1992; Simons, Lorenz, et al., 1992; Whitbeck et al., 1991a) in proposing that economic pressure links financial conditions to parents' emotional distress and marital conflict. Psychological problems, in turn, are hypothesized to exacerbate marital conflict and to disrupt effective parenting practices. The final part of this sequence of events is the direct path from conflict and hostility between spouses to disrupted parenting.

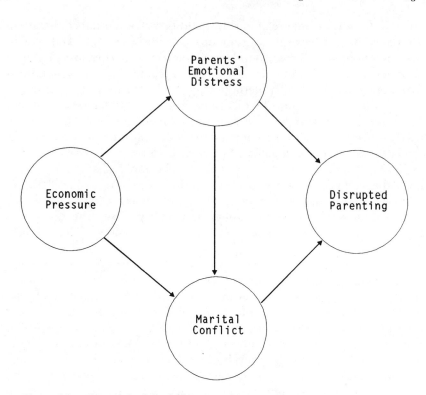

Figure 1.2.   A model of the influence of economic pressure on the moods
    and behaviors of parents.

Consistent with the model in Figure 1.2, contemporary research suggests that depressed mood may be a key psychological mediator between
stressful events or conditions and conflict in family relations (Downey &
Coyne, 1990); thus, we use it as our primary measure of emotional
distress in the following analyses. Especially important, this dimension of
distress may be critical to understanding women's response to financial
difficulties.

There is considerable empirical evidence to support the hypothesized
processes outlined in Figure 1.2. First, a number of studies have demonstrated that financial problems such as low income and work instability
are likely to affect emotional distress in both men and women through
the economic pressures or strains they create in daily living (e.g., Conger
et al., 1992; Conger, Conger, et al., 1993; Elder et al., 1992; Kessler et al.,
1988; Voydanoff & Donnelly, 1988). These findings are reflected in the
path from economic pressure to parents' emotional distress in Figure
1.2.

In addition, both experimental and naturalistic studies of emotional distress, and in particular research on depressed affect, have shown that negative mood is positively related to irritable or hostile behavior between intimates (Gotlib & McCabe, 1990). Emotional distress is also related to withdrawal from and reduced effort in socially skilled behaviors such as effective parenting practices (Berkowitz, 1989; Downey & Coyne, 1990). According to our conceptual model (Figure 1.2), the feelings of demoralization and depression associated with economic pressure will both exacerbate spousal conflict and reduce the level of investment in parenting. This line of reasoning also follows from Patterson and his colleagues (Patterson, DeBaryshe, & Ramsey, 1989), who have suggested that stressful family circumstances have their greatest impact on children and adolescents through their disruption of effective child-rearing practices.

From Parents to Children and Adolescents

Consonant with the developmental perspective proposed by Patterson et al. (1989), Fauber, Forehand, Thomas, and Wierson (1990) recently reported that for a sample of early adolescents, conflicts between parents influenced adolescent adjustment primarily through disruptions in parenting. Patterson (1991) has reported similar findings for boys living in intact families, and our research with rural adolescents suggests a similar process (Conger et al., 1991, 1992; Conger, Conger, et al., 1993). Thus, in our conceptual model we propose that marital conflicts will affect adolescent adjustment by diminishing or disrupting parents' child-rearing skills.

Parents distracted by ongoing antagonisms with a spouse likely have reduced time and energy for their roles as parents. Social control and the modulation of emotionality are undermined by parents who engage in recurring bouts of negativity and conflict. Moreover, hostility in the marriage may spill over into coercive interactions between parents and children and between siblings (Patterson, 1982).

We predicted that disrupted parenting would be the critical variable connecting earlier steps in the model to prosocial or problematic adolescent adjustment (Figure 1.3). The dimension of parental behavior of particular interest here relates to the noted hypothesis involving spill over from marital conflict and parental depression to hostile interactions and harsh discipline by parents toward children and adolescents. High levels of hostility and coercion by parents, which may include disciplinary practices that are both inconsistent and overly harsh, have been shown to intensify conduct and emotional problems of youth and to impede their development of social, cognitive, and emotional well-being. We expected

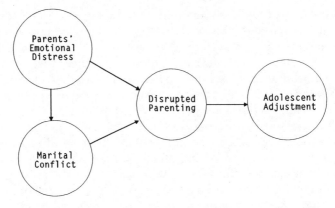

Figure 1.3.   Linking parents' emotional distress and conflict
            to adolescent adjustment.

that parents' hardship-related emotional and marital difficulties would
increase their irritability and harshness with their children. These parental behaviors, in turn, were predicted to increase risk for problematic and
less competent adolescent development (Larzelere & Patterson, 1990;
Laub & Sampson, 1988; Maccoby & Martin, 1983; Patterson, 1982; Patterson et al., 1989; Rollins & Thomas, 1979).

DEVELOPMENTAL AND MODIFYING PROCESSES

As illustrated in Figures 1.1 through 1.3, the discussion of our theoretical perspective thus far has dealt with the main and mediating effects of
variables thought to be important in the family experience of economic
hardship. A major focus of contemporary research on stress processes,
however, is the identification of personal or social resources that might
reduce the adverse effects of stressful life events or conditions (Coyne &
Downey, 1991; Kessler, Price, & Wortman, 1985; Rutter, 1990). An important component in research of this type, often referred to as the study
of *resilience,* is the investigation of developmental processes that reduce
the risk of experiencing distress or disorder even during stressful times.
Thus, a complete understanding of successful adaptation to life's stresses
and strains requires not only the identification of resources, such as
social support or a repertoire of effective coping strategies, that reduce
risk for emotional distress or behavioral disorder, but also the investigation of life experiences that promote the development of such resources.
    In the present study, we were particularly concerned with the quality
of social relationships both within and outside the family that might

affect the various linkages in our theoretical model of family economic stress. For example, we expected that social support from friends and family members might reduce the detrimental impact of economic pressure on psychological well-being. In addition, we were interested in certain aspects of the developmental histories of the parents in the study that might promote the establishment of close ties with others, relationships that were expected to foster resilience to economic hardship.

In the chapters that follow, we examine the degree to which the events and conditions in the lives of these Iowa families conform with these predicted theoretical processes. In many cases, we found the model was incapable of adequately capturing the richness of their experiences. In such instances, we depart as necessary from this beginning framework for the study.

OVERVIEW OF THE CHAPTERS

In these introductory comments, we have provided a brief description of the IYFP including its history and purpose, the participating families, our theoretical perspective, and some major elements of our methodological approach to the investigation. Each of these issues is addressed in much greater detail in the following chapters, beginning with Chapter 2, which provides a comprehensive description of the methodological procedures we employed to try to understand the hardship-related experiences of these Iowa families. Indeed, we believe that, in addition to advancing understanding of family adaptation to socioeconomic stresses and strains, the following chapters provide an important guide to a variety of methodological innovations that capitalize on advances in the measurement of family process. Especially important, later analyses indicate useful strategies for testing theoretical models using data derived from multiple study informants.

In Chapter 2, Lorenz and Melby review the general design and analytic strategies employed in the study. Readers interested in methodological details will want to proceed to this chapter immediately; others may wish to skip it and return to it as needed to understand analyses presented later in the book. In any case, Chapter 2 provides the logic of the inquiry and thus is essential for a complete understanding of the research.

Lorenz and Melby clearly explicate two major goals of the research methods employed: (1) to provide a respondent sample that adequately represents the variation required to understand individual and family adaptation to rural economic stress and (2) to generate the diversity of measures needed to maximize realism and minimize dispositional biases in the assessment procedures. The authors trace the reasoning behind the research strategies used and then show how structural equation modeling (SEM) with latent variables provides an appropriate analytic strategy for capitalizing on the rich system of multiagent, multiple-method measurements. They provide the essential background for understanding the analyses throughout the subsequent chapters in the volume.

In Part II of the book we consider the historical trends for rural communities and families that created the conditions we see today. In Chapter 3, which begins this section, Lasley traces the history of boom and bust cycles in agriculture. He notes that the crisis in the 1980s was especially severe for younger farmers, who were caught in a changing economic environment that first encouraged the acquisition of debt and then brutally turned the tables on farmers initially motivated to expand their operations. Difficulties in the farm sector produced an adverse ripple effect in the economies of rural communities that serve the farmer. Lasley documents how this chain of events led to severe outmigration and economic decline in the rural counties where our study families reside. He also speculates on the social and economic future of rural Iowa.

Elder, Robertson, and Ardelt operationalize the economic hardship and economic pressure constructs (see Figure 1.1) as they turn the discussion from rural communities in general to the lives of these Iowa families. In Chapter 4 they describe the measures of these constructs, highlighting the significance of adaptation to the economic losses that occurred during the 1980s. They note that families faced difficult choices in response to hardship such as cutting back expenditures and delaying necessary purchases. These multiple adjustments created significant pain for many of these families, as evidenced by the extreme distress among families who lost a farm as a result of the crisis.

Chapter 5 focuses on the farm origins and current relationships to agriculture for these families. Although a history of farming is common for parents or their immediate ancestors, only a minority (about 20%) of these rural families are significantly involved in farming today. About 13% of the families lost a farm during the past decade. The authors (Elder, Robertson, and Foster) trace the adjustments and adaptations of farm families to their changing world. In particular, they note the trend to off-farm employment for both husbands and wives and the disruptions it creates for a traditional way of life. The findings show that the cumulative, often adverse changes in agriculture have had important consequences for the psychological well-being of farm parents, particularly in relation to their attachment to the land.

In Chapter 6, Elder, Foster, and Ardelt turn their attention to the role of children in the household economy. They draw heavily on research with families of the 1930s to develop a set of predictions regarding activities that adolescents might undertake in response to economic hardship. Consistent with earlier findings, they demonstrate that these contemporary youth often contribute both to family income and to household labor in attempts to counter adverse economic circumstances. Farm boys, in particular, appear to benefit in the eyes of their parents from this industriousness. Indeed, the findings suggest that the rural context of adolescent work may have quite different developmental implications than adolescent work in urban settings.

In Part III, Husbands and Wives, we move from the unique histories of these rural families and communities to the more general lessons that may be learned from their hardship experiences. Chapter 7 asks how these parents' childhoods may have prepared or failed to prepare them for the crisis of the 1980s. Whitbeck, Lorenz, Simons, and Huck investigate the characteristics of the grandparent generation and how they influenced personality development for IYFP parents. In particular, they show that parents were at increased risk for disruptions in their own personality development when they experienced a child-rearing history that involved a mother or father with psychological problems or who engaged in ineffective child-rearing practices. The data show that low self-confidence and poor interpersonal skills in today's parents can be traced to family life in childhood. These contemporary deficits reduce success in enlisting social support during stressful times.

In Chapter 8, Lorenz, Conger, and Montague extend the analyses in Chapter 7 by showing that a parent's ability to gain support from others plays an important role in reducing the adverse psychological consequences of economic stress. The findings elaborate the theoretical model developed in Figures 1.1 and 1.2 to demonstrate that social relations within and outside the family are both affected by economic pressures and also help to attenuate their impact on parents' emotional distress. Most important, the results show that the basic theoretical model portrayed in Figures 1.1 and 1.2 is consistent with the data. That is, hardship conditions (family income, unstable work, debts and assets, income loss) were only indirectly related to psychological distress through the daily economic pressures they exacerbate.

Drawing on these findings, we extended our analyses in Chapter 9 by examining the impact of economic hardship, economic pressure, and parents' emotional distress on marital conflict and relationship quality (see Figure 1.2). In this chapter Conger, Ge, and Lorenz generate further support for the general theoretical model. They found, as expected, that economic pressure links hardship conditions to hostile interactions in marriage. Consistent with Figure 1.2, economic pressure was indirectly related to marital conflict through parents' depressive symptoms.

Not predicted was the finding that, once negative mood was taken into account, there was little direct association between economic pressure and marital conflict. It appears that the adverse emotional consequences of economic adjustments provide the primary avenue through which economic stress affects conflict in marriage. These conflicts, in turn, predicted feelings of unhappiness and dissatisfaction with the relationship for both spouses.

Figure 1.2 proposes that these accumulating emotional and relationship problems associated with economic stress will disrupt effective parenting practices. Part IV, Adolescent Development, begins by addressing this link in our Family Stress Model. In Chapter 10, Simons and his colleagues investigate the association between economic pressure and harsh, explosive parenting. Consistent with the model, they find that economic pressure is positively related to harsh parenting practices, especially through its impact on hostility and conflict in the marriage. The results also show that economic pressure diminishes a parent's support from his or her spouse, thus intensifying its adverse affect on parenting practices.

The final step in our theoretical model links disruptions in child-rearing practices to adolescent adjustment (Figure 1.3). Simons, Whitbeck, and Wu investigate this dimension of the economic stress process in Chapter 11. As we did in Chapter 8, they also consider how social support from outside the nuclear family might reduce the negative impact of economic problems on psychological functioning, in this instance for children rather than parents. Both economic problems and harsh parenting adversely affected the well-being of these children. Especially important, social support reduced the negative consequences of financial difficulties, but did little to decrease the developmental problems created by harsh parenting. Disruptions in child-rearing generated by economic stress appear to be especially harmful in the life trajectories of adolescents.

In Chapter 12 we note that our investigation of family economic stress would be incomplete without careful consideration of an often neglected family tie, the sibling relationship. Conger, Conger, and Elder report that disrupted parenting leads to conflict and hostility between siblings, aversive exchanges that lead to greater internalizing (e.g., depressed mood) and externalizing (e.g., aggressive behavior) symptoms for seventh graders in the study. Some of the results also suggest that close ties between siblings may attenuate the negative influence of these processes, but the findings are not definitive. The most important point of the chapter is that economically induced disruptions in the lives of parents threaten the emotional health of children both directly and indirectly through the turmoil they create in sibling relationships.

In the final chapter Conger and Elder review the empirical, theoretical, and practical implications of the findings reported in earlier chapters. They note the centrality of economic hardship in shaping family relationships and individual adaptation. They also discuss some limitations in the findings and identify important directions for future research. The discussion concludes by reviewing the salience of these results for families of the future, both rural and urban. In a society marked by dramatic, frequent, and widespread changes in economic circumstance, it is imperative that we understand the impact of these changes on the lives of families and individuals. Only in this manner will we be able to improve the capacity of people to cope successfully with stressful life change.

Chapter 2

Analyzing Family Stress and Adaptation: Methods of Study

Frederick O. Lorenz and Janet N. Melby

The study of the family has focused a need for distinctive research methods, since a family is neither simply a collection of individuals nor just another social group. Family researchers have identified specific issues dealing with theory and methodology that are unique to this particular enterprise.
—H. Grotevant in A. P. Copeland and K. M. White, *Studying Families*

The central purpose of the Iowa Youth and Families Project (IYFP) is to elaborate the relationships between economic hardship and specific developmental outcomes, including the psychological well-being of individual family members and the quality of family relationships. Consistent with the quote from Grotevant that begins this chapter, a second important purpose has been to develop methods and procedures that capitalize on recent advances in statistical and measurement techniques to more adequately evaluate family stress processes. This chapter presents the major methodological themes that directly affect how the research is organized and executed, beginning with a rationale for the research design and a synopsis of the data collection procedures. The material presented here describes the methodological and analytic strategies upon which the IYFP is based. For some readers, this information is important in its own right and they will profit from reviewing Chapter 2 before proceeding to subsequent chapters. Other readers may elect to skip this chapter until they reach analyses presented later in the book that are better understood after reading about our methodological approach.

As one reads the chapters that follow, two distinctive methodological themes will appear repeatedly: (1) our self-conscious attempt to obtain realistic measures of theoretical concepts, and (2) our concern to reflect accurately the relationships among concepts. Realism in measurement is especially important because it is only through the process of measurement that we can translate indirectly observed abstract concepts into empirical observation. From a design perspective, realism is advanced in the IYFP by obtaining measures of concepts from several sources, most remarkably by videotaping family members as they talk with one another about topics important in their lives. The section on observing families reconstructs how behavioral coding schemes were developed, how coders were trained to consistently rate videotaped family member behaviors, and how the consistency of the ratings is evaluated.

In Chapter 1 and in most subsequent chapters, the relationships among concepts are visually portrayed by theoretical models. These theoretical models are simplified versions of how researchers believe concepts are temporally ordered, and how they relate to their empirical indicators. Although a variety of statistical procedures is used to evaluate how well the models match with empirical data, we have found structural equation modeling (SEM) to be a powerful technique for evaluating many of the empirical processes of central interest.

As we evaluate theoretical models, realism in measurement again becomes an important theme. The threats to reliability and validity that initially motivated our concern for realistic measures of concepts reappear in the modeling process as measurement error—both random and systematic. In discussing SEM in this chapter, we elaborate the implications of both types of error, illustrate how these problems threaten causal inference, and suggest strategies for managing imperfect data. The chapter ends with a review of the criteria used to evaluate alternative models of family processes.

THE LOGIC OF THE STUDY DESIGN

Planning the IYFP required numerous design decisions, many of which had to do with what Kish (1987) has identified as the dynamic tension between the three Rs of research design: randomization (internal validity), representation (external validity), and realism, especially realism in measurement. Kish argued that these cannot be ranked hierarchically; instead, they represent goals that, when we are faced with scarce resources, require compromise. In the context of the IYFP, compromise meant balancing the demands for a sample large enough to construct and test complex models with the need for detailed information about families and family members.

Advancing Realism in Measurement

The traditional emphasis in sociological family research has been on representative sample surveys. Typically, a questionnaire is sent to a household to be filled out by the "head of household" or a designated family member. A respondent, perhaps the wife, may be asked for her opinions about, say, her satisfaction with her marriage. Her responses may contain measurement error, but if she responds independently of others, one can assume they are unbiased answers.

In many family studies, this respondent also may be asked about the attitudes or behaviors of other family members: Would you say your husband is hostile? Depressed? Are your children well-behaved? Delinquent? Collecting information about all family members from a single respondent may create systematic measurement error, specifically, "method-variance bias" (Bank, Dishion, Skinner, & Patterson, 1990; Cattell, 1957; Lorenz et al., 1991). The respondent's description of the attitudes and behaviors of other family members may reflect his or her own dispositions and attributions more than they describe the family member about whom the response was intended (Baucom, Sayers, & Duhe 1989; Sillars, 1985).

To counter the problems associated with both random and systematic measurement errors, we sought more realistic measures of family member attitudes and behaviors by obtaining multiple measures of concepts and by expanding our sample to include several members of each family. Decisions about who to interview were dictated by the kinds of relationships we were interested in studying. To examine intrafamily characteristics that promote well-being or exacerbate problem behaviors, however, required that certain structural characteristics of the family be held constant.

First, given our interest in the effects of economic hardship on adolescent behaviors, we wanted to interview adolescents. Because early adolescence is a pivotal age for many children, families were considered for selection into the study if they had a seventh-grade boy or girl. Second, to examine the effects of economic conditions on marital quality and stability, and the effects of marital interactions on adolescent outcomes, families were considered for selection into the study only if the seventh-grader lived with both biological parents. Finally, members of the research team hypothesized that the relationship between parents and children could be affected by the presence of a sibling who also would have an influence on the seventh-grader's thoughts, feelings, and behaviors. Hence, a third criterion for inclusion in the study was added: The seventh-grader had to have a sibling within 4 years of his or her age for the family to qualify to participate in the research.

From our Family Stress Model reviewed in Chapter 1, we argued that family member actions toward one another have important consequences for how social and economic changes affect family members; for example, economic stress has been shown to increase the likelihood of adolescent problem behaviors. But that outcome is not inevitable. To better understand the intervening conditions, we wanted to observe family members as they interact with each other. Are they respectful? Supportive? Or do they express contempt? Hostility? Do parents reason with their children or do they apply rules in an authoritarian manner? These intrafamily interactions have been shown to affect a variety of relationship and individual developmental outcomes such as marital quality (Conger et al., 1990) and adolescent behaviors (Patterson et al., 1989).

From a measurement perspective, observing family interactions is one way we can disentangle the biasing effects of self-report measures based on the views of a single family member. Trained observers provide an outsider's perspective that people in close relationships may be unable to see or unable to report themselves (Markman & Notarius, 1987). Yet behavioral assessments are seldom included in family studies, and they cannot be obtained from most self-administered questionnaires. One goal of our research design was to obtain realistic measures of these interactions, classify them according to an acceptable and reliable scheme, and incorporate the resulting behavioral scales into the statistical modeling process.

Implementing Advances in Measurement

The emphasis on realism in measurement, especially in observing and rating family interactions, focused our attention on a specific type of family structure in a limited geographic area. Because our data collection methods were labor-intensive, we limited the study to an eight-county area in north-central Iowa. This area, a socioeconomic "Three-Mile Island," was populated by prosperous rural families when the farm crisis hit in the mid-1980s. Many lost their farms or farm-related livelihoods; others are still farming but living in the shadow of severe debt. Thus it is an area particularly well suited for studying the effects of diffuse stressors, in this case economic pressure, on family functioning.

Although not everyone in the area suffered directly from the farm crisis, a greater proportion of families in this area suffered losses than in many other areas. Thus, the sample has many of the characteristics of an epidemiological community study (Kellam, 1990): It may not be representative of the population of rural people as a whole, but it is rich in the economic variation of theoretical interest. It contains a disproportionately large number of people who have had to respond to economic hardship.

Selecting families. Families selected for the study were identified, screened, and invited to participate through contacts with all of the 34 public and private schools located in communities of less than 6,500 population in the eight counties. From this sampling frame, 451 families, about 78% of the families who met our criteria for participation, agreed to be interviewed. Of these families, 34% lived on farms, 12% lived in rural areas but not on farms, and 54% lived in small towns. Among men, the most commonly reported occupation was farmer (22%). Other frequently reported occupations included manager or administrator, sales representative, skilled and unskilled factory worker, truck driver, and teacher. There was one physician.

About 22% of the women were identified as housewives, and another 17% were secretaries or engaged in office-related activities (e.g., bookkeepers). Other commonly reported occupations included teacher, registered nurse, medical/dental support, and child care provider. Median family income from all sources was $33,300 in 1988 and 11% of the families had incomes below the federal poverty line, about twice the proportion (5.6%) for married-couple families nationwide (U.S. Bureau of the Census, 1989). The median age for mothers and fathers was 37 and 39 years, respectively, and the median years of education for both was 13 years.

Interviewing families. After all four of the family. members—father, mother, target child, and his or her sibling closest in age—agreed to participate, they were visited twice in their own home by a member of the research team. During the first visit, a professional interviewer asked each participating family member to fill out a questionnaire, which asked for detailed information about family life and finances, friends, and physical and mental health. Family members independently completed the questionnaire so that they would not see one another's answers and so that they could be assured that all responses would be confidential. This took as long as 2 hours. Some of this information was quite sensitive, and interviewers were carefully instructed not to leave the house without first collecting and sealing each respondent's questionnaire.

Before leaving the family's home, the interviewer left behind a second questionnaire—affectionately referred to as homework—for each family member to complete before the second visit. In this questionnaire, parents were asked additional questions about work and family finances, life in their family of origin, and about their values and beliefs about a number of important topics. The two children were asked about their goals and values, performance in school, nonschool activities, and what they thought it would be like to be a parent.

Videotaping families in interaction. A second visit was made to the family, within 2 weeks of the first, during which time family members were videotaped in various combinations while participating in structured interactional tasks. At the beginning of the session, the interviewer asked each family member to independently complete a short questionnaire designed to identify sensitive issues about which family members disagreed (money, household chores, etc). Next, all four family members were gathered around a table and given a set of cards to read. These cards contained questions about parenting practices, schoolwork, household chores, and other important family events that they were to discuss (Task 1, family discussion). After explaining the procedures, completing a practice card with the family, and checking the video-recording equipment, the interviewer left the room for a distant part of the house. The family members then discussed the issues raised by the cards, and the video camera recorded the family's interactions. After 35 minutes, the interviewer returned, stopped the discussion, and described the second task.

A second interaction task (Task 2, family problem solving) was 15 minutes in length and also involved all four family members. For this task, the interviewer asked family members to try to resolve up to three areas of family disagreement, beginning with the issue that created the greatest amount of family conflict, selected on the basis of the questionnaires completed at the beginning of the visit. The third task (Task 3, sibling interaction), also 15 minutes in length, asked just the two siblings in the study to discuss their relationship and family life. While they were doing this task, the parents filled out yet a third questionnaire concerning their perceptions of the characteristics of other family members and recent important events in their lives.

The fourth task involved only the parents and lasted 30 minutes (Task 4, marital interaction). They were asked to discuss their history together, the current status of their relationship, and their plans for the future. During the marital task, siblings completed a questionnaire about important events in their lives. For their efforts, each family was paid $250, an amount that came out to about $10 per hour per person.

Observing Family Interactions

After completion of the interviews, the questionnaires were prepared for computer entry and behaviors occurring on the videotapes were rated by trained observers. Numerous procedures have been developed to assess family interactions. Some are designed to measure fine-grained behavioral events (McGillicuddy-DeLisi, 1985; Pellegrini, Brody, & Sigel, 1985), often using elaborate microanalytic time-sampling and event-sampling rating schemes to obtain sequential patterns of interaction (Dowdney, Mrazek, Quinton & Rutter, 1984; Mrazek, Dowdney, Rutter & Quinton 1982; Patterson, 1982).

In recent years, there has been renewed interest in global observer ratings, particularly in situations where general characteristics or dispositions of individuals and interactions are important (Bakeman & Gottman, 1986; Estrada, Arsenio, Hess, & Holloway, 1987; Hetherington & Clingempeel, 1986; Maccoby & Martin, 1983; Markman & Notarius, 1987; McGowan & Johnson, 1984). Generally, global ratings appear to reflect traitlike qualities of individuals and relationships, while more molecular, event-based coding schemes tap specific interactional processes of the moment (Cairns & Green, 1979; Hops et al., 1988).

Because we were interested in relatively stable personal and family characteristics, rating scales were appropriate to our observational research needs. They are also less labor- and time-intensive than microanalytic procedures, not an incidental consideration when a large number of families is being studied. Global rating of family interactions relies on the ability of trained observers to make discriminating judgments about overall characteristics of the individuals or groups being observed. Thus, careful initial and ongoing observer training and reliability assessment are particularly important in their application.

Iowa Family Interaction Rating System

To understand more fully the influence of economic events and conditions on the individual behaviors and interactional characteristics of these rural Iowa families, we used a global rating or macrolevel behavioral coding system to measure the quality of behavioral exchanges between family members. Our rating scheme borrows extensively from earlier work by Hetherington and Clingempeel (1986) as well as from other students of family interaction processes (Gottman, 1979; Hops et al., 1988; Markman & Notarius, 1987; Patterson, 1982).

The coding system includes 53 categories of behavior applied to 3 levels of analysis: individuals, specific dyads, and whole families (coding categories and brief definitions are provided in the Appendix). Thirty-two of the categories are general enough to be applied to all four family members in all four tasks. Of these 32 categories, some capture characteristics of the individual that may reflect a generalized disposition not necessarily directed toward any specific family member (e.g., use of humor, expressions of positive mood); others reflect actions of one specific family member toward another (e.g., husband's hostility toward his wife), while still others are dyadic characteristics (e.g., the observer's rating of the overall quality of the marital relationship based on the emotional tone of the couple's interactional style).

Among the remaining 21 categories, 11 are used to evaluate the child-rearing practices of each parent toward each of the two children in the study. These parenting behaviors were rated during Task 1 and they were primarily concerned with specific management strategies for guiding or correcting adolescent behavior (e.g., disciplinary style). During Task 2, observers rated family members using 5 scales that reflect individual problem-solving skills (e.g., solution quality, disruptive processes) and 5 scales that represent family-level problem-solving skills (e.g., family enjoyment, agreement on the problem).

For each of the 53 ratings, a scale was developed that focuses attention on both the frequency and intensity of verbal and nonverbal behaviors, as well as on the affective and contextual dimensions of the interaction. For most of the categories, the rating scheme ranged from 1 (not a characteristic of the individual or the behavior was not evident) to 5 (the characteristic is highly descriptive of the individual or behavior is frequent and/or intense). Thus, using the brief definitions in the Appendix, when the behavior of the husband was observed to be consistently angry, critical, disapproving, and rejecting of the actions or behaviors of his wife, he was rated a 5 for the category of hostility for that task. There were exceptions to this general scheme; for example, the category of relational quality ranged from 1 (poor) to 3 (neutral) to 5 (good).

Inasmuch as the coding categories are neither mutually exclusive nor exhaustive, many rating scales were expected to be correlated. For example, statements such as "you are wonderful" were coded as endearment as well as warmth/support, because the former is viewed as a special, extreme case of the latter. In many instances highly correlated individual ratings were combined to create a summative scale indicative of a more general interactional style such as the overall disposition to be warm and supportive toward others. Moreover, some behaviors that might occur in family interactions were not coded because no category existed into which they could be placed, i.e., they were not theoretically relevant to the conceptual framework for the study.

Coding observations from videotapes. The abbreviated definitions for each rating category shown in the Appendix have more elaborate counterparts that coders were required to master (see Melby et al., 1990). To learn and retain these definitions and keep them distinct from one another required extensive training. Each observer was instructed in the coding system and given 6 to 8 weeks of practice in rating interactions. Before actually beginning to code tapes, each coder had to pass written and viewing tests with scores that were at least 90% correct according to predetermined criteria.

After completing training, coders continued to participate in approximately four hours of training each week and to receive periodic retesting to inhibit "coder drift" from the original intent of specific definitions. These follow-up sessions reinforced distinctions and promoted consistent application of ratings. To promote coder effectiveness and facilitate ongoing training, all coders specialized in one of the four interactional tasks.

Coders for a specific task were randomly assigned to a family. After viewing the assigned task for that family one time to get an overall sense of the content, the observer randomly selected one of the family members to be the focal person. The coder then viewed the tape a minimum of two times for this family member and two times for each of the remaining members present in the task. During each of the viewings, observers stopped or paused at any time as they pleased, but were cautioned not to lose the flow or context of the interaction. During and after each viewing the observer could take notes and jot down tentative ratings. After finishing the viewing for one focal person but before proceeding to the next, the coder indicated on a scoring sheet a more or less final rating. The amount of time required for an observer to complete the ratings for all family members averaged a high of 8 hours for Task 1 to a low of 3 hours for Task 3; overall, each family required about 20 hours of coding time.

Evaluating observational data. To assess the consistency with which observers rated behaviors, 12% of the videotapes in each task were selected at random for consistency checks. Both interobserver and intra-observer reliability (internal consistency) for the interactional codes used in the following analyses are reported as appropriate in each chapter. Interobserver reliability refers to the extent to which two independent observers agree in their assignment of a score to observed behavior. Following Suen and Ary's (1989, pp. 115–129) recommendation, inter-observer reliability was measured using the generalizability coefficient, an intraclass correlation that may vary computationally depending on the design of the observational protocol.

This approach to evaluating observational data is grounded in classical test theory and requires that one meet the assumptions of the parallel test model as outlined in elementary psychometric texts (Nunnally, 1978). For pencil-and-paper tests, the assumptions of parallel forms can lead to several different strategies for estimating reliability, one of which is the equivalent-forms strategy. When two observers of family interactions are given identical training and identical sets of behavioral definitions, use an identical coding scheme, and are as similar as possible in many other respects, then they are analogous to equivalent forms of the same test. Under this condition, the interobserver correlation serves as an estimate of the intraobserver reliability. Interobserver correlations (i.e., intraclass correlations) can range from -1 to 1, with negative values indicating that the assumptions of the parallel test model have not been met (Suen & Ary, 1989, p. 126). For those instances in which ratings were summed within observers to create a more global measure of family interactions, the usual alpha test for internal consistency was used to estimate intraobserver reliability.

MODELING FAMILY DATA

The data collection procedures just described were elaborate and time-consuming. Our purpose in instituting them was to evaluate specific dimensions of our Family Stress Model, and related models as needed for the question at hand. In particular, we hoped to identify and describe how key family processes unfold in the face of economic stress.

The general approach used in many of the subsequent chapters to model the data is referred to under the rubric of "structural equation models (SEM) with latent variables" (Bollen, 1989), which combines the visual methods and calculus of path analysis with the indirect measurement of concepts from the classical psychometric tradition. This approach is appropriate when the sample size is relatively large and realism in measurement is of paramount importance. It is especially applicable in situations such as ours, where most concepts are conceived of as continuous and are measured from both questionnaire and observational sources.

In this section, elementary path models are used to show how theoretical relationships between variables can be elaborated, and then the conventions of path analysis are used to illustrate random and systematic measurement error and their effects on the modeling process.

The Path-Analytic Tradition

Our modeling efforts began with a priori theories whose causal order was justified on the basis of experimental evidence, previous literature, or prior attempts to model analogous processes. Our general Family Stress Model, and its specific application to economic stress, was presented in Chapter 1 and illustrated in Figures 1.1 through 1.3. Elaborations of this basic model, and the rationale for each variation, are articulated in subsequent chapters. The causal ordering of these path models is not ascertained from the data, yet these models are attractive because they make theoretical reasoning about causal mechanisms explicit and open to criticism, and they provide a framework within which statistical tests can be interpreted.

Path analysis refers to recursive models with the magnitude and direction of specific paths expressed as standardized regression coefficients (Duncan, 1975). By convention, path models distinguish between exogenous and endogenous variables. Exogenous variables, such as the four variables measuring economic conditions on the left side of Figure 1.1 in the previous chapter, are taken as given. All other variables are endogenous and presumably explained by combinations of exogenous variables and/or prior endogenous variables.

Over the years, the path-analytic tradition has been subsumed by a growing econometric literature to include nonrecursive "simultaneous" equations models and unstandardized "structural" coefficients (e.g., Judge, Griffiths, Hill, & Lee, 1988). Path analysis is frequently used to evaluate empirically one argument with another, especially when one model is a special case of, or "nested in," another (Bollen, 1989), and to evaluate direct and indirect effects of one variable upon another (Alwin & Hauser, 1975; Fox, 1980, 1985). In Figure 1.3, for example, the path model is asserting that parents' emotional distress affects their parenting behavior directly, but also indirectly through marital conflict. Figure 1.2 asserts that family economic pressure affects marital conflict both directly as well as indirectly through the parent's emotional distress. The relationship between economic pressure and parenting, however, is expected to be entirely indirect through parental mood and marital conflict, That is, the path linking economic pressure to disrupted parenting is hypothesized to equal zero.

Traditionally, direct effects have been evaluated by comparing the magnitude of coefficients to their standard errors. In recent years, advances by Sobel (1982, 1986) have made it possible to calculate the standard errors of indirect effects as well. In the following discussion we explicate these analytic strategies as they apply to theoretical models such as those outlined in Chapter 1.

Mediating variables in path models. Chapters in this book take advantage of path analysis to specify how previously established relationships can be elaborated by introducing theoretically important mediating and moderating processes (Baron & Kenny, 1986; Rosenberg, 1968; Wheaton, 1985). Mediating variables are important because they advance our understanding about how and why economic hardship and pressure have deleterious effects on important outcomes such as marital quality and adolescent behaviors. As examples, social support from within and outside the family are modeled as mediating mechanisms that affect the relationship between economic pressure and parents' depression in Figure 8.1 (Chapter 8). Similarly, Figure 9.2 (Chapter 9) shows that husband's hostile interactions with his wife provide a mediating mechanism to explain why a wife's marital quality is adversely affected by her husband's depressed mood and her family's economic pressure. In Figure 10.2 (Chapter 10) mother's hostility toward her husband is presented as an intervening variable that mediates the relationship between economic pressure and the extent to which she engages in harsh parenting practices.

Moderating variables in path models.   If a theoretically interesting relationship between an explanatory concept such as economic pressure and an outcome is contingent upon the value of a third variable, that third variable is referred to as a *moderator* (Baron & Kenny, 1986; Finney, Mitchell, Cronkite, & Moos, 1984; Wheaton, 1985). Moderating variables advance our understanding of family processes by specifying the conditions under which explanatory variables affect selected outcomes. In classical regression or analysis of variance, interaction variables are created as a product of the moderator and explanatory variables, and evidence of a moderator effect is given by the presence of a significant statistical interaction between the two.

When estimating the more complex models proposed in this book, the most insightful way to deal with interaction terms is to dichotomize the moderator variable and compare the resulting groups simultaneously. Evidence of moderator effects appears in Table 8.4 (Chapter 8), where the relationship between wives' depression and family and extrafamilial support is contingent upon family income: In families with low incomes, wives' depression is strongly related to family support, but in higher income families, depression depends more on extrafamilial social support. Moderator effects are also in evidence in Figure 10.4 (Chapter 10) where the magnitude of the relationship between economic pressure and mother's harsh parenting depends on whether the support she receives from her husband is relatively high or low.

Estimating Random Measurement Error

In the following chapters, the logic and algebra of path analysis is extended to express the relationship between theoretical concepts and their measures, or indicators. This application of path analysis is valuable because testing theories about relationships among concepts requires careful attention to the way in which concepts are connected to their indicators (Blalock, 1968). In our present study of Iowa families, the most important and interesting concepts (e.g., marital quality, spouse's hostility, parenting behaviors) are not always directly observable in their various manifestations, nor do they have obvious metrics (scoring schemes) linking them to the physical world. Instead, they are either indirectly or only partially observed, with no logical arguments or formulas to show exactly how the concept should be measured. The ambiguity this creates is manifest in the distinct problems of random and systematic measurement error. Although methodologists are developing new and better techniques for asking questions in ways that minimize response errors (Biemer, Groves, Lyberg, Mathiowetz, & Sudman, 1991), it remains the task of the data analyst to harness these sources of error in the modeling process.

The implications of indirect or partial measurement on random measurement error are traditionally understood in the context of classical psychometric measurement theory (Nunnally, 1978; Zeller & Carmines, 1980), which states that an observed score X is equal to the "true score" plus measurement error:

$$X = x + e$$

The observed score X could be an item from a questionnaire, an index constructed from multiple items, or a behavioral rating obtained from observing a videotape. Classical measurement theory argues that if the expected mean score for the error term is zero [$E(e) = 0$], if the error term is uncorrelated with the true score [$E(e, x) = 0$], and if the errors between two separate measures are uncorrelated [$E(e_i, e_j) = 0$], then the variance of each observed indicator, X_i, can be partitioned into "true score" and "error" variance:

$$\text{var}(X_i) = \text{var}(x) + \text{var}(e_i)$$

where var(x) is assumed to be the true variance, and the remaining variance var(e_i) is randomly distributed, with $E(e_i) = 0$. The reliability of an indicator is defined as the proportion of variance in the variable X_i that is explained by concept x (Bollen, 1989, pp. 206–209):

$$\rho^2_{Xx} = \text{var}(x)/\text{var}(X_i)$$

In simple regression, one important consequence of random measurement error is that it reduces, or attenuates, the relationships among observed variables. If the relationship between some explanatory variable X and its response Y is represented by the path coefficient β_{YX}, then the path coefficient is obtained from the equation

$$\beta_{YX} = \text{cov}(XY)/\text{var}(X)$$

However, to the extent that var(X) contains random error variance var(e), the denominator will be too large because the variance of X is

larger then the true variance var(x), and the resulting estimate of β_{YX} will
be too small. This consequence of random measurement error is commonly understood in the case of simple regression, but its consequence is
not as clear in the case of multiple regression or in path analysis, where
several regression equations are involved. As Bollen demonstrates alge-
braically (1989, pp. 159–175), collinearity between explanatory variables
means that all coefficients are affected by measurement error in one or
more of the explanatory variables, but not all in the same way: Some
coefficients may be smaller, while others may be larger.

Models for Random Measurement Error

Despite the implications of measurement error, a common situation in
modeling social science data is to ignore it. One argument for ignoring it
is that the relationship between the concept and its measure is obvious,
and the magnitude of the error is so slight that it is reasonable to assume
a perfect correspondence between the indicator (what you see) and the
concept itself. The status variable sex of respondent, for example, is
clearly understood and usually coded correctly. In our study, measurement error is ignored for concepts for which we lack the auxiliary information needed to estimate it. Examples include the four economic
exogenous variables described in Chapter 1 (Figure 1.1) and elaborated
in Chapter 4. Income, debt-to-asset ratio, work instability, and income
loss are all measured under the assumption that the error variance is
zero. Researchers do not really believe these variables are measured
without error, but the relationships between these concepts and their
measures are relatively clear and well-understood. We understand income per capita as it is expressed in dollar amounts, and we trust families
to give us their best estimate of it. For other measures, the linkage between indicator and construct may be less straightforward and additional
information may be used to evaluate the adequacy of measurement as
part of the modeling process.

Multiple indicators of concepts. The auxiliary information needed to
estimate measurement error may come from prior studies, from retesting, or by using multiple indicators of the same concept. Within the
context of the IYFP, we consciously developed multiple indicators of
concepts and systematically embedded them into our path models so that
we could estimate the magnitude of the error and correct for it.

The Interpersonal Social Evaluation List (ISEL), developed by Cohen
and Hoberman (1983) and used in Chapter 7 and 8 to measure perceptions of social support, provides a simple example of how measurement
error is estimated by incorporating multiple indicators into explicit mea-

surement models. Although taken out of context for purposes of illustration, Figure 2.1 shows four questionnaire items from the ISEL that were used as indicators of the belonging dimension of social support. The four items, presumed to have been sampled from a hypothetical population of items reflecting the domain of belonging (Nunnally, 1978), were "If I wanted to go on a trip for a day, I would have a hard time finding someone to go with me" (Y_1 in Figure 2.1); "I feel like I'm not always included by my circle of friends" (Y_2); "If I wanted to have lunch with a friend, I could easily find someone to join me" (Y_3); and "No one I know would throw a birthday party for me" (Y_4).

In the path model in Figure 2.1, the encircled variable η_1: Belonging is referred to as the latent variable, one that reflects the true score for the concept of belonging. The directed arrows (λ_{11}, λ_{21}, λ_{31}, λ_{41}) pointing from belonging to the four questionnaire items in Figure 2.1 imply that individuals' responses to the items are viewed as indications, or symptoms, of their true sense of belonging. Although the four items are presumed to measure the same concept, individual responses to each item may differ. These differences are attributed to a variety of reasons, summarized as the *unique variance,* or measurement error variance, of that item. This measurement error is presumed to be random as long as it remains uncorrelated with other indicators or concepts. The coefficients connecting each indicator to belonging can be interpreted either as factor weights in factor analysis or as standardized regression coefficients. Items with larger coefficients correspond more strongly to the underlying concept.

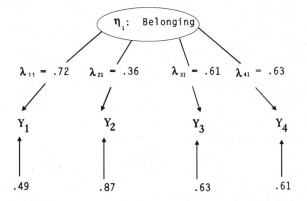

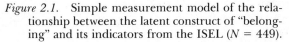

Figure 2.1. Simple measurement model of the relationship between the latent construct of "belonging" and its indicators from the ISEL ($N = 449$).

The proportion of variance in an observed indicator (Y_i) that is explained by the latent constructs provides a logically consistent way to estimate reliability (Bollen, 1989, pp. 218–221). For the simple model in Figure 2.1, squaring the regression weights gives an estimate of the variance in the observed indicator explained by the latent construct; the remaining variance is error variance. For Y_1, the coefficient of .72 means that about 51% of the variance in the first item is explained by the latent construct of belonging, and the remaining 49% is error variance.

Multiple indices of simple concepts.   The classical conception of random measurement error has been extended in several ways. First, many psychometric instruments contain too many items to effectively incorporate into a single model. One strategy to manage data in such instances is to create multiple indices of concepts, where each index consists of a number of questionnaire items either randomly assigned to it or assigned according to some criteria. The indices themselves are then used as multiple indicators to measure latent constructs (Newcomb & Bentler, 1986; Warren, White, & Fuller, 1974). Although some information is lost in combining questionnaire items, it reduces to a more manageable level the number of indicators you have to include in a model, and the new indices are more likely to have properties of "continuous" variables, especially when single items have limited response formats (e.g., Likert scales).

A second strategy for combining multiple indicators or concepts is to create "moderately similar" indices (Newcomb, 1990). In Chapters 7 and 8, for example, we combine three traditional aspects of perceived social support—belonging, appraisal, and tangible support—to show how they are affected by personal resources (Chapter 7) and how they mediate the relationship between economic pressure and depressive symptoms (Chapter 8). The justification for combining these three factors came, in part, from the second-order factor analysis shown in Figure 2.2. (These dimensions also have been examined separately to determine if they relate differently to important explanatory variables.)

The items on the right, labeled Y_1 to Y_{12}, are the 12 items measuring perceived social support. As demonstrated in previous research (see Cohen, Mermelstein, Kamarck, & Hoberman, 1985), the first four items represent the dimension of belonging, described in Figure 2.1, the second four represent appraisal, the extent to which you have someone who can help you make judgments about important decisions in life, and the last four reflect tangible support, the extent to which you have someone who will provide instrumental support when needed. As in Figure 2.1, the coefficients to the far right are the unique (error) variances. The first-order factor loadings link the specific items to the latent constructs of belonging (η_1), appraisal (η_2), and tangible support (η_3). These coefficients range from a low of 0.39 (Y_2) to a high of 0.78 (Y_{10}). Because the second-order factor scores linking the concept ξ: Social Support to belonging (.73), appraisal (.98), and tangible support (.82) are all quite high (Figure 2.2), we conclude that this second-order construct adequately describes the data and can legitimately be used in later analyses.

Multiple sources of information. A small number of family researchers has recently extended the ideas and logic of classical psychometrics even further to include multiple sources of information. We believe this work has major implications for both family research and the social and behavioral sciences in general. For researchers in the IYFP, a major impetus for us to move in this direction came from the work of Patterson and his colleagues at the Oregon Social Learning Center (Patterson, 1982; Capaldi & Patterson, 1989). They have argued that "a more generalizable model, using multiple indicators from different informants and

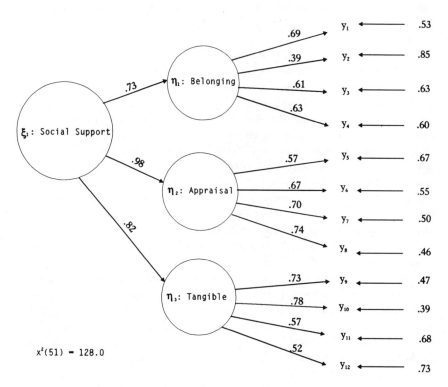

$x^2(51) = 128.0$

Figure 2.2. Second-order confirmatory factor analysis of three dimensions of father's social support ($N = 439$).

based on different methods, could be used to form latent variables," which in turn "ought to far more successfully predict theoretically important outcomes regardless of how each outcome was measured" (Bank & Patterson, 1991, pp. 2–3). This method of "triangulating" on an indirectly observed concept by combining indicators from several sources is repeated throughout this volume. Whenever possible, we attempt to construct latent variables by using reports from self, other, and observer, where *other* most often refers to the spouse of an adult, as in Chapters 8 and 9, or to the parent or sibling of the target child, as in Chapters 10 and 12. *Other* may also refer to the target's report of his or her parent's behavior, or vice versa.

As an example, husband's hostility can be measured by asking him how hostile he is, by asking the wife and/or the two children in the study how hostile he is, and by observing his behavior when he interacts with his family (Figure 2.3). This specific example is implemented in Chapter 9. Father's self-report of his hostility was based on items that recorded the extent of his discomfort during the past week because of his "temper outbursts that you could not control," "getting into frequent arguments," "shouting or throwing things," and "getting into arguments with my family or co-workers" (Derogatis, 1983). All items were measured on a 5-point scale from *not at all* to *extremely*, and summed to form a single index.

In a similar manner, indices were created for wife reports and observer ratings of husband's hostility. Wives were asked how often, during the past month, their husband had "criticized you or your ideas," "shouted or yelled at you because he was mad at you," "ignored you when you tried to talk to him," "threatened to do something that would upset you if you didn't do what he wanted," "tried to make you feel guilty," "got into a fight or argument with you," "hit, pushed, grabbed, or shoved you," and "argued with you whenever you disagreed about something." As a third source of information, observers used the categories discussed earlier in this chapter to rate husbands in both the second and fourth tasks on their overt acts of hostility toward their wives.

These different sources of information are not perfectly correlated because different informants are reporting on different aspects of husband's hostility. However, reports from these different agents may serve as multiple indicators of latent concepts because they converge on that element of common variance that is apparent to all observers and that may be salient to the theoretical relationships described in the model (Achenbach, McConaughy, & Howell, 1987; Furman, Jones, Buhrmester, & Adler, 1989). Figure 2.3 shows the results when this approach is applied to husband's hostility. The factor weight relating the latent variable, husband's hostility, to his own report is .39; the weights are .61 and .52 for spouse report and observer report, respectively. As in Figure 2.1,

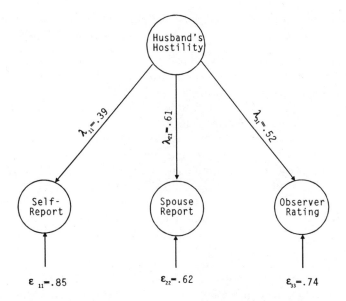

Figure 2.3. Multiple-indicator model of husband's hostility, using indices from self-reports, spouse reports, and observer ratings ($N = 430$).

squaring these coefficients provides an estimate of the variance in an indicator that is explained by the underlying concept.

Modeling Systematic Measurement Error

From a modeling perspective, a second reason for collecting data from multiple informants is that it provides researchers with an opportunity to examine certain kinds of systematic measurement error. Systematic measurement error reflects on the validity of one or more of our measures (Zeller & Carmines, 1980).

Traditionally, the validity of a concept is defined as the extent to which our items and indices actually measure the concepts they were intended to measure. In developing measures of concepts, IYFP researchers have had to be self-conscious and vigilant about the content of their indicators. Although content validity is the most intersubjective of all the validity criteria, it remains the one upon which measures of concepts ultimately stand or fall in the community of scholars. In developing new indices, authors of chapters had to demonstrate to themselves and others that selected questionnaire items or observer ratings tap the relevant domain of the concept, and that they do not tap competing or confounding concepts. In many cases content validity was best achieved by using indices previously developed by others and tested in earlier research.

Method variance. One particularly important manifestation of systematic measurement error is *method variance bias,* a problem that arises when the magnitude of a relationship between two or more concepts depends on one's source of information. One important advantage of using information from multiple informants is that it facilitates a careful examination of the systematic measurement error associated with method variance.

Although the problem of method variance is an old one, only since 1959 has it been cast in an analytically useful framework. Campbell and Fiske's (1959) multitrait-multimethod (MTMM) matrix provides a visual means to diagnose threats to the convergent and divergent validity of one's concepts, but it has not led to advances in managing the problem. As Bank et al. observed in their discussion of multiple traits and methods, no one since Cattell (1957) has

> systematically set out to deal with the method variance problem in a programmatic way. In fact, because efforts to deal within the multitrait-multimethod matrix have uniformly been less than clear successes, investigators have apparently removed the method-bias problem from the scientific agenda. (1990, pp. 259–260)

In recent years, scientific concerns about method variance have had a renaissance, perhaps for two reasons. Substantively, family researchers have been looking closely at intrafamily processes, which traditionally were assessed by reports from a single family member, usually the wife and mother. Increasingly, however, interest in a broader view of family life has led to the collection of data from husbands, wives, and siblings (Conger et al., 1990; Furman et al., 1989; Patterson et al., 1989). From a statistical perspective, MTMM matrices based on such multi-informant data can be estimated using methods of confirmatory factor analysis (CFA). Examining method variance within the CFA framework opens up the more optimistic viewpoint that if it can be modeled, it can be understood, and perhaps incorporated into a new generation of social science research.

As one example from our research, economic influences on husband's depression and hostility and wife's marital quality are modeled in Chapter 9. Each of the family process and mood concepts is measured using questionnaire responses from both husbands and wives, plus observer ratings. Self, spouse, and observer reports of husband's depression are developed in detail in Chapter 9. The self-report of marital quality was obtained by asking the wife how happy and how satisfied she is with her marriage. Husbands were asked to indicate "your wife's degree of happiness, all things considered, with your relationship." Observers rated a category labeled "relational quality" in the marital task, Task 4.

The confirmatory factor analysis of these three concepts is shown on the left side of Figure 2.4. Ideally, a 3-factor model—the 3 factors on the left side of the figure—should fit the data reasonably well, as indicated by strong factor loadings linking the three concepts to their indicators. However, only wife's report of husband's depression (.80) loaded strongly on the factor it was intended to measure; instead, husband self-report (.39) and observer report (.36) are relatively weakly related to his depression. The results for the hostility concept are similar.

Substantial improvements in the model were gained by fitting the Husband, Wife, and Observer factors shown on the right. These are the "method" factors because they link indicators of concepts to their source of the information. For husbands, the strong factor loadings relating to depression (.63) and hostility (.56) indicate that they have difficulty distinguishing their feelings of depression from their reports of their own hostile behaviors. Wives are able to distinguish husband's depression (.18) from his hostility (.44) and her marital quality (−.41), but the relatively large magnitude of these latter two coefficients suggests that they

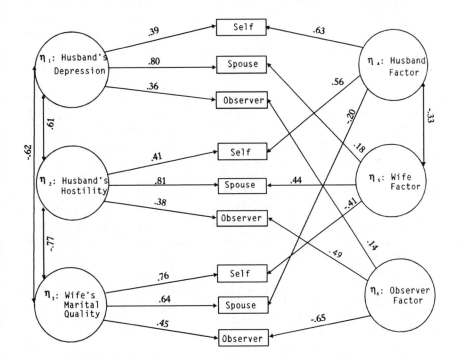

$x^2(14) = 18.7$

Figure 2.4. A MTMM matrix of husband's depression and hostility and wife's marital quality ($N = 439$).

are less successful in discriminating between his hostility and her assessment of the marriage. Similarly, observer ratings of husband's hostility (.49) correspond to ratings of relational quality (−.65). The presence of method factors in this model reflects the inability of individual respondents to separate and keep distinct conceptually important concepts. Psychologists have developed attributional explanations of this phenomenon (Sillars, 1985), but much work remains before researchers will be able to successfully anticipate and avert the modeling problems it causes. The important point here, however, is that analyses describing family stress processes must specifically model these reporter biases to improve our understanding of how they affect estimation of causal relationships. The following discussion illustrates the importance of this perspective.

Method variance in path models. Systematic measurement error due to method variance bias becomes a substantive problem when the source of information alters the relationships among concepts. The substantive importance of the method variance bias becomes obvious when measurement models are incorporated into path analysis. One can construct a simple model from the data used in Figure 2.4. In Figure 2.5, for example, the exogenous variable is economic pressure, measured with three indicators developed in Chapter 4, while the endogenous variables are, from left to right, husband's depression, husband's hostility, and wife's marital quality. The argument for this causal ordering derives from the Family Stress Model as elaborated in Chapter 9. The simplex model shown here is for expository purposes only.

Figure 2.5(a) is a monomethod model because all information is from a single source—in this case, from the wife. The resulting coefficients are strong: wife's marital quality is strongly related to her husband's hostility (−.65), which in turn is strongly predicted by his depression (.48). For this model the coefficients are probably inflated, especially for the path linking marital quality to husband's hostility, for reasons witnessed in Figure 2.4: Wives' responses to items indicative of husband's hostility and marital quality are affected by the wife's inability to differentiate these concepts, as captured by the presence of the Wife method factor.

In Figure 2.5(b), however, husband's self-reports are substituted for wife's reports of his depression and hostility, with the effect being substantially weaker, although still statistically significant, links between wife's marital quality and husband's hostility (−.16) and between his hostility and depression (.15).

In Figure 2.5(c), we configure a model in which none of the information on the endogenous variables is received from the same source. Wives report on their marital quality, husbands on their depression, and observers report on husband's hostility. The results are again different:

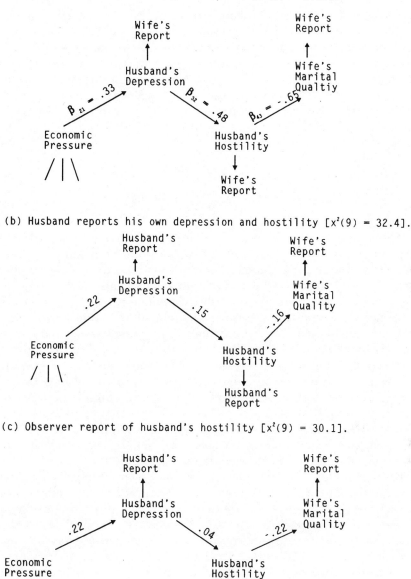

(a) Monomethod model: all wife reports [$x^2(9) = 37.7$].

Wife's
Report

Wife's
Report

Husband's
Depression

Wife's
Marital
Qualtiy

$\beta_{21} = .33$

$\beta_{32} = .48$

$\beta_{43} = -.65$

Economic
Pressure

Husband's
Hostility

/ | \

Wife's
Report

(b) Husband reports his own depression and hostility [$x^2(9) = 32.4$].

Husband's
Report

Wife's
Report

Husband's
Depression

Wife's
Marital
Quality

.22

.15

.16

Economic
Pressure

Husband's
Hostility

/ | \

Husband's
Report

(c) Observer report of husband's hostility [$x^2(9) = 30.1$].

Husband's
Report

Wife's
Report

Husband's
Depression

Wife's
Marital
Quality

.22

.04

-.22

Economic
Pressure

Husband's
Hostility

/ | \

Observer
Report

Figure 2.5. A comparison of effects of source of report on the magnitude of coefficients in a simplex model of husband's depression and hostility and wife's marital quality ($N = 439$).

the relationship between husband's hostility and wife's marital quality
(−.22) is stronger than in the previous frame (Figure 2.5b), but significantly weaker than in the monomethod model. In this last model, there is
no statistically significant relationship between husband's depression and
his hostility. The findings in Figure 2.5 suggest that the magnitude of
relationships between constructs can be over or underestimated depending on the source of information employed. In many instances this problem can be addressed by simultaneously using multiple reporting agents,
as demonstrated in later chapters.

MODEL INTEGRATION AND EVALUATION

These preceding analyses tell us that we must carefully consider the
psychometric properties of our measures, including their source, in evaluating our Family Stress Model. Thus, our first priority in modeling the
data is to relate analyses to theoretical arguments that capture the essence of
the process under investigation, while simultaneously considering the
influence of the reporting agent on model estimation. Taking both theoretical and measurement issues into account, findings are summarized as path
models that integrate realistic measures of concepts directly into the
network of relationships among variables. For some variables—especially
our measures of objective economic conditions—we had only single indicators of concepts. But for many others, we constructed multiple indicators of
concepts. Utilizing structural equation procedures allowed us to separate
random error variance from true score variance and thus to obtain estimates of relationships among concepts that, unlike ordinary least squares
regression, are corrected for attenuation (Bollen, 1989).

Perhaps most important, one of our goals in modeling data was to
manage the systematic measurement error associated with method variance. In some situations, we attempted to disentangle the pernicious effects
of monomethod models by alternating informants, as we did in Figure
2.5(c), so that no two adjacent concepts are measured using reports from
the same informant. This ad hoc procedure, first suggested to us by Bank et
al. (1990), eliminates the problem of the inflated coefficients we saw in
Figure 2.5(a), but it is an untenable strategy in models with dense networks
of interrelationships, and it does not encourage one to measure concepts
with the best indicators possible or with a complete complement of indicators.

Where it is clearly appropriate, we attempt to generalize a concept by
including information from multiple informants, often using the self,
other (spouse, child, parent), observer strategy mentioned earlier. This
does not rid us of method variance, but it does allow us to monitor it by
actually incorporating it into the modeling process. On several occasions in

subsequent chapters, we include method factors in the model; more often, the presence of method variance is incorporated by correlating errors between indicators of different concepts that are obtained from a common source.

Model Evaluation

Having hypothesized a model or set of models, how does one go about testing and evaluating them? Essentially, there are two overarching questions researchers ask when evaluating empirical tests of theoretical models: (1) How well does a specific path compare to its hypothesized value? (2) How well does the model, taken as a whole, fit the data? The presence of a path linking two concepts, or linking a concept to its indicator, is an assertion that a relationship exists, while the absence of a path between two concepts ($\beta = 0$) or between a concept and an indicator ($\lambda = 0$) implies that they are unrelated.

The hypothesis associated with each path is usually evaluated with a t-test. In addition, the credibility of each path, and ultimately the model as a whole, depends on whether specific paths have the expected sign, whether the standard errors are so large as to suggest misspecification or unusual multicollinearity, and whether there are inappropriate coefficients, such as negative values associated with estimates of variances (for discussion of Heywood cases, see Rindskopf, 1984). In Figure 2.5(a), the coefficients linking concepts are all significant and in the predicted direction, but Figure 2.5(c) provides little evidence to link husband's depression to his hostility because the path coefficient is quite small (.04) and the associated t-test is 0.80, much less than the customary 2.0 used to infer statistical significance in SEM (Bollen, 1989).

The answer to the second question, How well does the model fit the data? is usually couched in terms of the chi-square goodness-of-fit statistic. This evaluative strategy starts by noting that a model fits the data perfectly when the chi-squared statistic is zero, and then asks: How large of a departure from zero is permitted before we conclude that the model does not adequately fit the data? As an overall test of a model, the chi-squared statistic is computed by minimizing the difference between the observed covariance (or correlation) matrix S and the matrix Σ that is generated by estimates of the parameters of the model. Although there are numerous ways in which this minimum difference can be calculated, the procedure applied in most subsequent chapters is the method of maximum likelihood (Bentler, 1989; Joreskog & Sorbom, 1989).

A model is said to fit the data if the difference between S and Σ generates a chi-squared statistic that is small enough to be deemed due to chance. One problem with this approach, as well as other evaluative criteria, is that many models can fit the data, and selecting from among them is a substantive problem and not a statistical one (Berk, 1979).

Another problem with the overall chi-squared goodness-of-fit statistic is that it is difficult to reject a model if the sample size is small and difficult to accept if it is large. For this reason, several authors in this monograph use the *goodness-of-fit index* (GFI) to take sample size into account, but it remains sensitive to the number of parameters being estimated and it has no known distribution (Joreskog & Sorbom, 1989). An *adjusted goodness-of-fit index* (AGFI) attempts to adjust for the ratio of parameters estimated to degrees of freedom.

From a somewhat different perspective but still within the same framework, Hoelter's (1983) critical N represents an attempt to use sample size as a measure of fit. The idea is that if a model does not fit a large sample, what sample size would be necessary for the model to fit at .10? .05? etc. Or, if a model fits a small sample, how large a data set would be required to reject the model? Obviously in both cases, the better the model, the larger the sample size. Hoelter argues that a critical N of 200 or more suggests the model fits the data.

Comparing hierarchically related models. Despite these numerous attempts to fix the chi-squared statistic, most researchers are not satisfied with the results and have sought alternative approaches to model evaluation. Two related approaches that are gaining acceptance, described in this section and the next, attempt to place a theoretical model into a larger context by comparing it to hierarchically related alternative models. The first of these evaluative strategies is based largely on the procedures advocated by Bentler and Bonett (1980) and Anderson and Gerbing (1988, 1992), and yet is sensitive to the criticisms raised by Fornell and Yi (1992).

Hierarchically related models are often referred to as *nested models*, an idea that is best explained by examples. Referring again to the concept of perceived social support, previous researchers have raised questions about whether indices such as the ISEL tap a distinctive concept or whether they reflect just another aspect of one's cognitive structure or personality (Lakely & Cassidy, 1990). In Figure 2.6, Model A is constructed so that the three dimensions of perceived social support are viewed as part of a common personality factor, along with one's mastery (Pearlin, Lieberman, Menaghan & Mullan, 1981), self-esteem (Rosenberg, 1965), and coping ability (Costa & McCrae, 1985). Mastery is measured by a 7-item scale indicating the degree to which a person feels in control of life events. A high score on the 10-item self-esteem scale indicates a high sense of self-worth. The coping scale, which is the 8-item vulnerability scale (reverse-coded) from the NEO Personality Inventory, measures the degree to which a person perceives he or she can handle crises or emergencies. This model does not fit the data very well, as indicated by the large chi-squared statistic $[\chi^2(9) = 276.40]$.

Model A [X²(9) = 276.40]

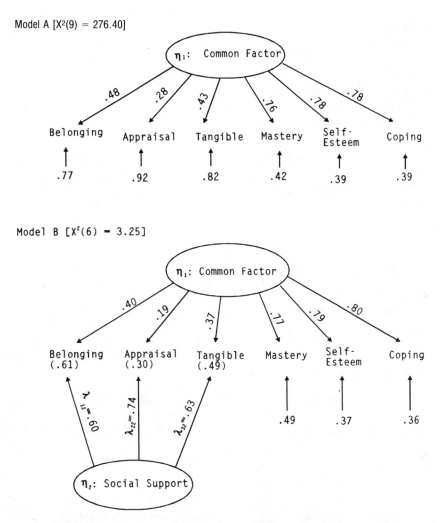

Figure 2.6. A comparison of dimensions of social support when modeled as (A) an indicator of a common personality concept and (B) a distinct subindex within the common personality concept.

Evidence for a distinct, separate concept of social support is provided by comparing Model A to Model B. In the language of SEM, Model A is said to be nested in Model B; that is, Model A can be seen as a special case of Model B, the case where paths λ_{12}, λ_{22}, and λ_{32} in Model B are set equal to zero. When two models are nested, one can directly compare chi-squared statistics. Under conditions that meet the assumptions of the chi-squared distribution, the change in chi-squared is itself distributed as a chi-squared statistic. For Model B, $\chi^2(6) = 3.25$, so that the change in chi-squared is large [$\chi^2(3) = 273.15$]. By nesting the three dimensions of social support as a subfactor within the more general personality factor, we were able to establish that the three traditional dimensions of the ISEL's social support represent something more than a repetition of these personality constructs.

By using nested models and by interpreting the change in chi-squared as a chi-squared statistic, certain theoretically interesting models can be compared. Figure 2.7 presents an array of nested models, beginning with a relatively restricted model in Figure 2.7(a). In Model 1, the four concepts of economic pressure, husband's depression, husband's hostility, and wife's marital quality are presented without arrows connect-

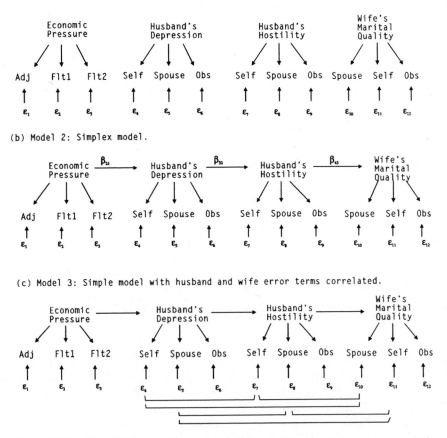

Figure 2.7. Alternative nested models linking economic pressure to marital quality ($N = 439$).

ing them, implying that they are independent and unrelated. Economic pressure is measured with the same three indicators as in Figure 2.5, which are described in Chapter 4. Husband's depression is measured by three indicators: the husband's self-report of his depression (Self), his wife's assessment (Spouse), and an observer's rating (Obs) of his depression as gleaned from videotapes of his behavior toward other family members (details of these measures are developed in Chapter 9). The concept of husband's hostility and wife's marital quality also are measured by indicators from each of the three sources.

In Figure 2.7, Model 1 is nested in Model 2; that is, Model 1 is the same as Model 2 except that paths β_{21}, β_{32}, and β_{43} are set equal to zero. Likewise, Model 2 is nested in Model 3, the difference being that in Model 3 the correlations among the error terms associated with the

(d) Model 4: Simple model with husband, wife and observer error terms correlated.

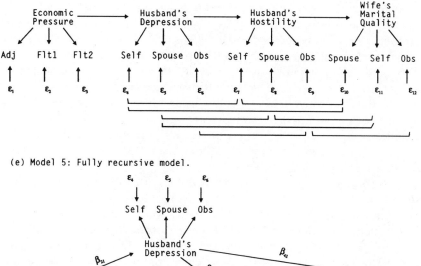

(e) Model 5: Fully recursive model.

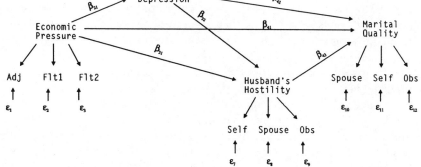

Figure 2.7.

husbands' and wives' responses are estimated while in Model 2 they are set equal to zero. Model 3, in turn, is nested in Model 4, a model in which the error terms associated with the observers' ratings are also correlated. Finally, Model 5 provides the fully recursive model, with each construct in the model predicting every construct to the right of it.

The relationships among these models are shown schematically in Figure 2.8. This figure suggests that Model 1 is not the most restrictive model one can imagine. Model 0 is even more restrictive, and represents the case where the 12 indicators of the four concepts are actually modeled as 12 independent concepts, each uncorrelated with the other. Models 0 and 1 will have interesting roles to play in model comparison: Model 0 represents the *null* model of independence suggested by Bentler and Bonett (1980), while Model 1 more closely reflects a theoretically interesting *baseline* model as proposed by Sobel and Bohrnstedt (1985).

The scheme in Figure 2.8 shows the hierarchical relationships among models, arranged so that the most restrictive models (Models 0 and 1) are presented at the top, and the least restrictive model (Model 7) is at the bottom. The scheme shows that Model 2 is nested in Model 3 and Model 3 in Model 4, but that neither Model 3 nor 4 is nested in either Model 5 or 6. Model 5, shown in Figure 2.7(e), is a *fully recursive* model in which all latent concepts are connected by a directed arrow. One can clearly see that Model 2 is nested in Model 5, the difference between Models 2 and 5 being that paths β_{31}, β_{41}, and β_{42} are set equal to zero in Model 2. Finally, Models 6 and 7 are also fully recursive models, but Model 6 has an error structure that parallels Model 3, and Model 7 has an error structure that parallels Model 4.

Each model in Figures 2.7 and 2.8 reflects a theoretically interesting situation. Model 2 is the researcher's dream: a parsimonious model with no significant structure to the error terms. Models 0 and 1 represent a researcher's nightmare: In Model 1, none of the concepts are related to each other, and in Model 0, not even indicators of concepts are correlated! Models 3 and 4 show the same parsimonious relationships among concepts as does Model 2, but they accommodate more complex arrangements among error terms. The least interesting model, because everything is related to everything else, is Model 7, which is fully recursive in its relationships among concepts, plus it has a complex arrangement of error terms.

Inspection of the chi-squared statistics associated with each of the models in Figure 2.8 implies that Model 7 fits the data best [$\chi^2(39) = 51$], and we conclude that since this chi-squared statistic is not significant, the model fit the data. However, we are also interested in knowing if any of the more parsimonious models also fits the data. By computing change in chi-squared, one can argue that Model 4 also fits the data, but Model 6

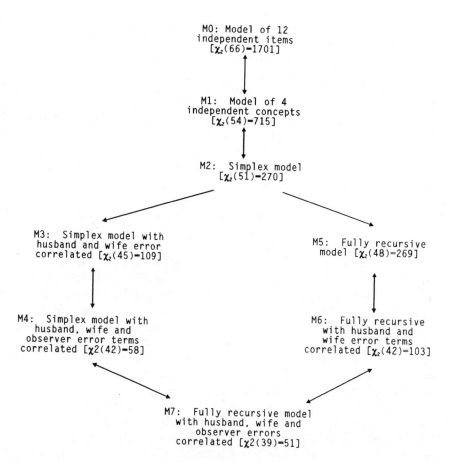

Figure 2.8. Comparing hierarchically related, nested models.

does not. The change in chi-squared associated with a comparison of Models 7 and 4 is $\chi^2(3) = 7$, which is not significant at the .05 level; hence, a case can be made for selecting the more parsimonious Model 4 over Model 7. However, other alternatives—alternatives that are appealing because they propose simpler error structures—are, according to this procedure of comparing models, remarkably inferior. We pursue a more extensive evaluation of Model 4 in Chapter 9.

Incremental fit indices. The change in chi-squared that results when two hierarchically related models are compared suffers from the same sensitivity to sample size as does the absolute value of the chi-squared statistic. To neutralize this effect and to give researchers better intuitions about the relative difference between two models, we have also compared models using incremental fit indices (Bollen 1989, pp. 269–281). The idea of an incremental fit index, as initially developed by Tucker and Lewis (1973), is roughly analogous to the R-squared statistic in regression. In regression, the implicit starting point, or baseline model, against which theoretically interesting models are compared is the null model of independence, expressed by the equation $y_i = \beta_0 + \epsilon_i$. This model, with $R^2 = 0$, argues in effect that the variable y is independent of all other variables $X_1, X_2, \ldots, X_k$.

Although several incremental fit indices have been proposed (Bentler, 1990; Bentler & Bonett, 1980; Bollen, 1989), we limit our discussion to the normed fit index, given as:

$$\delta_{hk|b} = \chi^2(h) - \chi^2(k)/\chi_2(b)$$

where $\chi(b)$ is a proposed baseline model with b degrees of freedom, $\chi(h)$ and $\chi(k)$ are two specific models being compared, and $\delta_{hk|b}$ states that we are comparing Model k to Model h, using Model b as a baseline.

An application of this evaluation strategy is demonstrated in Table 2.1, where the models referred to are those from Figures 2.7 and 2.8. In the second column of the table, the model of complete independence (Model M0 in Figure 2.8) is used as a baseline model because it represents the "most restrictive, theoretically defensible model" one can imagine (Bentler and Bonett, 1980, p. 600). Its chi-squared value of 1,701 becomes the denominator in the incremental fit index. When the model of independent concepts (Model M1) is fit to the data, the chi-squared statistic is 715, which according to the normed fit index is a reduction in the chi-squared of .58, or 58% when compared to Model M0. When the simplex Model M3 is compared to Model M1 using M0 as a baseline model, a further reduction in error of 26% is realized.

The third column of Table 2.1 uses Model M1 as a baseline rather than M0, a choice that was motivated by Sobel and Bohrnstedt's (1985) argument that the theoretically most restrictive model, rather than the most restrictive model one can imagine, should be used as a baseline. Using M1 as a reference point is based on the argument that the 12 indicators measuring the 4 concepts were purposely constructed to be interdependent, and to presume that they are not is artificial and deceptive. Thus, when using Model M1 as a baseline, the simplex Model M2 represents a relative improvement in chi-squared of 62% over M1; Model M3 represents an additional improvement of 23% over M2; Model M4 an additional improvement of 7%; and finally, Model M7 is an improvement of about 1% over M4. Since the proportional changes in chi-squared, calculated using these indices, is cumulative, we can also note in the third column that Model M3 represents an improvement of 85% over M1.

Using incremental fit indices to compare hierarchically related models provides a clearly different perspective on model fitting than is provided

Table 2.1. Model Comparisons Using Bentler's Normed Incremental Fit Index, Using Models from Figures 2.7 and 2.8

	Baseline model	
Model comparisons	*Model MO*	*Model M1*
Comparing models M1 and M0	$\delta_{01,0} = .58$	
Comparing models M2 and M1	$\delta_{12,0} = .26$	$\delta_{12,1} = .62$
Comparing models M3 and M2	$\delta_{23,0} = .10$	$\delta_{23,1} = .23$
Comparing models M4 and M3	$\delta_{34,0} = .03$	$\delta_{34,1} = .07$
Comparing models M7 and M4	$\delta_{47,0} = .00$	$\delta_{47,1} = .01$
Cumulative change	$\delta_{07,0} = .97$	$\delta_{17,1} = .93$

by the absolute value of the chi-squared statistic or even the change in chi-squared. Comparing Models M3 and M4 in Figure 2.8 leads one to note that the chi-squared statistic associated with M3 is about twice that of M4; certainly the change in chi-squared of 51 with 3 degrees of freedom is significant. But in relative terms, relative to Model M1, Model M3 represents an improvement of 85%, while the improvement of Model M4 over M3 is a relatively small, although perhaps nontrivial 7%.

CONCLUSIONS

As you proceed through this book, you will note that each chapter examines aspects of the Family Stress Model as applied to economic hardship in Chapter 1. Authors of these chapters elaborate the basic model by introducing theoretically interesting mediating and moderating variables, and then testing their models with data from our sample of 451 rural Iowa families.

The data used for testing these models were purposely collected to advance realism in the measurement of concepts. The detailed information we needed dictated that we get data from multiple family members and observe them as they interact with each other. One purpose of this chapter was to provide the reader with a rationale for the research design and a synopsis of the data collection procedures.

The credibility of the models examined in subsequent chapters depends on their proper specification, a theoretical issue that requires agreement and debate from within the community of scholars. But even with agreement about the specification of a model, there remain numerous threats to one's ability to test hypotheses, threats that result from random and systematic measurement error. The approach we have outlined in this chapter is to estimate and correct for random measurement error whenever possible by obtaining multiple indicators of concepts. In addition, obtaining multiple indicators from multiple sources serves to generalize our concepts, and in some situations it also allows us to model, and therefore manage, the systematic measurement error associated with method variance bias.

These attempts to address issues of random and systematic measurement error motivated us, in part, to think in terms of structural equation models (SEM) with latent variables. Certainly this approach to modeling data is not the only one, and it is easily abused. But our modeling efforts were theoretically driven and data-intensive, two characteristics that make SEM particularly attractive and relevant.

Although we hope that our efforts to obtain realistic measures of family member's attitudes, behaviors, and interactions will help to advance the discipline of family studies as a whole, we have only begun to penetrate some of the more difficult methodological issues that all researchers face, whether they systematically address them or not. Future waves of data collection on the IYFP will eventually enable us to extend our findings from cross-sectional results to the realm of a panel study. Multiple indicator data from multiple waves of data collection will permit more sensitive analyses than are currently possible, but they will also open up new methodological problems in need of solution. The pursuit of such solutions provides the grist for future advances in the understanding of family adaptation to the stresses and strains of everyday life.

In Chapters 1 and 2 (Part I) of this volume, we have provided some empirical, theoretical, and methodological background for this study of Iowa families during a time of rapid socioeconomic change. In Part II of the book, we change the focus to the historical context that helped to shape these families' recent experience and to a description of their past and current economic circumstances. These materials lay the groundwork for the later analyses linking economic hardship to family processes and individual behavior.

PART II

Rural Families and Communities

Chapter 3

Rural Economic and Social Trends

Paul Lasley

The Iowa economy is so poor and depressed that there is no use looking for a job locally. The state better look for ways to help keep people employed.
—IYFP father

Farming is both a business and a way of life. For many rural Iowa communities, farming is the primary economic base. The culture of these rural communities reflects their agrarian heritage. The blending of work roles into family life characterizes living in farm communities. Nearly everyone is somehow connected to farming. Those nonfarm jobs that exist are often in the agricultural supply or processing industries. The values and beliefs of the rural culture reflect a life-style and worldview that is shaped by the uncontrollable forces of nature.

Because farming provides both the economic and social basis of rural community life, changes in the financial conditions in farming hold important consequences for families and communities. Unlike other regions of the nation where rural communities often are dependent upon manufacturing, recreation, mining, or other industry, Iowa has a high dependence upon farming. Just as youngsters being raised on the prairie are conditioned to keep an eye on the horizon for ominous funnel clouds, residents in small towns keep close watch on commodity prices. Several times a day the local news reports on the futures market and farm prices at country grain elevators. Discussions in the local restaurants and coffee shops never veer far from the weather, prices, and crop conditions. It is well understood that farm prices hold consequences well beyond the farm gate.

Bender et al. (1985), in documenting the diverse socioeconomic conditions in nonmetropolitan counties, illustrate Iowa's heavy reliance upon farming. Their findings show that Iowa's counties draw heavily upon agriculture for their economic base. Many, though, view the state's heavy reliance upon farming as both a blessing and a bane. On the one hand, the rich, fertile land resources contained between the Mississippi and Missouri rivers has enabled the state to become the envy of the world in terms of food production. However, the heavy reliance upon farming has served to tie the future of many towns, and some would argue the entire state, to the prospects of farming. So long as the farm economy remains strong, the benefits flow across communities; but when the farm economy enters tough financial times or experiences a crop failure, the repercussions ripple throughout the entire economy.

As a major producer of field crops and livestock, Iowa consistently ranks among the top 10 producing states. This heavy reliance upon farming also affects the nonfarm employment structure. Major nonfarm employment exists in the supply and processing sectors of agriculture such as machinery, seed, milling, and slaughter houses. There is a close relationship between financial conditions on the farms and jobs and incomes in the nonfarm agricultural industries.

Perhaps, as some have argued, Iowa's relative prosperity in farming during previous decades has contributed to complacency about the need to diversify its economy. Prior to 1980 there was little perceived need to broaden the state's economic base and Iowa continued to rely upon the industry that made her great: farming. While some of the metropolitan areas actively recruited manufacturing and service industries, in the main, Iowa stayed the course and pursued agricultural development. Unfortunately, many small, rural, agriculturally dependent communities lacked either the resources or the will to change or diversify their economic structure. As the farm economy entered its worst financial decade since the Great Depression, agriculturally dependent communities were swept along in the flood waters of the farm crisis of the 1980s. The families in the present study are representative of those residing in these small rural towns. This chapter describes what happened in these agriculturally dependent communities as the farm crisis emerged and engulfed the state.

HISTORICAL PATTERNS

Farming is a risky business. Much of the imagery surrounding farming reflects the struggles of fiercely independent farmers trying to make a living in a hostile environment. Drought, insects, disease, and a host of uncontrollable natural forces have always created uncertainty in farming. Economic hardship and financial distress in farming are equally prominent and predictable as natural disasters.

The history of American agriculture is a series of recurring farm crises. Farming is characterized by periods of prosperity followed by periods of stagnation and economic hardship. Agricultural historians have noted the cyclical nature of farming (Cochrane, 1979). However, social scientists and farmers have tended to ignore the economic cycles. Given the length of the economic cycles in farming, perhaps individual farmers can be excused from ignoring these macrolevel historical forces. However, social scientists cannot be so easily excused. Following each burst of prosperity has been a period of recession or depression leading to readjustment. An often neglected component of these crises and adjustments has been their impact upon farm families and rural communities.

The boom-to-bust pendulum in farm economics is well established in agricultural history. Increasingly, as agriculture becomes integrated into the global economy, more risk and uncertainty are introduced. The events that heavily influence or determine farm prices lie beyond farmers' control. Crop failures halfway around the world or international politics far removed from farmers' daily activities exert much influence on price levels and who will be able to farm next year. What is much less understood is how these global external forces that determine farm profitability are reflected in the values and beliefs of rural people and how they become part of the culture of rural communities.

Events Leading Up to the Farm Crisis During the 1980s

Since 1950, there has been a substantial shift in the nature of rural America. Prior to World War II, much of rural America was synonymous with farming. In 1950, over 2,000 of the 2,443 nonmetropolitan U.S. counties were classified as farm dependent, defined as deriving at least 20% of total county earnings from farming. By 1980, only 505 nonmetropolitan counties were considered farm dependent (Bender, Green, Hady, Kuehn, Nelson, Perkinson, & Ross, 1985). The consequences of this transformation have not gone unnoticed. In 1940, nearly one-third of the nation's population lived on farms, compared with only about 2% in 1980. During this same time, farm numbers declined by over 60%, the average size of a farm more than doubled, and much of rural America diversified into nonagricultural industries. Economies based upon manufacturing, government services, recreation, and retirement replaced agriculturally dependent economic structures at the county level (Bender et al., 1985).

These national trends were quite pronounced in the Midwest, often viewed as the breadbasket of the world, as suggested by the fact that 859 of the 1,054 midwestern counties are classified as nonmetropolitan. Using Bender's typology, 38% of the midwestern nonmetropolitan counties are classified as farm dependent, 19% as manufacturing dependent, and 3% as mining-dependent. Thus, midwestern nonmetropolitan counties are more likely to be economically dependent on agriculture than similar counties elsewhere in the United States. Thus, they are especially vulnerable to financial downturns in farming.

The 1970s: Sowing the Seeds for the 1980s Farm Crisis

The seeds of the farm crisis of the 1980s were sown during the 1970s. Several events emerged during this decade that set the stage for the farm crisis in the 1980s. In the early 1970s, there was much concern about world hunger. In 1972, world food production declined by 33 million metric tons, the first decline in 20 years. The United Nations World Food Conference met in Rome in 1974 to consider the gloomy prospects of millions of hungry people across the world. Although world food stocks were sufficiently low to cause great concern at the World Food Conference, the United States was attempting to hold down domestic production through set-aside programs.

At the same time, global economic growth and population increases were creating new demands for food. New, rich, oil-producing countries and other industrial nations were actively searching for new sources of food stocks. Coinciding with these events, the Soviet Union purchased huge quantities of U.S. grain in 1972, marking the beginning of long-term trade agreements with the Soviets. In response to these multiyear trade agreements, U.S. agriculture entered into a period of expansion. Federal government set-aside or conservation policies were relaxed, and in some cases eliminated, to facilitate growth in the agricultural economy. Exports became increasingly important to offset trade deficits in other areas, particularly in oil imports. As the energy crisis deepened, there was heightened interest in using agricultural crops as alternative energy sources, providing additional impetus for increased farm production.

Farmers were once again optimistic about the future and responded to Secretary of Agriculture Butz's call to plant "fencerow to fencerow." Enormous amounts of capital were needed to finance the expansion of agriculture. Some farmers had personal funds to invest in their farms, but for the vast majority of farmers, this expansion was financed through borrowed capital. The farm debt increased from $11.2 billion in 1950 to about $60 billion in 1972, but then skyrocketed to $216 billion in 1983 (Harl, 1987). Farm income rose from about $25 billion in 1967 to $60 billion in 1983, and these profits were often reinvested in the agricultural industry.

In response to the renewed prosperity and nearly unbridled optimism, land values rapidly escalated as farmers bid up the prices of land to expand their operations. For example, in 1969, just preceding this boom period, the average value of an acre of Iowa farmland was $400, a figure that escalated to $1,700 by 1982. The value of the average farm during the same period increased from $94,000 to $471,000, a fourfold increase in only 13 years (Lasley & Goudy, 1982).

Reflecting the prosperity in farming, the general economy was growing and inflation rates were high. Inflation became an accepted part of the economy and was soon incorporated into investment decisions. It made sense and was economically rational to be in debt as long as the inflation rate exceeded the nominal interest rate. It was logical to borrow heavily and repay those debts with cheaper dollars in the future. Farmers were not alone in discovering the benefits of being in debt during periods of high inflation. Consumers, home buyers, and businesses purchased more on credit because it was assumed that "it will cost more next year." And government policies made borrowing money easier by keeping in place liberal monetary practices and allowing interest payments to be deducted from federal income taxes.

Farmers and lenders discovered the newfound source of wealth in property values as another method to borrow additional capital to finance even more expansion. Leveraging property at inflated values as collateral against loans to purchase machinery and new facilities was a frequently employed growth strategy. After all, property values continued to escalate and borrowers and lenders felt sure that land and real estate were good investments.

The renewed optimism about the future of rural America that was created by the prosperity in farming was contagious. Farmers had improved incomes, which were spent on new machinery, automobiles, houses, and other durable goods. This in turn created more jobs in manufacturing and business. As tax revenues increased, small towns and communities were able to make new investments in public buildings and utilities. For the first time in several decades, nonmetropolitan growth rates exceeded metropolitan rates and there was renewed faith in the rebirth of rural America. With increased preference for rural living, communities that had lain dormant for many years began to build additional housing and schools. Some people talked of a new rural renaissance that was occurring as urban people fled metropolitan areas and moved to small towns and villages.

The prosperity of the 1970s is reminiscent of the prosperous period during 1910–1914, often called the Golden Age of Agriculture. During this period, farm prices were high relative to the prices of nonfarm goods and this fueled belief in the agrarian ideology that hard work, frugality, and optimism would lead to the good life. Often the price ratio that existed in 1910–1914 is used as the standard called parity. However, with the close of World War I, farm prices began a decline and the agricultural economy slumped into a recession in 1920 that continued unabated throughout the depression years of the 1930s.

Similarly, the prosperity of the 1970s ended as policy changes occurred that were outside the control of agriculture. In response to what was termed runaway inflation late in the 1970s, the federal government was forced to act. In October 1979, the Federal Reserve Board attempted to curb inflation by raising the discount rate, thus raising interest rates to borrowers. In addition, indexing the inflation rate into retirement programs and other government programs contributed to higher inflation rates, which had an adverse influence on agriculture and other capital-intensive industries (Harl, 1987, 1990). Harl points out that the Economic Recovery Act of 1981 was responsible for massive federal budget deficits that also led to substantially higher interest rates for borrowers. The combined impact of these policies was to reduce the rate of inflation by restricting credit and creating high real interest rates. For heavily indebted farmers, higher interest rates posed a substantial problem in at least two ways: (1) they strengthened the value of the dollar relative to other world currencies and therefore reduced the demand for U.S. farm exports, and (2) they raised farmers' production costs.

Record high real interest rates, where the interest rates paid by borrowers exceeded the inflation rate by as much as 8–10%, led to substantial declines in farmland values. Farmers who had heavily leveraged inflated land values to buy additional land and equipment were faced with rapidly deteriorating financial conditions. They were forced to pay for expensive land and equipment with crops and livestock that were substantially reduced in value. In addition, many lenders began to call in risky loans to protect their positions. Credit dried up and soon the impact of these economic charges was visible along main streets across rural communities.

Where possible, farm families postponed purchases and made do with what they had, often repairing old farm machinery rather than replacing outdated equipment. In other cases, getting by meant buying less merchandise in general or shopping for lower prices even if quality was sacrificed. Soon farm equipment manufacturers found their inventories growing, and layoffs in agribusiness began to occur. Rural store owners and shopkeepers experienced declines in retail sales and often became financially distressed. Price cutting, promotions, and bargain days appeared as merchants tried to increase sales by offering discount prices. As this cycle continued, the entire state was soon caught in its worst financial condition since the 1930s.

*What Made the 1980 Farm Crisis Unique From Previous
Agricultural Recessions?*

Historically, farm families adjusted to tough economic times by reducing their expenditures. These belt-tightening efforts generally included spending less money for purchased goods. However, farming for the past 50 years has increasingly relied upon purchased inputs. Whereas pioneer families could hunker down by spending less money, farm families in the 1980s lacked the ability to cut expenses. The substitution of purchased inputs such as seed, fertilizer, fuel, and chemicals for farm-produced inputs such as labor and feed has been dramatic. The volume of purchased inputs nearly doubled between 1930 and 1970; farm machinery use increased by 212%; purchased feed, seed, and livestock products increased by 270%; fertilizer and chemical use increased by 1,800% (Cochrane, 1979). The dramatic shift of substituting purchased inputs for nonpurchased inputs has reduced farm families' abilities to reduce cash outlays. When the bulk of farm inputs such as seed, energy, and machinery must be purchased, there are few options available to reduce expenditures necessary to maintain a farm operation.

The life-style of farm families in the 1980s was quite similar to the lifestyles of nonfarm families. Insurance, taxes, auto repairs, and food are things that require cash and few options exist to greatly reduce these living expenses. As farmers postponed or reduced purchases, agribusiness and main street businesses became victims of the farm crisis. Many farm families sought off-farm jobs to supplement their incomes. However, few jobs were being created in the community and additional workers served only to depress wage rates. Often the jobs that were available were seasonal, minimum-wage jobs that frequently had few if any benefits. As conditions worsened, sales tax revenues declined and property tax collections fell, leaving fewer tax revenues to support local services and facilities.

In the early years of the farm crisis there was a lack of consensus that problems existed in agriculture. Federal and state governments often denied there was a problem or attempted to minimize its seriousness (Harl, 1990). As a result, farm families were often viewed as victims of poor management. In addition, the national economy, particularly in the Sunbelt and on the West Coast, was growing, inflation rates were low, the world was at peace, and many urban people could not understand what was happening in the heartland. As the trends continued, the formation of a dual economy began to take shape. It was difficult for nonfarm people to understand what was happening on farms.

Part of the difficulty in communicating what was happening in rural America was due to poor terminology: The term *farm crisis* was not very descriptive. First, its impact was much wider than just farms, and the ripple effect soon engulfed the small towns and agriculturally dependent communities. Further, what was happening was not a crisis, but rather a return to long-term historical trends. The situation was more accurately described as a chronic condition. Davidson (1990) refers to the 1980s as the rise of rural ghettos. Making intervention difficult was the inability to identify victims—they were not readily visible to the media. Unlike victims of natural disasters, it was very difficult to identify the victims of financial distress. Oftentimes victims were unwilling to admit they had a problem, or if they stepped forward, they were stigmatized as "abnormal" or "bad managers."

Victims of the farm crisis were very heterogeneous and often reflected differing degrees and stages of economic distress. The diversity of victims in terms of farm enterprises, debt load, commodities produced, the availability of off-farm employment, and other sociodemographic traits made intervention difficult. Where substantial numbers of farm families were faced with serious financial problems, the traditional community support structure was either not in place or offered very limited support. Unlike previous farm crises that tended to level out differences among farmers, this crisis widened the gap and disparity among farmers. Those with little or no debt were generally immune from the crisis; however, farm families with modest to high debt loads were severely affected. This widening gap was also evident among nonfarm families. Those with more years of seniority in employment were often able to keep their jobs; young workers with families who were the last hired were often the first fired.

Harl (1987) notes that the crisis had little to do with efficiency and that some of the most efficient producers were often among the casualties of the crisis. Especially hard hit were young farm families, in their 30s or early 40s, who were in the establishment phase of their farming operation. The families in the present study typically fall into this age group. Rural families at this stage of life often had borrowed heavily to establish their farming operations and also were in the early years of beginning their families and creating their own households. Bultena, Lasley, and Geller (1986) found that the farm families most vulnerable to displacement were younger, had more years of education, farmed larger operations, and had more dependent children. Thus the 1980s found a widening gap between farm families who had high debt and those with low levels of debt. Young people who attempted to get started in farming during the late 1970s and early 1980s, and who followed the same paths used by their parents and older siblings to enter farming, found the economic doors to farm entry slammed shut. Many farm families caught in this window of vulnerability were forced out of farming by financial distress (Rosenblatt, 1990; Friedberger, 1989).

Indicators of Economic Distress in the Study Area

The families participating in this study live in eight counties in north-central Iowa, an area recognized as containing some of the best farmland in the world (see Figure 3.1). In 1987, the eight counties produced a total of $830,732,000 in agricultural sales, an average of $103,841,000 compared to a statewide average of $90,170,000 (Table 3.1). Average value of farmland is another commonly used measure of productivity. In the eight counties, the average farmland values ranged from $1,349 per acre in Marshall County to $1,722 in Wright County. The average value of farmland in each of the eight counties was considerably higher than the statewide average of $1,214.

The economies of these counties are heavily dependent upon farming as shown in Table 3.1. All but one county in the study area have a higher proportion of farm earnings as a percentage of total county earnings than the statewide average of 6.7%. In Butler, Franklin, Humboldt, and Wright counties, farm earnings account for 25% or more of the total county earnings and thus exceed the criterion used by Bender et al. (1985) to define agriculturally dependent counties. Only one county (Marshall) had less farm earnings as a percentage of total earnings than the statewide average of 6.7%.

Each of these counties has been hard hit by the farm crisis as witnessed by the steep declines in their economies. From 1975 to 1990 in the study counties, the number of farms declined by a low of 14.7% in Webster County to a high of 27.3% in Wright County, compared to a statewide average decline of 20.0%. The decline in average land values from 1980 to 1990 ranged from 39.6 to 46.0%. The faltering local economies resulted in increased business failures. Between 1980 and 1990, the number of businesses declined in six of the eight counties. The business declines ranged from 1% in Webster County to 13% in Hamilton County. In Hardin and Marshall counties, where the increases were very modest (1.4 and 0.2%, respectively), the economic gains were not adequate to compensate for jobs lost in other businesses. The decline in the number of businesses triggered substantial reductions in employment opportunities for both farm and nonfarm residents.

Declines in employment levels are useful indicators of financial hardship and a shrinking economy. Between 1980 and 1988, total employment declined in each of the eight counties. The declines ranged from 0.2% in Wright County to 11.7% in Franklin County. During this same period, the state's employment increased by 3.6%. Farm employment declined from 10.7% in Humboldt County to nearly 18% in Franklin County. Wage and salary employment also declined across the eight counties, ranging from a 1.0% decline in Wright County to 16.2% in

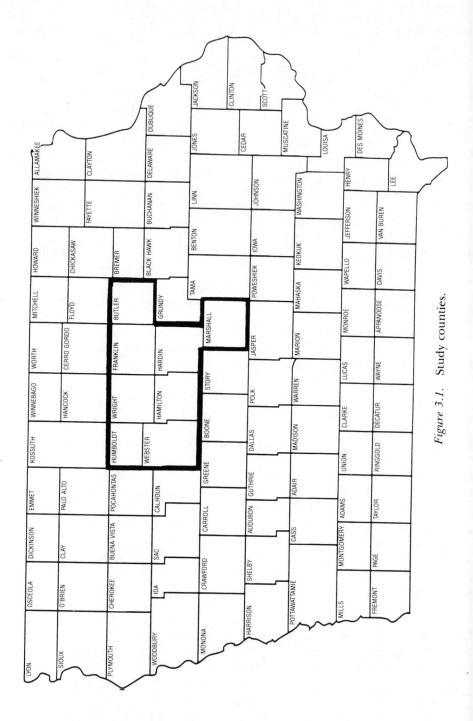

Figure 3.1. Study counties.

Table 3.1. Economic Indicators in the Eight-County Study Area

Indicators	Study counties								Iowa average
	Butler	Franklin	Hamilton	Hardin	Humboldt	Marshall	Webster	Wright	
Market value of agricultural products sold (1987)[a] ($000)	105,209	110,938	133,865	115,469	77,786	90,288	112,144	85,033	90,170
Average value of farm land (1990)[b] (per acre)	1,385	1,532	1,717	1,578	1,669	1,349	1,681	1,722	1,214
Farm earnings as percentage of total county earnings (1988)[c]	30.9	34.8	15.4	11.2	29.6	4.2	9.0	24.9	6.7
Change in land values (1980–1990)[b] (%)	−46.0	−45.0	−40.8	−41.3	−45.2	−39.6	−41.6	−41.0	−41.2
Change in number of farms (1975–1990)[b] (%)	−19.4	−23.7	−24.1	−18.6	−20.7	−19.7	−14.7	−27.3	−20.0
Change in number of businesses (1980–1990)[d] (%)	−8.4	−12.5	−13.0	1.4	−6.3	0.2	−1.0	−7.6	0.5
Change in total employment (1980–1988)[c] (%)	−7.3	−11.7	−10.4	−7.8	−2.1	−5.6	−10.5	−0.2	3.6
Change in farm employment (1980–1988)[c] (%)	−12.8	−18.0	−16.8	−13.4	−10.7	−14.2	−14.3	−13.0	−14.7

(continued)

Table 3.1. Economic Indicators in the Eight-County Study Area (Continued)

Indicators	Butler	Franklin	Hamilton	Hardin	Humboldt	Marshall	Webster	Wright	Iowa average
Change in wage and salary employment (1980–1988)[c] (%)	−16.0	−16.2	−13.3	−11.1	−2.8	−8.6	−13.5	−1.0	2.0
Change in net earnings (1980–1988)[c] (%)	−5.0	−1.6	−3.0	−7.5	−3.0	−5.9	−9.2	−3.1	−3.8
Change in average farm earnings (1980–1988), adjusted by CPI[c] (%)	36.5	82.9	−17.9	−19.2	40.0	−18.8	−24.4	8.8	39.9
Average farm earnings (1988)[c] (dollars)	16,420	26,231	18,141	11,499	28,651	12,349	20,620	32,273	13,841
Per capita personal income 1988[c] (dollars)	13,106	14,209	16,306	14,305	14,758	14,862	14,022	16,669	14,662
Change in per capita income (1980–1988) adjusted by CPI[c] (%)	6.5	11.3	8.8	2.4	12.6	1.4	−1.2	14.4	9.0
Recent change in retail sales (1980–1990), adjusted by CPI[d] (%)	−46.0	−53.6	−36.5	−43.7	−38.1	−15.6	−19.7	−46.3	−15.0

[a] Market Value of Agricultural Products Sold in Iowa Counties: 1987, Iowa State University, Community Resource and Development 303, June 1990.

[b] Iowa's Counties: Selected Population Trends, Vital Statistics and Socioeconomic Data, 1991 edition.

[c] Iowa Employment, Earnings and Income, Rural Development-01, Iowa State University, June 1991.

[d] Iowa Retail Sales, 1980–90, Rural Development-02, Iowa State University, June 1991.

Franklin County. However, for the entire state, wage and salary employment increased by 2%.

Between 1980 and 1988, net earnings fell in each of the eight counties, and ranged from a 1.6% decline in Franklin County to a 9.2% decline in Webster County. The percentage change in average farm earnings showed a wide variation across the counties between 1980 and 1988. Four of the counties experienced a significant increase in average farm earnings. (Franklin County had an 82.9% increase.) On the other hand, four of the counties had declines in average farm earnings that ranged from 18 to 24%. Average farm earnings for 1988 ranged from $11,499 in Hardin County to over $32,000 in Wright County.

Per capita incomes in the counties in 1988 ranged from $13,016 (Butler) to $16,669 (Wright). Four of the counties had per capita incomes less than the state average of $14,662. When the per capita incomes are adjusted by the consumer price index (CPI), only modest changes occurred between 1980 and 1988. Webster County experienced a 1.2% decline in per capita income, while Wright County had a 14.4% increase. Five of the eight counties had less than the statewide average of a 9.0% increase in adjusted per capita income.

The declines in numbers of farms and businesses, coupled with the declines in net earnings, employment, and incomes, contributed to substantial declines in retail sales in each of the counties in the 1980s. When retail sales are adjusted by the CPI to remove the effects of inflation, each of the counties experienced retail sales declines greater than 15%. Four of the counties (Butler, Franklin, Hardin, and Wright) had adjusted retail sales declines in excess of 40%. Two counties (Hamilton and Humboldt) experienced retail declines between 35 and 40%. Marshall and Webster counties, the most populous counties in the study area, had retail sales declines of 15.6 and 19.7%.

CONSEQUENCES OF ECONOMIC STAGNATION

Stagnant economic conditions are readily visible in labor force and population changes (Table 3.2). In five of the eight counties, the labor force declined between 1980 and 1990. The labor force declines were greatest in Franklin County, a 20.2% decline. Hamilton County experienced the greatest increase in the labor force, 13%. Franklin County experienced a 21.2% decline in the number of people employed between 1980 and 1990. Three counties (Hamilton, Marshall, and Wright) experienced slight increases in the number of employed, but only Hamilton County's increase was greater than the state average of 6.1%.

Table 3.2. Population Changes in the Eight County Study Area

Indicators	Study counties								Iowa average
	Butler	Franklin	Hamilton	Hardin	Humboldt	Marshall	Webster	Wright	
Change in labor force (1980–1990)[a] (%)	-9.7	-20.2	13.1	-12.2	-2.2	3.1	-10.6	0.7	4.5
Change in number of employed (1980–1990)[a] (%)	-11.2	-21.2	13.3	-12.9	-0.2	5.1	-9.8	1.9	6.1
Total population (1990)[b]	15,731	11,364	16,071	19,094	10,756	38,276	40,342	14,269	28,000
Population change (1980–1990)[b] (%)	-11.0	-12.8	-10.0	-12.3	-12.2	-8.1	-12.2	-12.6	-4.7
Population change (1980–1990)[a]	-1,937	-1,672	-1,791	-2,682	-1,490	-3,376	-5,611	-2,050	-137,053
Estimated net migration (1980–1990)[c]	-2,342	-1,944	-2,313	-3,032	-1,945	-4,918	-7,406	-2,238	-293,569
Change in school enrollment (1980–1990)[a] (%)	-15.9	2.1	-12.4	-17.3	-18.3	-15.3	-16.7	-14.1	-9.7
Change in female-headed households, children present (1980–1990)[a] (%)	55.3	9.4	12.6	23.4	11.2	22.6	26.6	25.3	26.2
Change in population 65+ (1980–1987)[d] (%)	10.0	6.9	9.3	6.6	9.0	12.6	8.2	5.0	8.4
Population 65+ (1987)[d] (%)	19.6	20.0	17.8	19.9	19.5	16.5	17.4	21.0	14.9

(continued)

Table 3.2. Population Changes in the Eight County Study Area (Continued)

Indicators	Study counties								Iowa average
	Butler	Franklin	Hamilton	Hardin	Humboldt	Marshall	Webster	Wright	
Population living below federal government poverty level[a] (%)	12.3	13.2	11.3	13.5	10.1	10.4	12.2	10.6	11.5
Residents receiving food stamps (1989) (%)	4.9	4.7	4.5	4.8	4.5	6.1	8.3	4.2	5.9
Residents eligible for Title 19 (Medicaid) (1989)[f] (%)	5.5	5.1	5.1	5.2	5.2	6.3	8.6	5.1	6.4
Transfer payments as percentage of total income (1988)[c] (%)	16.8	15.1	14.1	18.2	15.6	15.5	18.3	15.4	15.0

[a] Iowa's Counties: Selected Population Trends, Vital Statistics and Socioeconomic Data, 1991 edition.

[b] Iowa's Counties in 1980 and 1990: Initial Census Counts on Population, Race, Hispanic Origin and Housing Units Census Services 91-2, February 1991.

[c] Iowa Employment, Earnings and Income, Rural Development-01, Iowa State University, June 1991.

[d] Estimates of the 65 and Older Population in Iowa Counties, 1980–1987, Iowa State University, Community Resource and Development 290, 1989.

[e] Des Moines Register.

[f] Iowa Counties: Selected Population Trends, Vital Statistics and Socioeconomic Data, 1990 edition.

Six of the counties in the study area had populations of less than 20,000 compared to the statewide average of 28,000. In response to economic decline, each of the counties lost a significant proportion of its population during the 1980s. The eight counties lost over 26,000 residents during the 1980s, an average of 3,200 per county. While the state lost 4.7% of its population during the 1980s, each of the counties lost more than 8% of its population. Five of the counties lost more than 12% of their population during the 1980s.

The loss of population is also evident in school enrollment declines between 1980 and 1990. The public school enrollment in seven of the counties declined by more than 12%. The number of female-headed households with children increased from 9.4% in Franklin County to 55.3% in Butler County. As a consequence of young families migrating out of the counties in search of jobs, the proportion of 65 and older residents increased from 5.0 to over 12% in the eight counties. In 1987, nearly one-fifth of the population in the eight counties was over the age of 65. Over 10% of the population in each of the counties had incomes below the federal government poverty levels. Food stamp recipients ranged from 4.2% in Wright County to a high of 8.3% in Webster County. At least 5% of the residents in each of the counties were eligible for Title 19 support (Medicaid). Transfer payments as a percentage of the total income in the counties for 1988 ranged from 14.1 to 18.3%.

WHAT DO THESE STATISTICS SUGGEST ABOUT THE FUTURE?

Two conclusions from the data in the preceding tables stand out: The counties in the study area have not recovered from the financial shock wave of the 1980s, and the ripple effects continue to reverberate across the landscape. While the farm crisis has faded from the newspaper headlines, there is substantial evidence that financial hardship continues to grip the local economies. In the aftermath of the farm crisis are socioeconomic conditions that are reminiscent of the Great Depression. Davidson (1990) described conditions during the farm crisis as a "sinkhole" that is responsible for the rise of rural ghettos. Davidson finds many similarities between rural Iowa during the 1980s and the conditions described by Bender, Green, and Campbell (1971) in Ozark communities when a mine or manufacturing plant closed.

The rise of rural ghettos in the Ozarks resulted from three interconnected processes according to Bender et al. An economic shock wave, such as a mine closing or plant shutdown, begins a pattern of inter-generational poverty that families have profound difficulties breaking. This intergenerational passing-on of diminished life chances has been described by others studying rural poverty. From her study of rural poor in New York, Fitchen writes,

> What all the chronically poor nonfarm people have in common today, then, is that their parents or grandparents made an unsuccessful transition from agriculture or agriculture-related occupations, in which insufficient resources, unfortunate timing, and large scale economic trends all worked against their making an advantageous adaptation to nonagricultural pursuits. (1981, p. 214)

A second trend that contributes to the emergence of rural ghettos is a selective migration in which more prosperous and upwardly mobile residents migrate. The loss of opportunities and poor future prospects contributed to outmigration, leaving behind an older, less mobile population in which poverty becomes more concentrated. These impacts are documented in the data presented in Tables 3.1 and 3.2.

And finally, the socioeconomic structure of the communities responds in ways that contribute to deteriorating social conditions. In acts of desperation, communities often engage in competitive bidding to attract new employers. Because poor communities are more likely to attract low-wage industries, an available supply of labor willing to work at minimum wages further contributes to a cycle of poverty. This scenario is reflected in a recent critique of Iowa's economic development strategy of building upon the meat-packing industry. This report, entitled Shattered Promises (Prairiefire Rural Action, 1991), examines how meat-packing industries in Iowa and elsewhere have turned to recruiting non-English-speaking minorities who work in packing houses at low wages and under dangerous working conditions, live in crowded and substandard housing, and experience language and racial barriers that contribute to the development of rural community ghettos.

This downward spiral in Iowa's rural communities, triggered by a sudden financial disruption, reverberates across the rural population, infecting the social and economic fabric that binds the community together. However, the most insidious part of this process is that it begins to build upon itself. Davidson (1990) argues that the processes that gave rise to rural ghettos in the Ozarks and Appalachian areas, vividly described by Fitchen in rural New York, are at work in the rural heartland.

IMPLICATIONS OF THE FARM CRISIS FOR RURAL IOWA

There are at least five major areas of concern about the probable impacts of the farm crisis: the structure of farming, community life, social relationships, and individuals and families.

Structure of Agriculture

Since the turn of the century, the number of farms in the state has declined from 225,000 to 105,000. However, the decline has not occurred evenly among farms of differing size. What has occurred is the formation of a dual structure of agriculture with increased numbers of small farms and an increase in the number of large farm units (Lasley & Goudy, 1989). The decline in farm numbers has come primarily from a rather steep decline in the number of midsize farms. Between 1969 and 1987, the number of farms with less than 50 acres increased 24%, farms with 50–179 acres declined by 43%, and farms with 180–499 acres declined by 41%, but farms with 500–999 acres increased by 61%, and farms with over 1,000 acres increased by 268% (Lasley, 1990). The farm crisis hastened the movement toward a bimodal structure of agriculture.

The financial crisis has contributed to the separation of land ownership from labor. For many farmers, land ownership is not possible even at the depressed land values. It is likely that more tenancy and sharecropping will occur as financially strapped families try to stay in farming by renting or leasing more land. Over one-fifth of the farmers in a statewide sample of Iowa farmers indicated they were planning to rent more land in the next 5 years (Lasley, 1990). In this same study, only about 16% were planning to buy additional land. The farm crisis accelerated historical trends to fewer and larger farms, further reducing the opportunities for new, young farm families.

Community Consequences

The declining number of farms also means further declines in the farm population. The loss of farm population contributes to declines in retail sales, which result in main street commerce and agribusiness failures. Thus, the small towns in the study area that were primarily dependent upon farming have become more dependent upon the elderly and the poor. The decline in the number of businesses indicates the loss of purchasing power and the declining demand for goods and services. Another consequence for the rural community business sector has been the proliferation of discount stores that have cropped up across the farm belt. In response to financial distress, families have become more price conscious and as a result often travel long distances to purchase goods at lower prices. Stone (1985) has reported a direct positive relationship between the size of the community and retail sales. Throughout the 1980s, smaller towns lost a higher proportion of their retail business than midsize and large communities.

Not only have these socioeconomic changes of the 1980s forced many farm families out of farming, but they also have discouraged many young people from entering farming. The number of farmers under age 24 declined by 55% between 1978 and 1987 (Lasley & Goudy, 1989). Based upon the age distribution of Iowa farmers in 1987, it is predicted that farm numbers will decline by 9.5% by 1997 (Lasley, 1990). In the 1991 Iowa Farm and Rural Life Poll, 56% of the statewide sample of farmers indicated they would like one of their children to take over the farm when they retire; however, 22% indicated they would not like one of their children to take over their farm (Lasley & Kettner, 1991).

It appears that across many rural, agriculturally dependent counties, further institutional consolidation is likely to occur. The declines in school enrollments reported in Table 3.2 suggest that many of the schools will be forced to deal with a substantial reduction in number of students through further school consolidations and school closings. Other community institutions such as churches and hospitals also are struggling with the consequences of outmigration. Local community organizations such as civic, social, and fraternal groups are also adversely affected by declining memberships and participation. The entire social structure of many rural communities has been greatly affected by the decade-long farm crisis and the subsequent ripple effect.

Social Consequences

A tearing of the social fabric of farm-dependent counties is reflected in the deterioration of social relationships. Brown's (1989) depiction of the Lone Tree tragedy and *Farming Is in Our Blood* (Rosenblatt, 1990) offer vivid accounts of what happened when people were pushed to their psychological limits. While the tension between lenders and farmers received much publicity, the tearing of the social fabric also occurred between landowners and tenants and between friends and neighbors as people struggled to make ends meet. In some cases, tensions became so great that communities became divided, and people withdrew from community affairs and turned inward. Diminished satisfaction with community life and feelings of less integration, community cohesion and participation have been reported among small-town residents as well as among farmers (Ryan, 1991).

The diminished levels of community pride and attachment resulting from heightened financial stress contributed to a voting No syndrome. School bond issues and referenda on tax levies to replace or restore community facilities often failed at the polls because residents were unwilling or unable to pay higher taxes. In addition, as residents lost pride in their communities, they were less willing to make necessary investments in local institutions and agencies. As a result, many communities postponed investments for the future, which further contributed to unsatisfactory public services and facilities. Outdated and inadequate public services and facilities contribute to making communities less attractive for potential employers who are searching for new locations. Without adequate support services and infrastructure, oftentimes local communities are not attractive for new residents or businesses.

Ironically, at the very time that communities needed to be pulling together, it was evident that community social support networks, long thought to be a primary attribute of rural community life, were fragile and fragmented. As more people needed public assistance, fewer resources were available. With fewer people remaining to support local services, many communities face the need to either raise local taxes or cut services. Unlike state and federal governments, local governments do not have the ability to run budget deficits. Local budget constraints forced many communities to cut services, not because they were not needed, but because of declining revenues.

Another complication during the farm crisis that exacerbated the reduction in public services was the New Federalism of the Reagan administration. This political perspective cut federal programs and shifted additional responsibilities to state and local governments. Revenue sharing, community block grants, and other forms of federal aid were reduced under the new initiative to give communities more control over and more responsibility for funding local services.

Individual and Family Impacts

Discrimination against poor people is neither new nor unique to the farm crisis. Poor people, regardless of the circumstances surrounding their financial status, are stigmatized. For farmers, this stigma involved labeling them bad managers or high rollers. For the unemployed or displaced, the stigma was to define them as lazy or as taking advantage of the welfare system. Blaming the victim was a frequent justification for explaining the financial difficulties of farmers and nonfarmers alike. This labeling process further contributed to the financial strains experienced by individuals and families. The deterioration of social relationships in rural communities led to diminished levels of participation in social affairs and further eroded perceptions of the quality of life in small communities. In many cases these processes socially isolated economically stressed families.

Bultena, Lasley, and Geller (1986) explored how farm families adapted to financial distress by reducing expenditures and making household adjustments. A recent 12-state survey conducted across the north-central region documents the pervasiveness of the farm crisis and its effects on farm families (Lasley & Fellows, 1990). Taking off-farm jobs, holding multiple jobs, deferring expenses, postponing medical care, and other short-term and often risky behaviors are strategies that families have used to make ends meet.

The despair and sense of hopelessness resulting from financial uncertainty have contributed to heightened levels of interpersonal and familial stress. Throughout the decade, rural mental health agencies have struggled to meet the increased demands from farm and rural residents. Consistent with research on economic downturns in urban areas (McLoyd, 1989), chronic economic depression among families in the study area has led to higher rates of spouse and child abuse.

Within the eight target counties, child abuse increased from 291 cases in 1982 to 416 cases in 1988 (Table 3.3). This growth in absolute numbers of cases of family violence is even more telling in that it occurred in the face of a declining population. Other social pathologies such as substance abuse and suicide also increased during the crisis years (Davidson, 1990). Families who lost their jobs or lost their farm or business often were forced into bankruptcy. These financial crises were associated with a loss in identify and self-esteem. Losing one's job and means of support is both an economic and emotional shock. Blundall (1990) points out that many farm operators have feelings of guilt that they violated an inter-

Table 3.3. Official Reports of Child Abuse in the Study Area

Study county	1982	1983	1984	1985	1986	1987	1988
Butler	10	13	11	16	11	10	32
Franklin	7	16	14	19	10	10	22
Hamilton	25	23	31	24	26	27	34
Hardin	28	24	22	32	34	27	41
Humboldt	20	21	32	13	13	10	7
Marshall	54	81	86	88	116	112	135
Webster	135	129	161	130	109	102	131
Wright	12	30	23	20	30	21	14
Total for study counties	291	337	380	342	349	319	416

Note: Iowa Department of Human Services, Official Statistics, 1990.

generational trust because they would not be able to pass the farm down to their children.

Unlike other periods of economic stress in agriculture, farmers who lost their operations in the late 1980s often could not find employment in the community and were forced to relocate. Studies of displaced farmers consistently report that farm families want to remain in the local community (Heffernan & Heffernan, 1986). However, staying in the community often meant accepting a reduced standard of living, working at minimum wage jobs that offer few or no benefits, and accepting employment with little chance of long-term advancement.

The remainder of this book will explore in more detail the consequences of the farm crisis for families in these counties. In the next chapter, we review important dimensions of family economic life as the decade of crisis came to a close. These analyses demonstrate the end results of the previously discussed historical trends as they are reflected in the financial troubles of this contemporary group of rural Iowa families.

Chapter 4

Families Under Economic Pressure

Glen H. Elder, Jr., Elizabeth B. Robertson, and Monika Ardelt

It's incredible! Families have fallen apart and businesses as well.
—Small businessman, 1989

From a general picture of economic decline in rural Iowa during the 1980s, we turn to the circumstances of our Iowa families at the end of the decade. We address the current status of the Iowa families by describing their economic variations and links to the older generation. Consider the men who were born on a farm: Why did some enter farming while others pursued nonfarm employment? Were there distinguishing characteristics of the farm itself and the farm family that pulled men into farming? What about the men who lost the farm? Were intergenerational influences important in this failure? As we shall see, men who stayed in farming are among the most prosperous heads of households in the Iowa sample.

The circumstances of many hard-pressed families at the end of the decade pose questions concerning their efforts to survive. Ways of responding to the constrained circumstances of family needs can be thought of as socioeconomic strategies (Elder, 1974; Moen, Kain, & Elder, 1983). We view strategies of this kind as outcomes of decisions on matters of production and consumption. This is a family process in which scarce resources (income, time, skills) are allocated among competing needs in order to maximize family well-being. Effective management of the household economy entails an optimum use of resources for reasonable needs, a synchronization of income with living requirements and other considerations. Planning, with its attention to timing and schedules, is a core element of this process. The issue is whether, how, and when to generate additional income, to economize, and to purchase furniture or medical insurance.

79

In theory, families that have insufficient income to meet their needs can seek to reduce economic pressure by employing one or more of the following strategies. They can reduce the need or demand by cutting back on consumption and/or they can attempt to increase family income through multiple earners or a change in jobs (Conger et al., 1990; Elder et al., 1992). A third strategy makes no change in level of income or in family need. Instead it minimizes any major decline in living standards by mortgaging future income through the use of loans, credit, and savings. Families that follow this course of action are "living beyond their means" at the time and postponing a lasting solution to the economic crunch or hardship.

Transactions that mortgage future income (use savings, loans, credit) can serve as the first line of defense in hard times and are commonplace in the agricultural world of farm families. They become problematic when outstanding debts build across the years and approach expectable income. An "unchanging dark cloud," as one Iowa woman put it, heavy indebtedness can exact a costly toll in feelings that one's life is out of control. The ultimate objective of cutting back on expenditures is to achieve a more balanced relation between income and outgo, but the short-term experience is likely to be one of loss and its hard choices. Reduced expenditures on household utilities, food, and medical care represent a painful decline in living conditions, which increase the risk of depressed feelings and demoralization (Kessler et al., 1988), at least over the short term.

In the last half of this chapter we focus on these socioeconomic strategies and their relation to income-generating efforts, and then we explore some key antecedents, such as indebtedness and unstable work. The felt economic strains of families and their adaptations depend on the local economy, in farm and nonfarm communities alike. For this reason, we compare sources of strain and adaptation in these communities and identify important differences. But, as we shall see, both family and personal consequences of economic strain and adaptation are similar in psychological mood for both farm and nonfarm settings.

One of the most important differences concerns off-farm employment among husbands and wives and its survival role among farm families. By the end of the 1980s, approximately half of all Iowa farm operators held jobs in the off-farm market, a notable increase since the immediate postwar era. Likewise, the mounting budgetary pressures of the 1980s brought increasing numbers of women into the off-farm market. In the next chapter, we explore the pressures underlying off-farm employment on matters of farm survival, loss, and adaptation, and investigate some material, social, and emotional strains among families that lost a farm.

IOWA'S FAMILIES AT DECADE'S END

The winter of 1989–1990 was mild as winters go in Iowa and the economic crisis of the decade had moderated some, but none of this could obscure the trail of heartbreak for many families. A father who lost a farm in the 1980s spoke to us about two very different times in his life, before and after:

> We had everything going our way—maybe 11 or 12 years ago.
> Thought you knew it all, you knew how to farm, you knew how to make money, and you were financially secure, and you paid your own bills.
> Twelve years later and you're borrowing the money to make ends meet.
> You kinda feel like you're going backwards.

In another family that had given up its farm during the mid-80s, the mother reflected on how their lives had changed: a move to town, her return to college and the credentials to teach (followed by a substitute teacher appointment in the local schools and a part-time job in the public library), and her husband's employment as a truck driver in an agribusiness firm that provides fertilizers, insecticides, and seeds for local farmers. She recalled that when they were first married, "We spent all our time together. We both had a common goal on the farm because we were working as a team." In contrast, the husband's present job has seasonal peaks in spring and fall when he spends as much as 20 hours per day at work. During these times, in particular, "We live on notes." But as she put it, "We do make it a point to say 'I love you.'" Though very unhappy about her public library job, she makes do because "it is a job." Also, she appreciates her husband's support, as when "he comes into the library with a cup of coffee or a donut or an apple for me."

Less than half of the 451 study families had entered farming (44%), though only 30% of the fathers currently defined themselves as farmers (see Figure 4.1). Half of the men who left farming hold blue-collar jobs and a slight majority managed to find work that had something in common with farming, such as truck driving, feed sales, and farm equipment repair. The loss typically occurred from 1981 through 1987, a good many years ago in most cases, but to most families the event seemed like yesterday, so vivid and painful.

One of the men who now works for a meat-packing plant spoke of his "quitting farming" in answer to a question on recent family changes of importance. His wife quickly noted that the interview card said *recent* changes and that the farm loss was a long, long time ago. He replied that it "seems not long to me." His wife noted, "Well, it's been 8 years." But he continued to insist that it wasn't long ago: "Twenty years ago wouldn't be that long."

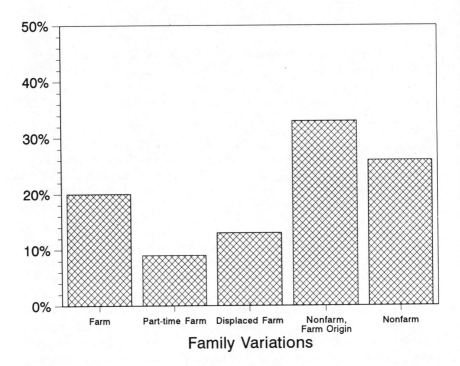

Figure 4.1.   Family variations in Iowa study, 1989.

She moved on to a question about whether the changes had been for the better or worse and concluded that in her mind they had been for the better, "considering how farming's been." Turning to her husband, she asked how he felt, believing that he would no doubt agree. After a moment's pause, he replied, "Terrible."

Of the families still actively engaged in farming, one-third occupied a borderline position, partly in and partly out. The men in these families did not regard themselves as farmers when asked and they were typically employed in nonfarm jobs along with their wives. Another one-third of the families included one or more parents whose sole contact with farming occurred in childhood, many years ago. They are now employed in nonfarm careers, from professional and managerial to semiskilled. The remaining families, one-fourth of the sample, were literally generations removed from farming. Neither spouse in these families had even spent his or her childhood on a farm. Half of the nonfarm men had white-collar employment at the time of our initial survey.

Three issues bear upon the socioeconomic standing of the Iowa families as we found them at the end of the decade. The first concerns the socioeconomic standing of families in each of the types just discussed: farm, part-time farm, displaced farm, farm origins only, and nonfarm. How do these families compare at the end of the crisis decade? The second issue concerns family history in relation to success and failure in farming. What role did the parents' own family background play in determining their socioeconomic activity and position? The third issue concerns memories of the bad times experienced by farm and nonfarm families, and the stresses they continue to live with.

Socioeconomic Variations

From the standpoint of total family income, the farm (median family income $40,076) and part-time farm families were doing better in 1988 than families out of agriculture, but this partly reflects a tortuous process in which financially troubled operators are forced out of business (see Table 4.1). Current farm operators were clearly better off than families that had recently moved out of farming (median family income $32,000), both in terms of income and indebtedness. For example, the debt-to-asset ratio was .48 for farm families compared to .58 for displaced farmers. Rural families that had not been involved in farming, however, were the most disadvantaged in terms of median income ($29,050), debt-to-asset ratio (.67), and work instability (24% of these families).

Despite their overall economic well-being, some farm families remained in serious straits, even on the verge of losing the farm. One farmer with a debt-to-asset ratio of .72 for a farm operation of nearly 500 acres

Table 4.1. Socioeconomic Status of Iowa Families by Economic Types

| | | Socioeconomic status, 1988 | | |
| | Total family income ($ median) | Debt-to asset ratio | Unstable work[a] last year (%) | Wife employed (%) |
Economic types				
Farm (N = 90)	40,076	.48	7	72
Part-time farm (N = 40)	46,076	.42	12	68
Displaced farm (N = 59)	32,000	.58	22	80
Nonfarm with farm origins (N = 148)	33,721	.66	15	85
Nonfarm (N = 116)	29,050	.67	24	75

[a] Score 1 to each family who experienced any one of the following events in 1988: reduced hours, spell of unemployment, demotion, change to unrelated job.

somehow managed to remain optimistic about his financial recovery, despite a doubtful prognosis:

> It is getting a little bit easier, the light is getting a little bit brighter at the end of the tunnel, I think. Another three to four years will be fairly tight as far as income versus expenses is concerned.

The economic downturn of the 80s had major consequences for the economic level of the nonfarm families through a dramatic shrinking of skilled blue-collar employment and a corresponding decline in wage levels. The closing of meat-packing plants, machine shops, and sundry businesses frequently initiated a downgrading of wage levels through reemployment at lower-level service jobs. The minimum wage at $4.65 per hour frequently replaced a $13- to $15-per-hour job in the trades among workers who had never been dependent on public assistance, but now faced the dreaded prospect of such help "as the only way out." Losses of this kind typically forced Iowans to add many hours and additional part-time jobs to their workday, including mothers and children. An Iowa mother expressed satisfaction with her job in a food processing plant, despite its minimum wage: "Like I said, it may not be the best job or the best paying job, but that's income. It's better than nothing" (Naples, 1992, p. 12).

Downward pressures on family budgets across the 1980s, reflecting the increasing inequality of income, placed a much greater burden on the earnings of wives and mothers in this midwestern region. As Tilly put it more generally, "the trend toward inequality has assigned women a pivotal role in the struggle to maintain a family's standard of living" (1991, p. 754). Since the inequality of rural and urban families has increased dramatically in the Midwest, this assigned role is most acutely experienced by rural women and most especially the mothers and wives in this study. Over the past 30 years, the paid employment of rural women in the United States has steadily risen to match the employment level of urban women. In the Iowa study, well over 70% of the mothers reported paid employment for an average of 37 hours per week.

Three out of five working mothers were engaged in white-collar jobs—such as teacher, social worker, bookkeeper, librarian and service work. Women's earnings amounted to one-fifth of the total family income for the sample as a whole, but it ranged upward to one-third or more among lower income families. We shall return to matters concerning the dramatic level of gainful employment among these Iowa women when we take up strategies of making ends meet in this chapter and then again in the next chapter's examination of farm families and their varieties. We turn now to the influence of family origins on the current standing of the Iowa families.

To Farm or Not

Most of the Iowa families in 1989 had personal links to the farm, and thus felt close to the agricultural crisis. Three out of five fathers grew up on a farm, and the same proportion chose to enter farming. A start in Iowa farming generally depended on access to a farm through parents or the wife's parents. In fact, only two self-defined farmers in our sample did not grow up on a farm. What factors distinguished between these different life paths? Once engaged in farming, did family origin and influences play any role in determining the likelihood of survival and success through the farm crisis?

A farmer's son's entry into farming depends upon many factors from motivation to opportunity, with opportunity being greatest when the father is a full-time owner operator of a farm (Lyson, 1984). Motivation has much to do with past experience and family influence, such as the attractiveness of father as a career model. Modeling is unlikely when the family home represents a battlefield between parents or when father is harsh and erratic. Opportunity is indicated by the economic success of the farm operation and by the absence of brothers.

Both opportunity and motivation turn out to be influential in shaping a young man's entry into farming, as expressed across the generations in the Iowa study. The fathers who entered farming, typically in the 1960s and 1970s, came from families with fewer male children and a more viable farming operation (Elder, Robertson, & Conger, 1993). The fathers of these men had a higher standard of living, more education, fewer incidences of unemployment, greater farm involvement (owned and operated, etc.), and more years of farming, when compared to the fathers of nonfarm sons. All of these data were obtained from the sons in 1989.

Family farms typically involve the labor of many family members in maintaining efficiency, especially in planting and harvesting times. Boys growing up on owner-operated farms would be more likely to have first-hand experience with farm work than those whose fathers managed or labored on farms owned by others. Anticipatory influences, such as working on a farm, a parental emphasis on son's work role, the personal value of hard work, and parents' approval of son's farming all have been found to be related to aspirations on farming. In combination, they suggest a link between role-playing and the modeling of parental behavior in relation to farming careers.

We expected accounts of parents and of father as a parent to tell us something about the power of family ties in shaping occupational preferences. However, only one memory stands out in this regard, that of marital conflict and discord. Men who followed their fathers in farming were less likely to report conflict and discord in their parents' marriage, when compared to men in nonfarm communities (Elder et al., 1993). However they were not less likely than men in nonfarm careers to describe parents as rejecting and harsh.

It is true, of course, that memories of parents in one's childhood may not be accurate from the vantage point of childhood. Indeed, they may tell us more about adult life than about childhood. However, it is also plausible that opportunity and its pressures are the controlling influence. Whether a son feels kindly toward his father or not may be irrelevant when he is faced with the pressures of intergenerational succession on the farm. A viable farm operation, indexed by standard of living and investment in farming, represents the single most important determinant of entry into farming among the Iowa fathers when judged by a discriminant function analysis, and it should also represent one of the most important indicators of farming success (see Elder, Robertson, & Conger, 1993).

Other analyses showed that these economic differences in the family of origin did not predict which farmers would be displaced from the occupation. Displaced farmers in the Iowa study reported a slightly lower standard of living on their father's farms ($p < .06$), but no other economic differences in early life distinguished current from displaced farmers.

Are there any indications that men who gave up farming (the displaced families) came from more troubled homes and parents? Recollections of the parental marriage are similar by group on marital affection and marital conflict. We also find no difference on the quality of parent behavior from the retrospective accounts of sons, as in the use of harsh discipline, consistent discipline, reasoning, supportiveness, monitoring, explanatory communication, and feelings of parental rejection. Lastly, the men in farming and nonfarm occupations do not provide a different account of their own father—whether hostile or not, depressed, mastery-oriented, or neurotic. Overall, we find no basis for concluding that the men who lost their farms were brought up in more unstable homes.

Farm survival during the 1980s crisis seems to have had much to do with what Barlett (1993) calls managerial style. The depression generation of American farmers was distinguished by a resistance to indebtedness and risky ventures. By contrast, expansionary pressures during the 1970s undermined the wisdom of this managerial style. Young farmers in particular turned away from the cautionary ethos of the depression and the older generation to a risk-taking mode that accepted heavy risks and indebtedness for advancement. Rosenblatt (1990) describes cases where young farmers were actually encouraged by bankers during the 1970s to take out larger loans for the expansion of landholdings. Expansionary operations soon ran aground in the farm financial crisis when land values declined by one-third or more. A young farmer in the study sample observed that when land values collapsed, his "net worth dropped abruptly and went from a fairly decent positive figure to a negative figure."

We do not have any way of assessing the managerial style of the Iowa farmers in our study, though it may have something to do with life stage. Young men who were just getting started were no doubt open to the persuasiveness of an expansionary logic, much more so than the older farmer with a well-entrenched operation. Even so, the displaced farmers are not younger than men who are still farming.

Remembering the Bad Times

The hard times of the 1980s were often bad times for men, though more women recalled periods of emotional distress. We asked a series of questions about emotional strains over the past decade. Did the couples have periods of emotional depression or of anxiety that lasted at least 2 weeks and did they seek help for emotional problems in the past? The Iowa wives were more likely than their husbands to report such experiences, 42% versus 30% on depression episodes, 22 versus 17% on anxiety, and 26 versus 16% on seeking help.

The report of men on depression and seeking help tends to be concentrated among displaced farm families, an F ratio of 4.3 ($p < .01$) for depression and a ratio of 3.5 ($p < .05$) for seeking help. Figure 4.2 shows the overall configuration for men by family types. A survey of displaced farmers in North Dakota (Murdock & Leistritz, 1988, p. 136) obtained an identical percentage on depression episodes. Both of these findings are consistent with reports of an elevated suicide rate among midwestern farmers during the 1980s. Reported episodes of anxiety show no variation by family type.

Women do not vary by family type on their personal health experience during the 80s, according to their report. However, husbands and wives in displaced farm families show the smallest sex difference on their accounts of the past. The average difference is less than 4%. The intense emotional experience of losing a farm produced a shared trauma that has no match among other couples in the Iowa study, though some of the farm families came within an eyelash of seeing their own farm taken over by the banks.

Couples who had lost their farm typically identified this experience as among the most traumatic events in their life. When asked about such experiences, the wife of a displaced farmer noted many searing events of this kind, including the major illnesses of their children, but concluded that the year her husband "went bust in farming" was the worst of all,

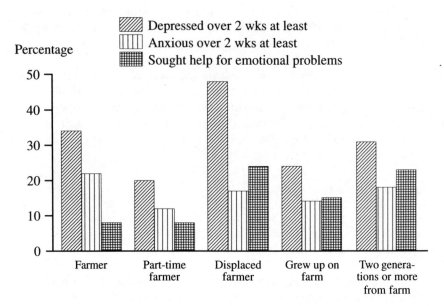

Figure 4.2. Mental health problems of men in the past by family types, in percentages, as of 1989.

both the agony of giving up the farm and the aftermath. She seldom had time with her husband after the loss, though she was desperately needful of support. His new work schedule required frequent travel and days away from home. "That year really sticks out in my mind as being horrible." Her husband added some recollections of the farm sale:

> I was numb up to the sale and then after the sale I was just so depressed. I wasn't really angry but I just didn't know what to do with myself. It influences us today—I'm sure it does.

Giving up a farm that had been in the family for generations was especially difficult to accept. It is hard, as one displaced farmer put it, to

> lose something that's been in one's family for generations, to watch others come in and pick it up and take it over. Things you've worked hard to preserve and carry on, to see that crushed and gone.

The loss is not merely a personal failure, but a failure magnified across the generations—from the son who will no longer have the chance to farm to the father and grandfather who saved the farm in the 20s and 30s. What is it like to fail the stewardship expectations of most everyone you deeply care about? This rhetorical question was asked in different ways by families that had lost family farms and thus family legacies in the 80s crisis.

An uncertain future after the loss added to the emotional distress. Devoting what seemed to be a lifetime to building up a farm, a couple vividly recalled the prospect of being separated from their identity and thrust into a totally different situation. They "went broke on the farm in 83," bankruptcy and all. The husband remembered well the struggle during legal proceedings and seeing "them come and take the farm away and not knowing what you were going to do."

This was "the hardest thing we've ever faced," he observed. He began drinking heavily as the farm's economic fortunes turned sour, but with his wife's support he somehow maintained the faith "that I could go out again and start over. And today I have a good job and a lot of responsibility." Though times were tough, the couple seemed to have come out stronger. As the husband put it, "We were standing there together."

In this farm state, the 1980s decline amounted to a general crisis that touched most lives, especially outside the large cities. Listen to a small businessman in the study reflect upon the changes in his community. When asked about the effects of the farm crisis, he exclaimed:

> It's incredible. People who were sound financially, prior to the early 80s, happy, lost entire farms. Families have fallen apart and businesses. I have a business just off Main Street, and I have watched business after business after business go out. We've lost industry.
> There hasn't been anything left unaffected by this.

Still Feeling the Strain

During the winter of 1989, three types of Iowa families had different stories to tell about their plight: families that were still in farming, the families that left farming, and the nonfarm families that had child-hood roots in farm culture. The farm families had managed to survive the 80s, if only barely, a survival that may reflect in part the adaptive value of an agrarian outlook that played down the value of materialism. Displaced families resembled the nonfarm households on income, but a past of life disruption and deprivation gave them a distinctive legacy. Is this legacy still felt in terms of financial strains, emotional distress, and family discord?

To answer this question, we focus on the three types of families in a series of multiple classification analyses. Each analysis obtained devia-tions from the sample mean for each type. To measure financial strain, we summed and averaged the responses of husband and wife to questions about difficulty paying bills and not having money left at the end of each month (5-point responses). A second index of family strain involves ineffective problem solving (see footnote b to Table 4.2). Each spouse was asked eight questions regarding the ineffective problem solving of the other spouse. These include "ignores the problem," "has poor ideas for solving the problem," and "blames others for the problem." The depressed mood of mother and father, reported by the other spouse, was measured by three 5-point items: unhappy, tense-irritable, and sad/depressed (see footnote c to Table 4.2). Lastly, the support of each spouse toward the other was measured by observational ratings that are based on videotaped interactions in the household. Table 4.2 shows the results of a comparison of the family types on these measures.

Without any doubt, the displaced farm families remain families in trouble. No other type of family comes close to the financial strain reported by parents in these households. Nonfarm families are clearly better off in terms of this subjective account and farm families appear to be even better off. It is among the displaced families that wives were most likely to describe their mate as ineffective in problem solving, as unwilling to listen or to address issues. The ineffectiveness could be part of the problematic history of these families, as well as a consequence of the emotional trauma and marital discord associated with family losses and hardships. Only the farm families rank above the sample average on marital support.

It is apparent that the experience of losing a farm, perhaps one that had been in the family for generations, still weighs heavily upon the displaced farmers, though less upon their wives. We asked each spouse to describe the mood of their mate in terms of three questions on unhappiness and irritability. The wives of displaced farmers still see their husbands as more troubled than the wives of farmers or nonfarm men. However, the husbands in displaced families do not describe their wives as more unhappy than wives in the other two groups.

This difference is highly significant and relates to the emotional history of men who lost their farm. Displaced farmers who reported a period of emotional depression during the 1980s were more likely to be described as depressed by their wives than were men who did not report a troubled history (t-ratio = 2.62, $p < .01$). The difference also applies to men who are currently farming. Those who claimed to have been depressed in the 1980s are more likely to be more depressed than other men today, as reported by wives.

Children are typically influenced by how their parents respond to the stresses in life, and we see suggestive evidence of this in Table 4.3 and its comparison of farm, displaced farm, and nonfarm families. The study children from displaced farm families rank well above children in the

Table 4.2. A Comparison of Parents in Three Types of Families—Farm, Displaced Farm, and Nonfarm—in Multiple Classification Analysis

		Deviations from grand mean			
Parents' strain, health and family relations	Grand mean (X)	Farm (N=90)	Displaced (N=59)	Nonfarm (N=148)	p value
Can't make ends meet[a]					
(low = 2, high = 10)	5.07	−.19	.54	−.10	.01
Ineffective problem solving[b]					
Mother, report by father	2.18	.00	.04	−.02	NS
Father, report by mother	2.28	.03	.24	−.11	.05
Depressed mood[c]					
Mother, report by father	2.11	−.03	.05	.00	.74
Father, report by mother	2.09	−.12	.24	−.02	.00
Marital support[d]					
(low = 2, high = 10)	4.72	.25	−.11	−.11	.04

[a] Both spouses reported whether they have difficulty paying bills each month (1, *no difficulty at all;* 5, *a great deal of difficulty*) and whether they have money left over at the end of the month (1, *more than enough money left over;* 4, *not enough to make ends meet*). The two items were highly correlated for mothers and fathers (av. r = .61). Each spouse's responses were standardized and summed. The correlation between parent reports for the summed scales was .65; therefore, the father and mother scales were combined and averaged to produce a single indicator.

[b] Ineffective problem solving for mother and father was measured from the perspective of the other spouse. The index for father represents the average of eight 7-point items (1, *never;* 7, *always*): just seems to get angry, criticizes you or your ideas for solving the problem, ignores the problem, has poor ideas for solving the problem, seems uninterested in helping to solve the problem, refuses to work out a solution to the problem, blames others for the problem, and insists that you agree to his solution to the problem. Alpha equals .85 for the mother's report on father, and .83 for father's report on mother.

[c] Measured as the simple average of three items (unhappy person; sad/depressed; tense/irritable), with a score from 1 (*strongly disagree*) to 5 (*strongly agree*). The alpha coefficient is .79 and .82 for mother's and father's depressed moods, as reported by the spouse.

[d] Marital support represents an observational measure that was derived from the family problem-solving task as well as the marital interaction task. For each task, father's support for wife and mother's support for husband were added first, and then the average of the sums was taken across the two tasks. The resulting index has a range from 2 (low) to 10 (high).

other groups on feelings of economic hardship, emotional distress, rejection by parents, and quarrels with parents over financial matters. Parents beset by many problems are not likely to be attentive to children's needs, and this would be especially true of depressed parents with problems. The adolescents who scored high on feelings of rejection were most likely to be exposed to such neglect. These results do not vary between girls and boys.

Table 4.3. A Comparison of Adolescents in Three Types of
Families—Farm, Displaced Farm, and Nonfarm—in Multiple
Classification Analysis

Target child's strain, health, and family relations	Grand mean (X)	Deviations from grand mean			p value
		Farm (N=90)	Displaced (N=59)	Nonfarm (N=148)	
Felt economic pressure[a]	−.03	−.13	.26	−.03	.01
Quarrels with parents over money; child report (1, *always*; 5, *never*)	4.17	.09	−.19	.02	.12
Emotional distress[b] (subscales, SCL-90-R)	6.09	.08	.58	−.28	.01
Feels rejected by father[c]	1.76	−.04	.19	−.05	.03
Feels rejected by mother[d]	1.69	.00	.18	.07	.02

[a] Child's *Felt Economic Pressure* is measured as the average of three items: Problem family has because parents do not have enough money to buy things; how often parents argue about money; how often you argue with parents about not having enough money. Each item is standardized first and then averaged. A high score indicates high strain. The alpha coefficient is .68.

[b] Four components of the SCL-90-R scale were summed to index emotional distress: anxiety (trembling; suddenly scared for no reason;) spells of terror or panic; thoughts and images of a frightening nature); somatization (headaches; faintness or dizziness; pains in heart or chest; . . .); depression (feeling low in energy; thoughts of ending life; feelings of being trapped or caged; . . .); and hostility (feeling easily annoyed or irritated; temper outbursts; urges to beat, injure, or harm someone; . . .). Each item is measured on a scale ranging from 1 (*not at all*) to 5 (*extremely*). The alpha coefficient for the four components is .83 for anxiety, .80 for somatization, .87 for depression, and .81 for hostility.

[c] Parental rejection is measured as the simple average of 5 items (my dad/mom really hurts me; my father/mother really cares about me; . . .). The scale ranges from 1 (*strongly agree*) to 5 (*strongly disagree*). The alpha coefficient is .76 for mother's rejection and .80 for father's rejection.

[d] Marital support represents an observational measure that was derived from the family problem-solving task as well as the marital interaction task. For each task, father's support for wife and mother's support for husband were added first, and then the average of the sums was taken across the two tasks. The resulting index has a range from 2 (low) to 10 (high).

The most obvious casualties of the farm crisis are families that lost their farm, and the extent of this legacy is compelling. But hard-pressed families can be found in all of the family types, from farm to nonfarm. We turn now to income variations in family responses to hardship and to the identification of sources of economic pressure among farm and nonfarm families. These sources among nonfarm families include a history of displacement, unstable work, indebtedness, and level of income.

Among farm families, the size and sales of the farms play a role in determining the economic pressures they faced.

TO MAKE ENDS MEET

More indebtedness, additional earners or work hours, and pulling in one's belt a couple of notches exemplify prominent alternatives or strategies among hard-pressed families in the study. Indebtedness up to a point enabled families to postpone painful adjustments that could reduce the gap between income and outgo. An additional earner illustrates a strategy to generate more income, whereas belt tightening refers to getting along on less, a cutting-back strategy that directly affects the family's standard of living. Most Iowa families, at one time or another, have used each of these options.

By the end of the 1980s, however, indebtedness had become more of a problem than a promising solution. In the final analysis, observed a woman from a displaced farm family, we "just plain need to get the financial burden taken care of." But the question is how to do it. She and her husband were unwilling to bring the problem to a financial counselor, at least not now. To be "debt free" was the overriding wish of a displaced farmer who had just experienced the same "dark valley" of uncontrollable circumstances. Despite all of this, some kind of borrowing, whether from kin or others, remained a possibility.

When asked whether the family drew upon savings, obtained a short-term loan, or used available credit last year (1988), nearly 40% of the Iowa couples claimed they drew upon savings, 29% reported that they borrowed from relatives, and 25% said they used more credit. As might be expected, the poorer Iowa families were most likely to take such actions, from 36 to 44% of the households with a total family income of $24,000 or less in 1988. In most cases, this total figure came from the earnings of two parents. The most well-to-do families in the upper fourth of the sample, with a reported income of $46,000 or more in 1988, were generally 20% lower in use of credit, a modest but consistent difference.

This is the only income category of families in which reported debts for the household do not exceed assets. Table 4.4 assigned the Iowa families, farm and nonfarm, to one of four income levels. Self-defined farmers are most likely to be in the highest income category, but this status does not bear upon household indebtedness. Indebtedness due to farming is quite another matter among farm families. By definition, self-employed farmers could be more stable in work than the nonfarm, a

Table 4.4. Social, Economic, and Subjective Aspects of Iowa Families by Total Income Level, 1988

Social, economic, and subjective factors	Total (%)	Total family income, 1988 (1,000s)				F-Test of income (I) & farm (F) effects
		≤$24 (N=112) (%)	$24–34 (N=113) (%)	$34–46 (N=113) (%)	≤$46 (N=113) (%)	
Social & economic status						
Lives in town	54	54	64	59	41	5.5**
Farmer by definition	29	27	14	26	49	
Debt/asset ratio (% above median)	55	69	56	58	38	
Unstable work (husband)	16	25	18	12	10	I: 3.1* F: 4.9*
Financial strain						
Less $ than most families (mother only)	26	49	25	17	13	I: 16.4**
Difficulty paying bills (mother only)	18	35	17	15	6	I: 10.8**
$ Left at end of month	17	33	17	12	5	I: 11.7**
Not enough $ (both parents) (% above median)[a]	57	78	61	57	32	I: 17.3**

*p ≤ .05. **p ≤ .001.

[a] An index of "not enough money" centers on material standards. Each parent responded to seven items, which asked if they agreed or disagreed on a 5-point scale that their family had the money they needed for a home, clothing, household items, a car, food, medical care, and recreational activities. The summed scales (alpha = .89 for mothers, .89 for fathers) for each parent were highly correlated (r = .54) and thus were averaged to create an index of material needs.

difference that clearly emerges from the tabular analysis. Lastly, low income represents a powerful source of financial strain. The lower income parents were most likely to have experienced difficulties in making ends meet.

By comparison, income level tells us very little about the employment status and work week of the Iowa women (Table 4.5). Three out of four of these women reported paid employment in 1989, and this applies to women at all levels of income. Among men, a second job reflects economic pressures on the farm more than family income. Indeed, their additional earnings were often plowed back into the farm operation, no matter what the family need at the time. Consistent with the historic trend of increasing off-farm employment, farmers were more likely to hold second jobs than men in nonfarm occupations. The difference is most evident among families that are below the median income for the sample, but it is also present among high-income families.

Hard-pressed parents were not putting in longer work weeks than better-off families. Only the men in farming had claim to the longest work week, a figure that runs from 50 to 90 hours. However the mothers in low-income situations were most likely to have added hours or another job over the past year, generally in response to a worsening economic condition. A good many fathers claim to have added to their work week as well, and they were more likely to do so than women (44 vs. 58%), but family income was not a consistent determinant. Other economic factors played a role, such as the returns from farming.

Along with efforts to borrow and generate money, a large number of families were engaged in an economizing strategy at the time. The most popular direct reduction on consumption was entertainment—half of the Iowa couples mentioned this cutback, in contrast to only one-fifth for transportation, a critical activity in the open country of Iowa (Table 4.6). The most popular postponement concerned the purchase of a costly household item (47%). Next in line were postponed vacations and bill paying. Without exception, these reductions increased in popularity as income decreased. Very few of the high-income families engaged in any of the practices. Reduced expenditures for entertainment and the postponement of bill payments and medical/dental care show the strongest association with lower income.

As shown in the far right column, we tested for the main effects of income and farm residence, as well as for their interaction effects. Only one of the cutbacks, on insurance, varied significantly by farm residence, with farmers showing less inclination to lower expenditures on insurance than nonfarm men. The high risk of accidents in farming may well have something to do with this different perspective. Overall, socioeconomic strategies in the lower strata reflect an inability to make ends meet, a

Table 4.5. Income-Generating Strategies by Total Family Income

	Total family income, 1988 (1,000s)				F-Test of Income (I) & farm (F) effects
Income strategy	≤$24 (N=112) (%)	$24–34 (N=113) (%)	$34–46 (N=113) (%)	≤$46 (N=113) (%)	
Employment status (%)					
Wife	75	77	84	74	NS
A second job (%)					
Husband	32	24	30	42	IxF: 4.1**
Wife	20	21	22	16	F: 22.7*** NS
Work hours per week (%)					
Husband	52	49	49	51	IxF: 3.0*
Wife	32	34	33	36	F: 17.7*** NS
Added Hours, Job[a] (%)					
Husband	58	34	46	35	I: 6.2***
Wife	44	36	33	19	I: 5.3***

[a] Either the addition of a job, more hours, or both.

* $p \leq .05$. ** $p \leq .01$. *** $p \leq .001$.

Table 4.6. Strategies That Reduce Consumption by Total Family Income: Test of Income and Farm/Nonfarm Effects

Strategies that reduce consumption costs	Total (%)	Total family income, 1988 (1,000s)				F-Test of income (I) & farm (F) effects
		≤$24 (N=112) (%)	$24–34 (N=113) (%)	$34–46 (N=113) (%)	≤$46 (N=113) (%)	
Cutbacks						
Charitable contributions	27	41	22	26	19	I: 5.5***
Food	26	36	31	22	17	I: 4.5**
Transportation	19	29	21	13	12	I: 4.3**
Entertainment	47	71	48	41	27	I: 17.2***
Household utility costs	25	39	28	21	12	I: 7.1***
Insurance	23	38	25	13	15	I: 9.7*** F: 4.9*
Postpone outlay						
Major household purchase	45	57	47	44	33	I: 5.2***
Vacation	32	46	31	33	19	I: 6.3***
Property tax	15	22	17	16	5	I: 3.8*
Payment of bills	30	49	30	28	12	I: 13.0***
Medical and dental care	24	41	30	18	8	I: 12.7***

$* p \leq .05.$ $** p \leq .01.$ $*** p \leq .001.$

point well documented by reports of difficulties in paying bills and of the lack of money left over at the end of each month. Virtually none of the high-income families made such statements in contrast to slightly more than one-third of the lowest income parents.

A family's total income level at the end of the decade tells us a good deal about the need for economizing measures and the degree of financial strain. But it provides little insight into the income strategies of families. For example, income level does not tell us anything about the average length of the work week among Iowa fathers nor about whether they had a second job. As noted, farmers ranked substantially higher in both respects than nonfarm men. Neither income nor farm status made a difference in the employment of wives.

If observed over time, Iowa families under economic pressure would tend to economize through lower expenditures and to engage in efforts to produce more family income. One way to measure such pressure is through questions about insufficient money for family needs and the inability to make ends meet. Two interrelated questions were averaged to produce a measure of "can't make ends meet" (see Table 4.2) and seven questions were averaged to index a belief that the family does not have enough money for family needs (see footnote a to Table 4.2). To assess the relation between felt pressure and family strategies, we considered three types of actions as elements of a cutting back strategy: borrowing and using savings, reducing expenditures, and selling property. Efforts to generate more income were indexed by reports of husband and wife on adding hours and jobs. Values range from 0 to 4.

Figure 4.3 presents the three constructs in a measurement model derived from a polychoric matrix with weighted least squares. The model, as proposed, fits the data reasonably well. Couples who reported efforts to generate more income over the past year were also likely to claim that they had tried to economize in various ways. Both strategies are highly related to perceptions of economic pressure.

The strong correlation between subjective economic pressure and cutting back suggests that both domains tap the experience of families under economic pressure. The inability to make ends meet may stem from high material standards and the tendency to live beyond available resources, as well as from a failure to make sufficient economic adjustments that lower expenditures. We summed all actions listed under cutting back in Figure 4.3 to produce a summated index of economic adjustments and included it as one of the three indicators of economic pressure: cannot make ends meet, not enough money, and economic adjustments.[1]

What conditions most dramatically increased the economic pressure of Iowa families? The answer depends in large part on whether we are

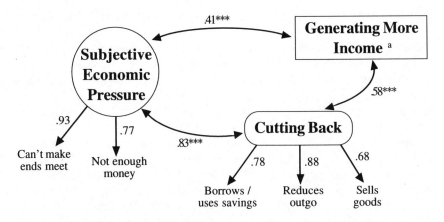

Figure 4.3. Subjective economic pressure and family adaptation strategies: a measurement model, 1989 (N = 451). This analysis (LISREL 7) used a polychoric matrix with weighted least squares since we treated the indicators for *cutting back* and *generating more income* as ordered categories. *Generating more income* was indexed by husband and/or wife report on adding hours/job (scores from 0 to 4). $\chi^2{}_7$ = 8.58, P = .29, GFI = .998, AGFI = .994, *p < .10.. **p < .05.. ***p < .01.

speaking about farm or nonfarm households. Farm families join family life and firm, and thus elements of the business had direct implications for the pressure they experienced. The market value of the farm is one such indicator. The historical trend is toward larger farm operations, and yet a good many of the largest farm operations encountered hard times through expansion and indebtedness in the 1970s and 1980s (Barlett, 1993). This risk also applies to the smallest farm operations, including many well under 300 acres. The return on capital investments is profitable among Iowa farms that are larger than 400 or 500 acres.

The debt-to-asset ratio on family farms provides a measure of indebtedness and viability, a proven index of a farm family's economic survival and independence during a general financial crisis (Bultena et al., 1986).[2] Values above .40 identify operations that are at some risk of economic failure. This outcome is more likely when the value exceeds .75. In a survey of farm operators from the state of Iowa, Bultena and his colleagues found that emotional distress and major financial setbacks increased sharply across the above data points. One of our Iowa couples illustrated this connection by noting how much they wished they could take their minds off income and their financial problems. With both spouses working long hours, they spoke about having to talk about "our problems when we go to bed at night and then we end up being awake half the night." The wife noted, "It just sets us back several days because we're so tired."

To the debt-to-asset ratio, we add the income-to-needs ratio, a well-established measure of a family's level of living. The ratio adjusts total family income for size of family in relation to the poverty line. A score of 4 refers to a level of living that is four times the poverty line for a particular size of family. We excluded unstable work from the analysis because it does not apply to farmers who are self-employed.

In analyses to estimate the effects of the income-to-needs ratio, the debt-to-asset ratio, and farm value on economic pressure, we found that pressure was not linearly related to farm value. Both low and high levels of farm value increased the risk of economic pressure, much as Barlett's work (1993) indicates. To fit the model to data, we followed Bollen's (1990) prescription and included two measures of farm value, squared and unsquared, as shown in Figure 4.4. Among farm families in the sample, economic pressure increased with indebtedness, low income, and both large and small farm operations, defined by market value.

A greater variety of economic circumstances appears among nonfarm families (see Figure 4.5). Level of living differences capture some of this variation, as indicated by the income-to-needs and debt-to-asset ratios. Some form of unstable work was reported by over one-fifth of the non-farm men, including episodes of unemployment, underemployment, and demotions. Any evidence of work instability was sufficient to identify men with unstable work. Income loss could not be measured satisfactorily within a single wave of data, though displaced farm families had

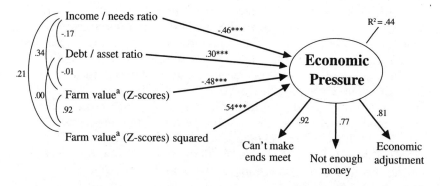

Figure 4.4. Antecedents of economic pressure for farm families ($N = 129$). Approximate current market value of farm, including land, machinery, buildings, and livestock. *Farm value* squared was included in order to model its curvilinear relation to economic pressure. $\chi^2_8 = 10.65$, $P = .22$, $GFI = .977$, $AGFI = .919$, $*p < .10.$ $**p < .05.$ $***p < .01.$

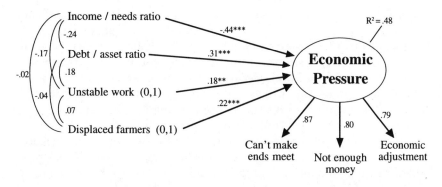

Figure 4.5. Antecedents of economic pressure for nonfarm families (N = 320). Since *unstable work* and *displaced farmers* are dichotomous variables, a polychoric matrix was analyzed using a weighted last squares estimator. χ^2_8 = 7.86, P = .45, *GFI* = .999, *AGFI* = .995, *p < .10.. **p < .05.. ***p < .01.

such losses over the past decade. With this in mind, we defined displacement as an index of income loss.

Relatively low income and heavy indebtedness account for most of the economic pressure experienced by nonfarm families. However, men with unstable work and those who lost their farm in the 1980s were clearly at greater risk of such pressure than other men. In both farm and nonfarm families, we account for approximately 45–50% of the variance on economic pressure.

How were hardships expressed in the experiences of Iowans and their families, farm and nonfarm? Even with indebtedness, low income, and unstable work in the picture, it is clear that the displaced farm families remained more deprived than other nonfarm families at the end of the decade. We know from Tables 4.3 and 4.4 that this deprivation included substantial social and emotional costs for boys and girls. In particular, children from displaced families were most likely to have fathers who were depressed and ineffective in problem solving, and consequently unlikely to assume a nurturing role as a parent. The children of these men scored relatively high on felt rejection by parents and on emotional distress. In later chapters we consider in more detail the relation between economic pressure and individual and family well-being.

THE FARM CRISIS AND IOWA FAMILIES, 1989

Iowa families had experienced the worst economic decline since the Great Depression when we began to carry out fieldwork in the winter of

1989. The "worst of times" had passed, people believed and hoped, and Iowans were looking forward to better times in the years ahead. In our sample, we identified three types of families that had very different stories to tell about the 1980s: farm, displaced farm, and nonfarm families.

The families still in farming had survived the crisis, if only barely, and they made up one-fifth of the sample. Some would eventually end up in both worlds, running a small farm and working off the farm (one-tenth of the study families in 1989). Slightly more than 1 out of 10 families in the study sample had moved out of farming by the end of the decade, a loss most fully revealed in their extraordinary level of economic strain and hardship. For a number of the farmers and displaced farmers, memories of the 1980s were memories of exceedingly painful times, coupled with family support, occasional regrets, feelings of bitterness, and valuable lessons. Displaced families, in particular, demonstrated a legacy of continuing emotional and family distress.

Families not engaged in farming, whether before or after the farm crisis, were not doing as well economically as families still in farming. Wage levels had declined across the decade for a good many of these Iowans, and most were striving to make ends meet through a strategy of multiple earners and jobs. Nearly four out of five women in nonfarm households, displaced and other, were holding paid jobs. This plus different work schedules for husband and wife, and the husband's second job had markedly increased time pressures in Iowa families and diminished what one wife called their "time together."

Hard-pressed families were trying to make ends meet through loans and borrowings, through the reduction of consumption, and through the generation of additional income, as in the wife's employment and that of the husband's second job. We used the reduction of consumption as evidence of economic pressure and identified key sources among farm and nonfarm families. In both sectors, farm and nonfarm, low family income and heavy indebtedness markedly increased the level of economic pressure. In addition, both large and small farm operations, defined in terms of farm value, were linked to economic pressure among farm families. For the nonfarm families, the hard-pressed were most likely to have a history of unstable work and the loss of a farm. Both of these factors significantly increased their level of economic pressure. We turn in the next chapter to a more detailed account of the Iowa farm and displaced farm families in terms of strategies of survival and recovery.

NOTES

1. Economic adjustments were indexed by reports from both parents concerning changes they made in response to financial difficulties over the past year.

Each spouse noted (1 = yes, 0 = no) whether their family had made any of 17 possible cutbacks in expenditures or assets during the past year (e.g., giving up medical insurance, reducing utility costs). Parent responses were combined into a single index. If either or both parents responded yes to an item, the index increased by 1 (range = 0–17). Separate parental reports of adjustments were significantly correlated ($r = .59$).

2. We divided the estimated value of all debts by total family assets to obtain a debt-to-asset ratio. Because of skewness in the distribution of the resulting coefficient, we used a natural log transformation of the original variable in the analyses.

Chapter 5

Survival, Loss, and Adaptation: A Perspective on Farm Families

Glen H. Elder, Jr., Elizabeth B. Robertson,
and E. Michael Foster

Over the last three years farming has not made a living for us.
—Iowa farmer, winter, 1989

Farm survival and loss experiences during the 1980s identify contrasting states of family well-being. A good many Iowa families managed to survive in farming, whether full- or part-time, and came out of the decade with an economic advantage when compared to nonfarm families as a group. By comparison, the legacy of farm loss seemed to offer little more than disadvantages of one kind or another. However, survival and loss experiences were by no means uniform. Some farm families encountered very difficult times, "living on the edge," as one couple put it, whereas other farm operations were remarkably successful in escaping the recessionary cycle (Barlett, 1993). Still, other families, living under a black cloud of farm indebtedness, were beginning to see a ray of light ahead. Families that lost a farm are likely to include the deeply distressed and those on a path of economic recovery through nonfarm employment.

This chapter explores the survival adaptations and lessons of farm families and the psychosocial experience of loss and recovery among the displaced. Unlike the prior chapter and its comparative thrust, this chapter attends to variation in experience and adaptation within the farm and displaced farm groups. We also investigate some implications of life changes for parents and children. These include the quality of marital support, intergenerational ties, and emotional health.

SOCIAL TRENDS AND THEIR LOCAL IMPLICATIONS

The driving force behind the economic and social changes of the region has much to do with the declining profitability of farming. As discussed in Chapter 3, gross farm income increased dramatically from the early 1970s in the state of Iowa, but most of it was absorbed by the soaring expenses of farm production, as in fuel and equipment, fertilizer, seed, and pesticides. Iowa farmers have been earning more but gaining less over the years to support their families and to reinvest.

Pressures to borrow have been restrained in many cases by the desire to get out of debt. As a young farmer put it, "I'd hate to live the rest of my life under this financial cloud of gloom. Part of it might be good for us [in terms of the lessons learned], but I'm sure it's taken years off our lives." Indebtedness cause people to place many things on hold and to question the wisdom of anything other than hard work. Vacations often proved to be a distant memory. Living a good life, as several farmers put it, became something they could look forward to in retirement, rather than something in the present. Some of these pressures were evident in the comments of a middle-aged man with more than 500 acres: "Farming has been tough and a strain on all of us. I'm sure we've all been a little short-fused, but it still is a fairly good place in which to raise kids."

These pressures have mounted rather dramatically among farmers with relatively small landholdings. Farms and operations with up to 200 acres have capital expenses (equipment, etc.) similar to much larger farms, but they could not match the same level of return. Cash flow problems and nearly overpowering levels of indebtedness had become almost chronic states in this segment of Iowa farm life. As the wife of a young farmer explained with exasperation, "We can't pay back our farming debt with a hundred acres of farm to run. So our biggest concern is, 'how are we going to be coming out of this.'"

The couple responded by attempting to increase family income through off-farm employment. The husband started working as a local trucker and the wife picked up a clerical job in the nearby town. Historically, farmers and their wives have turned to off-farm employment as a survival strategy in dismal economic times (Pfeffer & Gilbert, 1991) and we see evidence of this strategy in Iowa over the past decades. Off-farm employment has been adopted with increasing frequency by farm operators in the state. Over half of the farm operators currently hold jobs off the farm, and the percentage of wives with off-farm jobs is even higher.[1] Murdock and Leistritz conclude that the high rates of farm failure in the Great Plains and Midwest are due in part to this region's limited opportunities for off-farm work "to supplement farm income and defray operating expenses" (1988, p. 178).

In the Iowa study, the dual goal of farm survival and family well-being often placed wives in conflict with their husbands, especially when women brought home a substantial paycheck. In troubled times, farmers tended to plow as much as possible of the farm's earnings back into the operation, hoping to make it more viable, whereas their wives understandably sought more money for the family in terms of food, housing, clothing, and school expenses.

New furniture for the home versus new machinery for the farm symbolized the dilemma that generally led to resolution in favor of the farm. Wives often complained about inadequate support from the farm and husbands insisted on the necessity of capitalizing the farm operation, even during hard times. In some cases, separate savings and checking accounts for the family were set up to handle the wife's earnings.

We turn now to the off-farm employment strategy of the Iowa families and to its implications for family and farm. As a rule, this strategy meant, as one wife put it, "much less time to be together," a change greatly regretted by couples in the study. But the merger of family and business in the farm family also had its costs in the difficulty of separating out these concerns.

Farmers had trouble putting aside the cares of the farm at night and spoke about their inability to get away mentally and for family vacations. Especially in hard times and busy seasons, farm needs controlled the day, dictating responses to family needs. These dual considerations of business and family are expressed in the human experience and strains of off-farm employment for many families in the region.

WORKING OFF THE FARM AS A SURVIVAL STRATEGY

Iowa farm families (in which father defined himself as a farmer) can be viewed according to their economic reliance on off-farm employment. At the most conventional end of the distribution are farm families (Type I in Table 5.1) in which the husband still works full-time on the farm and the wife may be employed up to 30 hours off the farm. Two out of five of the self-defined farmers were coping with their unpromising economic situation in this manner as the 1980s came to an end. At the other end of the off-farm employment continuum we find 12 families (Type III) in which both husband and wife held jobs off the farm. The wife is employed for 30 hours or more. Type II families fall between these modes of off-farm employment.

Forty families living on a farm were headed by men who did not define themselves as farmers. Men who operated at least 100 acres in 1988 and

Table 5.1. Iowa Families Involved in Agricultural Operations by Off-Farm Economic Activity, 1988–1989

Type of family	Average acreage	Percentage of income from farming	Debt-to-asset ratio, farm-related[a]
I Farm families—male head does not work off farm, wife may work up to 30 hours (N = 36) ↘	445	90	.43
II Families with extensive off-farm employment (N = 42) ↘	497	71	.58
III Dual career on and off farm—both husband and wife work off farm, but also substantial acreage (N = 12) ↘	430	40	.58
IV Part-time operation—male head does not think of self as farmer, nonfarm job (N = 24) ↘	277	28	.68
V Hobby operation—lives in country but works off farm (N = 16)	9	0	.25

[a] Median values

did so with a primary nonfarm job were defined as heads of a part-time farm family, Type IV. Men in the last group, Type V, typically lived in the country on a small parcel of land. They generally fit the term *hobby farmer,* though some were involved in a subsistence life-style. As shown in the table, economic dependence on farming sharply declines across the five categories of farm families.

Of those reporting a significant proportion of agricultural income, Type I families scored lowest on a farm-related index of indebtedness, the debt-to-asset ratio: .43. By comparison, the other two family types ranked above this figure and much closer to the critical line of survival (.43 vs. .58; Stover & Clark, 1991). As a group, the Type I families managed the largest number of acres, whether owned or rented in; and they were most likely to be doing so with the additional responsibility of livestock (Table 5.2). They were clearly more invested in their farming operation and less tied into the off-farm labor market, when compared to other farm families. One consequence of this strategy is a more modest income than that of other farm families.

Table 5.2. Socioeconomic Status of Iowa Farm Families by Type of Operation, 1988

Farm type	Total family income, median	Acreage		Livestock		Employed off-farm		Percentage of income from wife (%)
		Owned & operated (X)	Rented (X)	None (%)	Hogs (%)	Husband (%)	Wife (%)	
Large farms								
I N=35	$35,200	153	320	17	61	0	59	8
II N=43	$41,750	80	328	17	45	41	77	30
III N=12	$52,250	110	293	50	25	100	100	33
Small farms								
IV N=24	$48,840	40	160	52	26	100	71	16
V N=16	$41,874	9	0	31	31	100	63	24

What did Iowans in each of these farming operations think about the farm economy and their farming prospects? We asked such questions of the men and compared their answers across the four types (Table 5.3). The last type (Type 5) includes farm operations that are too small to be considered more than a hobby, and thus it was excluded from the analysis.

Nearly one-third of the men felt that Iowa farmers were still in very serious condition and slightly more drew the same conclusion about their own operation (Table 5.3). By and large, the men were satisfied with farming as a way of life but not as a way to make a living (46 vs. only 18%, very satisfied). Indeed, over 30% claimed to be waiting for the opportunity to leave farming.

The wait in one case reflected the contrary pulls of family tradition and obligation, on the one hand, and economic realities, on the other. A farmer with a debts "from here to there," as he put it, reflected on his still painful quandary: "Every other week I have to deal with the folks who loaned me money and I find it awfully difficult. I am left with less desire to farm because it doesn't look as if there is any future." The continual problems of making a living conflict with incentive to retain the farm as a family tradition. The real prospect of losing it made him feel guilty with regard to his father: "I feel as if I let him down, even though he has been dead many years." When asked how he is handling the problem (crisis first occurred in 1983), he replied,

> Not very well. It definitely influences us today. I think about it every day. One minute I think I should quit farming, sell and get out for health reasons. And the next minute I think I can't give up yet.

Waiting for the opportunity to leave farming also had much to do with the loans and collateral posted by kin in an effort to help the family get started. In an era of diminished land values, the sale of a farm had little chance of recovering the money invested in the place during more prosperous times. One farm couple was haunted, in particular, by the prospect of saving their own situation while losing nearly $100,000 that their parents had invested in the farm. Another couple who had tried most everything to stay afloat reported a plan to cut their farm losses after a drought and low feeder pig prices and try to support themselves with off-farm employment alone for a period of a year or so. They hoped to maintain control of the family farm, their livelihood over the past 15 years, but they were not sure they could.

Type III men represent a small but strategic group relative to matters of survival in farming. They most completely exemplify the use of off-farm employment as a mode of economic survival and appear to rank well above other family types on the sale of family land and assets in

Table 5.3. Attitudes Toward Farming by Type of Family Farm

	Total (%)	Large farms (%)			Small Farms (%)	Probable
Attitudes	Types I–IV (N=11)	I (N=36)	II (N=42)	III (N=12)	IV (N=24)	significance level (%)
Iowa farmers in very serious condition	33	31	33	50	25	NS
Own farm in very serious condition	35	36	33	42	33	NS
Farming a way of life, very satisfied	46	58	40	75	21	$\chi^2 = 12.9$*
Farming as way to make a living, very satisfied	18	25	21	0	13	NS
Would leave farming if given opportunity, very likely or likely	34	17	38	17	63	$\chi^2 = 15.4$*

* $p \leq .10$.

order to meet the demands of creditors. We asked whether the husband and wife added another job, declared bankruptcy, and/or sold land and assets in the 1980s. The most common response was an added job for either husband or wife (36%), followed in frequency by the selling of land and assets (35%, and by declaring bankruptcy (8%). To a great many families, bankruptcy represented an immoral solution to the economic crisis.

Figure 5.1 compares the first four family types, along with the displaced families, on these economic actions. Judging from the prevalence of each response, Type IV families appear to have been least affected by the farm crisis. They were least dependent on farm income and ranked low on indebtedness at the end of the 80s. They seldom report any response to the crisis, except for the off-farm employment of the wife. The Type IIs show more evidence of a troubled past, but the most troubled by far are the Type III families, who closely resemble the displaced families on measures of economic adaptation.

Type III men do not equal the displaced farmers on actual losses; they are still farming, if only holding on by a thread, and they less often report a lengthy bout with depression during the 80s (34 vs. 48%). However, their emotional costs show up in accounts of earlier periods of

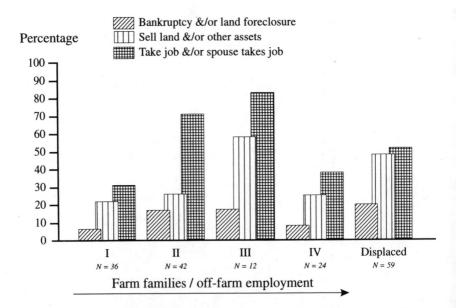

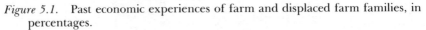

Figure 5.1.   Past economic experiences of farm and displaced farm families, in percentages.

anxiety and in reports of efforts to seek help with personal problems. Periods of extreme anxiety are consistent with the uncertainty of farm survival in the 1980s crisis. As one farmer put it, "not knowing what would happen" was difficult to deal with. Forty-two percent of the men reported a period of extreme anxiety during the 80s, in comparison to slightly less than one-fifth of all other farmers. The latter percentage also applies to the displaced farmers. Both the Type III men and the displaced farmers reported unusually high rates of seeking help for emotional problems in the 80s, from 18 to 22%.

Not having experienced such hard times before, the couples in Type III families experienced much anxiety over the course to follow. Their advisors did not always agree. A case in point for one family was the bankruptcy option; in the wife's account, "We didn't know for sure exactly what to do, to do it or not to do it." The culture was against it and the realities of the situation. The husband had trouble with the bankruptcy option because it did not allow him the time or option to pay back the borrowed money. "They won't let you pay it back and I guess that's kind of like stealing."

Reflecting on the land sales and past trauma, a middle-aged farmer concluded, "We ended up better than some. We ended up staying here, and not in the road with a suitcase in our hand." His wife agreed, but she noted how concerned she was about the emotions he held back: "I'm the kind to scream and screech and bawl about it. But you didn't. I worried about you for about a year and a half." That time was a "bad news deal," as the husband put it, and he quickly changed the subject. What evidence do we have that the "bad deal" remains a personal problem for certain farm couples?

Let us consider reports by wives on husbands in the winter of 1989. As noted in Chapter 4, displaced farmers ranked highest on depressed mood and ineffective problem solving (reported by wives) when the comparisons included all farm and nonfarm families. However, we find no significant differences on these measures across the farm types, I through V. This result also applies to the wives, as described by their husbands. Off-farm employment in the farm types is not linked to psychological well-being among fathers or mothers. However, men who reported an episode of depression in the farm crisis were more likely than other men to be described by their wives as melancholy or depressed (t-ratio $= 2.20, p < .05$). One of the farmers with a history of depression claimed that he was smiling more now, but his wife replied, "Still not enough." "Yes," he concurred, as if he had heard that before, "not enough."

The trials, stresses, and losses of family farming in the 1980s assigned little if any promise to a future in farming for young boys in farm families. Farming meant long hours, very hard work, and a stressful existence in which income was usually modest and uncertain. The farm mothers were typically against such a future for their sons and a good many of the fathers expressed the same views (Elder et al., 1993). At the ripe age of a seventh-grader, a surprisingly small number of boys were looking to farming as a future (seven sons of farmers).

A farmer with a large operation of some 400 acres noted the age-old tradition, "You always want your oldest boy to follow in your tracks and be a farmer. But I don't want my boy to be a farmer. . . . In some ways, I might even discourage him." He well appreciated the disadvantages of farming, from low pay to endless hours and economic uncertainty, and he did not want the responsibility of making someone else's decision. Another large-scale farmer who did want his sons to consider farming (and would not say anything about it), laid out the harsh realities: For one, "they have got to learn to do without a lot of material things if they want to farm."

Types of Family Strategy

When we put all of the pieces of information together on these families, the Type I families appear to have survived the 80s by employing a cautious management style. In response to a series of questions on family history and experiences, the couples tended to stress the tighter economic situation they had experienced and the need for a more conservative use of money. Financial crises and close calls in the 1980s reinforced the wisdom of this strategy.

Barlett describes this style as one in which farm operators "avoided debt, preferred direct control over farm tasks, accepted a more modest standard of living, and expected hard manual labor and personal attention to detail" (1993, p. 138). Several of these farmers talked about the necessity of eliminating all hired help. On one farm, two hired hands had been released. Family members, particularly maturing sons, became the replacements. With a very tight budget to contend with, the couples generally looked forward to the day when they would not "have to think about income all the time," or worry about a debt that seemed endless.

When wives did not work in these households, husband and wife typically managed different worlds, farm and household. For example, a mother of two boys who once taught school expressed no desire to do so again, and described her marital arrangement as very traditional. If the issue concerns the farm, her husband decides. "If it concerns the house or the kids, I decide." She added, "I have the typical farm wife's complaint that there's never any cash to spend on us. I think any farm wife has the same complaint. It's not a big problem."

Looking at her husband, she observed, "You make the money so you decide how to handle it. We don't have any big disagreements. If you say we need something for the farm, we get it." Though family money seemed to be short all the time, she felt that they had enough to support the children. Their need was not great enough to force a return to teaching against her wishes, especially since she valued the family time that would have to be sacrificed.

These families had less in the way of income, when compared to other farm families, but their material desires were less as well. We asked the wives and mothers about their material goals and the materialistic demands of their children. Three item scales were constructed on both of these topics, with alpha coefficients of .60 and .72, respectively.[2] The Type I mothers scored lower on both scales, when compared to the other farm families, but the difference was not statistically significant. However, all farm women in the three groups do rank significantly lower on materialism, as measured by the two indexes, when compared to the nonfarm women ($p < .05$). Among some families that had been on the edge of insolvency, the lessons of hardship were shared with children in order to reinforce the importance of living within the family's means. One mother acknowledged that her children "remember those years" of great hardship and "are aware of money" and of "how we are doing."

Whatever the material aspirations and resources, other women who centered their lives around the household (Type I) insisted that the "typical farm wife complaint" did represent a notable problem. Their husbands defined spending on the farm as an investment or a form of savings, whereas they could only see this action in terms of what it took away from the household life-style and the children. Husbands who excluded wives from the farm's business facts and decisions thus invited *uninformed* criticisms of farm expenditures: "Why do we need a new John Deere or repairs on a machine we don't use?" Similarly, husbands were frequently ill-informed on family or children needs, and thus resented expenditures of this kind.

The distinctive features of the farm family (such as a business and home in one location) ensured that husband and wife would "see a lot of each other," as a young farmer noted, but it did not ensure shared understandings and priorities in many cases. The wife's off-farm employment undermined the shared life-style and made more problematic a shared knowledge and understanding. In Types II and III families, wives were contributing, on average, one-third of the total family income, a contribution that helped to raise concerns about the fairness of a marriage in which the husband's earnings from the farm were reinvested in the business and the wife's earnings were the sole economic base of the household.

Consider the tension in the marital relationship of a midlife farmer and his wife who are both employed in jobs off the farm (Type III). Indebtedness remains high, and the farm operation barely pays its way. When asked what they disagreed about, the husband replied, "Money and farming, always farming's to blame. It is just a never-ending battle." His wife took issue with this interpretation by claiming, "We don't disagree about how money is handled, except that I don't like you spending it on farming when we have other bills to pay. I wish you'd help me pay some bills." On two occasions involving other families, purchases (a new tractor or farm truck) were delivered to the farm even before the wife had learned about the decision.

Finding Work and Time

The decision of men and their wives to seek off-farm employment is typically linked to a belief that it will enable the family to live on and operate the farm. In one case, a woman from a Type III family explained that she went to work full-time as a bookkeeper when they finally realized that it had to be done in order to permit them to continue "living on the farm and operating it." Apart from the profitability of farming, the value of this goal stressed life-style preferences, such as the responsibility experiences of farm children in caring for animals, the ease of supervising children on a farm, and the shared family experience of farm life.

One-third of the farm women in the work force managed to obtain professional jobs, such as teaching; one-third entered lower white-collar jobs in stores and firms; and one-third obtained low-paying jobs. One of the wives asked her husband whether he liked the way she earned money, making doughnuts. When he diplomatically replied "Yeah," she promptly objected, "I don't." The job seemed more acceptable to her after he noted the limited options: "What choices are there in a small town in Iowa?"

At the time of our family visit in 1989, the average work week for the men ranged from 57 to 66 hours. Among working wives, the weekly average increased sharply from Type I to Type III families and then decreased for families on small farms. The off-farm employment of women led to some changes in household responsibilities as father and children shouldered more duties, according to the evidence at hand.

The most useful index of this adjustment compares Type I versus Types II and III. Forty-one percent of the fathers in Types II and III households, where most mothers worked off the farm, reported helping out on matters of child rearing, as against only 17% of the fathers in Type I families. A similar difference appears on household chores in general. When the mothers were asked whether their children were involved in household chores, nearly 60% of the women in Types II and III families reported they were, in comparison to one-third of the mothers in full-time farm households. The off-farm employment of mothers thus appears to represent an important force in shaping the household roles of children, our topic in Chapter 6.

Time pressures for the Iowa couples stand out among the dual-career families (Type III). They reported long hours on the job in town and in operating a large farm. How were they able to handle both worlds? One strategy involves the reduction of labor- and time-intensive livestock, such as dairy animals and hogs. For example, Type I families are mainly operators of farms with livestock, whereas only half of Type III and IV families have livestock. Moreover, the latter families tend to have a smaller number of animals. The pressures of managing both worlds are well stated by a young farmer:

> The daily schedule is really tough on our lives because we both get up early in the morning and go all day and then come home at night and go over and do chores. In the summer I try to do my own field work and that kind of thing. We (my wife and I) just don't have a whole lot of time together. By the time we get any time together it's supper time and shortly after that it's bedtime. When we were first married it wasn't so bad because we weren't each working a job in town and then trying to farm. I sure hope it gets better.

With this couple in mind, one might expect support for the notion that work interferes with family life. However, less than 10% of the farm wives with jobs claim that this interference occurs often in their life. Farm husbands are more likely to report such interference, a percentage that is relatively constant among all three groups of farm families, Types I, II, and III (28%).

We also find no evidence that job dissatisfaction among husbands and wives is more common in dual-career families. The Iowa couples were asked to rate their job satisfaction on a scale from 1 to 5. Mean values across all categories of farming are typically close to 4.00. Self-defined farmers are more satisfied with their work than small farm operators who define themselves in terms of an off-farm job ($p < .01$), but we find no indication that off-farm employment diminishes the satisfaction of men with large farm operations. The off-farm employment of women in a large farm unit is coupled with less job satisfaction than we find among women from smaller operations, but the difference is too small to be reliable.

Whatever the demands of off-farm employment, the five types of farm families have much in common on economic pressure and marital support (discussed and measured in Chapter 4). Perhaps reflecting the lower significance of material resources among farm families (cf. Salamon,

1992), the economic pressure reported by parents and children in the Type I families resembles that experienced by more affluent families in Types III through IV. All of these families are better off than those who lost their farm.

LEAVING THE FARM

A good many displaced farmers remember the past as a bad time, "five years of hell," as one put it. For most of these men, the loss occurred between 1981 and 1987, and yet the costs persist in economic pressures and disadvantage. What factors have enabled some men and wives to put the crisis behind them and move on with their lives?

Two general considerations establish a context in which to address this question: (1) the male-oriented culture and social structure of Iowa agriculture, and (2) the special properties of farm work and life. The turning wheel of life on Iowa farms typically involves a transfer of management and ownership from father to son or sons (Friedberger, 1988, chapter 5, p. 21). In some cases, the transfer involves the wife's father and husband. Nearly one out of five men who gave up their farm did not grow up on one and a majority ran farms that were initially owned by their wife's father. Though Iowa women often play major roles in the farm operation (see also Rosenfeld, 1985), they seldom play the lead role. As Deborah Fink concludes, on Iowa farms "only men are recognized and supported as farmers" (1986, p. 232). This observation clearly applies to farm families in our study.

The gendered nature of farming suggests that attachment to farming and depressed feelings over the lost farm should be more common among men than among their wives. What might this psychology be like among displaced farmers? Consider the words of Marc Fried on urban relocation. The emotional states in "grieving for a lost home" seem likely to be common among the displaced farmers. In Fried's study, half of the men and women who had been moved out of an urban area reported emotional distress and even severe depression.

> Grieving for a lost home includes the feeling of painful loss, the continued longing, the general depressive tone, frequent symptoms of psychological or social or somatic distress, the active work required in adapting to the altered situation, the sense of helplessness, the occasional expressions of both direct and displaced anger, and the tendencies to idealize the lost place. At their most extreme, these reactions of grief are intense, deeply felt, and at times, overwhelming. (1963, p. 151)

To understand the significance of a lost farm, we need to appreciate the intergenerational meanings of the farm as a family legacy. Another consideration involves the special properties of farm work as it is integrated into family life: the blending of farming and family roles, of work and leisure, and of self-direction with cooperative endeavors. The bond of work and family with place reinforces a sense of attachment to land (Barlett, 1993). The work of a farmer entails elements of independence and connectedness, both with people and with the spiritual essence and biology of nature. To many fathers and mothers in displaced farm families, farm life is remembered as an ideal environment for children and their development, for teaching responsibility through the care of animals, and for bringing family members together. However, off-farm employment has eroded some of this favored quality.

From the standpoint of leaving the farm, loss of autonomy or self-direction is one of the most expectable and powerful changes for men. Approximately half of the displaced farmers found jobs that bore some relation to their work in farming, such as a mechanic and feed dealer, but neither of these occupational roles offered men the same degree of independence. Mooney quotes a marginal farmer on his work as a meat-packer: "Sure it's good money, can't beat the money and the benefits, but I'm not made for that kind of work. I just don't have it in me. I hate every minute I'm there" (1988, chap. 5, p. 23). Having a boss was one of the more onerous features, along with close supervision and rigid scheduling. Especially in rural Iowa, one-time farmers in blue-collar employment should be especially resentful of current circumstances while remaining attached to the old farm and its memories.

In the Eyes of Men and Women

When we combine the gendered nature of farm life with the distinctive features of farm work, loss of the farm highlights differences between husband and wife. Men are likely to view the loss in terms of the farm itself and to dismiss any positive aspects of the transition. A quality job may have little to do with how they feel about their departure from farming. With more investment in the well-being of children and less in the farm operation, women are apt to look to a future out of agriculture while their husbands retain the dream of returning to farming and their old farm. If this is so, the adjustment of women will have much to do with their economic well-being. They should feel the least amount of distress over the loss when their level of living is much improved.

A North Dakota family that moved to Iowa after losing the farm in the mid-1980s illustrates this cleavage between husband and wife. Family life had improved on time together and on income since the loss, but the lure of the farm remained strong in the husband's mind. When asked about disagreements, he said to his wife:

Sometimes we disagree about what to do with the farm in North Dakota, and on how I would really like to go back and farm and you wouldn't. Although I'm not set on doing that type of thing now, if things were in the right position, I might and I think you wouldn't care.

His wife had just complained at great length about the hard, endless hours of work on the Dakota farm and the lack of money. She responded by asserting:

The farm still influences us today because you don't like it here and want to go back. Yet we left there to have a better life. It is hard for the kids and me because we don't understand why you want to go back.

An answer to the question Why go back? has much to do with culture and upbringing. As a farmer put it, "Farming gets in your blood. It is almost like a disease, I think. It's the eleventh commandment; thou shalt farm" (Rosenblatt, 1990, p. 10). This point is consistent with the responses of displaced farmers and their wives to a set of questions on the transition out of farming. One question concerns the desire to return to farming. On a scale from 1 to 5, we find very little marital consensus on this objective, a correlation of only .30. Over four out of five men had higher scores than their wives, a difference expressed in the significantly higher mean score of men (3.5 vs. 2.8, $p < .01$). Only a half-dozen wives expressed more attachment than their spouses.

We also asked the couples whether they felt bitter about the way they had been treated, thought their future had lost its promise, and felt angry and depressed over the experience. The last two items were combined into a single index of unhappy and angry feelings. All of these items and the question on attachment were averaged to form a summary index which we call *depressed feelings*.

Except for bitter feelings and the perception of a bleak future, we find more distress reported by men than by wives (Table 5.4). Men were more attached to the idea of returning to the farm and felt more depressed and angry over the loss. Couples tended to agree most on whether they were ill-treated, a correlation of .52. In some cases, this sense of ill-treatment evolved into a grievance culture.

The experience of bankruptcy fueled such emotions. One woman, still irate over the unfairness of the system, thought it outrageous that some debts were forgiven and theirs were not. They paid all their debts in town, except for their debt to the agency (FMHA), and now feel unfairly stigmatized by the bankruptcy course they had to follow. People other than friends "don't know that we didn't stick everybody in town. When you take out bankruptcy people automatically think that you came out smelling like a rose. We didn't."

Table 5.4. Farm Attachment and Mood of Displaced Farm Couples, in Means

Farm attachment and mood	Correlations Husband/wife	Mean scores Husband	Mean scores Wife	Probability level Husband vs. wife
Attachment to farm, land[a]	.30	3.5	2.8	H > W, p = .001
Bitter, resentful[b]	.52	2.6	2.6	NS
Unhappy, angry[c]	.34	2.9	2.5	H > W, p = .07
Bleak future[d]	.35	3.1	2.8	NS
Depressed feelings, summary index[e]	.56	3.0	2.6	H > W, p = .002

[a] "You would return to farming if you could." Responses range from *strongly agree* (1) to *strongly disagree* (5). Scores reversed for means.

[b] "You feel bitter and resentful about how you have been treated." *Strongly agree*, 1; *strongly disagree*, 5. Scores were reversed.

[c] A two-item index of unhappy and angry: "You are angry that you were forced out of farming" and "You are unhappy or depressed about no longer farming." For both items (r = .75), *strongly agree*, 1; and *strongly disagree*, 5. Scores were reversed and averaged to form the index.

[d] "Your future does not hold the promise you thought it would." *Strongly agree*, 1; *strongly disagree*, 5. Scores were reversed.

[e] All of the items above were included in a general measure of depressive affect regarding loss of the farm. Scores on each item were averaged to form the index: alpha = .76.

Both differing and similar views among displaced farmers and their wives could reflect their social origins on a farm or elsewhere. Over 80% of the men came from a family farm as did approximately 60% of the wives. We compared couples who shared a farm background with those where only the husband came from a farm. For the most part, marital differences were not larger or notably smaller between the two types of family backgrounds.

Still Grieving for a Lost Farm

Not all displaced couples feel strongly about their loss, and differences in social origin and destination may account for this variation. For example, the farm origins of displaced farmers tell us about their socialization into farming and, most importantly, about the nature and meaning of the farm loss itself (Elder et al., 1993). Attachment to the idea of farming should be most fully developed among men with a farm childhood. Such attachment would also be a factor in the persistence of emotional distress over the loss. A second factor of potential importance involves the status level of the job they now hold. The higher the job's status, other things being equal, the greater the prospect for some autonomy in the work process, a quality men experience in farming. Three out of five men reported white-collar jobs during the winter of 1989.

To explore these hypotheses, we compared three categories: no farm origin, farm origins with white-collar job, and farm origins with blue-collar job. Only the farm origin group is large enough to permit analysis of occupational variations after the farm loss. Using analysis of variance, we obtained significant differences ($p < .001$) across all measures except "bitter and resentful." Men who ended up in blue-collar work are the most distressed by the loss experience and the nonfarm origin group is least distressed. Blue-collar men who grew up on farms remain more committed to the idea of a return to farming than any other group, and they also rank at the top on unhappiness and anger over the loss.

Figure 5.2 shows the mean scores on men's attachment and depressed feelings by these categories. Not surprisingly, we find no corresponding pattern among the wives. Their attachment to farming and depressed feelings are not related to farm origins generally, whether husband's

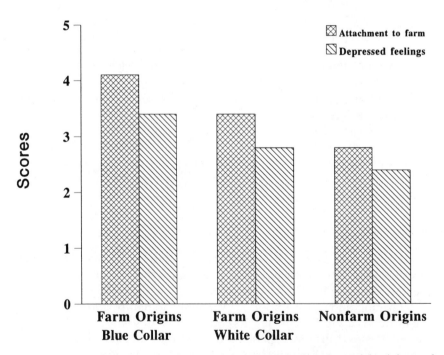

Figure 5.2.   Men's attitude to farm and depressed feelings by social origins and current occupation, in means. (a) Attachment to farming: F ratio = 5.1, df = 2.54, $p < .01$. (b) Depressed feelings, summary index: F ratio = 8.8, df = 2.54, $p < .001$.

or their own, and husband's occupational standing is not an important source either. Both attachment to the farm and farming as well as depressed feelings over the loss depict a continuing preoccupation with the past on the part of some displaced farmers.[3] We have argued that wives are more invested in the present and future, both for their children and for the family as a whole. Assuming this to be the case, current economic conditions should make a difference in their sentiments regarding farming and unhappiness over the farm's loss. The more successful the family's adjustment after the loss, the less they should be attached to the family farm and troubled by its loss.

To identify successful and unsuccessful families, we used three economic measures: debt-to-asset ratio, economic adjustments, and income-to-needs ratio. Successful families were defined by a debt-to-asset ratio of .50 or less (the sample average is .50), by reported economic adjustments of less than 7, and by an income-to-needs ratio of 2.45 or greater (nearly half of the families in the sample fit this specification on income-to-needs). The unsuccessful families had a debt-to-asset ratio greater than .50, eight or more reported adjustments, and an income-to-needs ratio less than 2.45. All remaining families were placed in a mixed category. Ten families met the criteria of economic success, 12 families ended up in the unsuccessful category, and 35 families are in the mixed group.

Families so classified differed strikingly on economic well-being in 1989. For example, the mean debt-to-asset ratio for successful families is .23, as against a value of .95 for the unsuccessful families. The successful families reported, on average, only 3 economic adjustments for the past year, in contrast to 11 adjustments for the unsuccessful families. These large differences in economic well-being make more of a difference in the attitudes and mood of wives among displaced farm families than in the outlook of their husbands. Across all measures in Table 5.5, the variation is greater among women than among men.

Economic success has little to do with how either spouse views farming and the transition out of agriculture. The bleakness of the future has more to do with the loss of a farm among men in the displaced group than with economic well-being. This is not true for wives, however. Economic troubles shape a more dismal future among women. The results on "bitter and resentful" for women suggest that differences in their contemporary well-being also color how they interpret the past. The worse they are doing, the more bitter and resentful they are about past treatment during the economic crisis. In this respect, they resemble husbands whose attitude toward farming and the loss experience have much to do with their occupational status. The lower the status, the more attached they are to the premise of a return to farming at some point in the future.

Table 5.5. The Farm Attachment and Mood of Displaced Farm
   Couples by Relative Economic Success Since the Economic Loss,
   1989, in Means

Farm attachment and mood	Unsuccessful (N=12)	Mixed (N=35)	Successful (N=10)	p level
Attachment to farm, land (5=*strong*, 1=*weak*)				
Husband	3.8	3.5	3.3	.55
Wife	3.4	2.7	2.7	.23
Bitter and resentful (5=*bitter*, 1=*not*)				
Husband	2.8	2.7	2.0	.07
Wife	3.4	2.5	1.8	.00
Depressed over loss (5=*depressed*, 1=*not*)				
Husband	3.3	2.7	2.5	.10
Wife	2.9	2.5	2.0	.07
Sees bleak future (5=*bleak*, 1=*not so*)				
Husband	3.3	3.0	3.0	.82
Wife	3.3	2.7	2.6	.32
Depressed feelings, summary index				
Husband	3.3	2.9	2.7	.15
Wife	3.2	2.6	2.2	.02

From the evidence we have examined, displaced farmers and their
wives express very different temporal perspectives. A larger percentage
of the men are invested in the past and look forward to the day when
they can return to farming. This is especially true of farm sons who are
now in blue-collar jobs. Their wives are more invested in a nonfarm
future that promises a way of life that offers more material resources.

CONCLUSION

Iowa families at the end of the decade reflect the great diversity of life
experience during a time of unparalleled change. Some of the farm
families lost their farm, others survived major setbacks but remain on the
edge of profitability, and still others have turned mainly to off-farm
employment to make ends meet. Families that were still in farming enjoyed the highest income level of all families in the study, whereas the
loss of a farm placed a number of families at the lowest level.

In this chapter we have examined the diverse paths followed by farm
and displaced farm families in their survival and loss experiences. The

variable off-farm employment of farm families identified three socio-economic strategies: full-time farming with minimal employment off the farm (Type I), farming with more involvement in work off the farm (Type II), and the involvement of both husband and wife in work off the farm (Type III). Type I families tend to represent a conservative strategy of survival with lower overhead and indebtedness, compared to other families. Type III families have survived by committing much time to off-farm employment and by selling land and other assets. Both of these farm types entailed substantial acreage, and, in many cases, livestock as well. Smaller operations were managed by men who defined themselves in terms of nonfarm employment. These included farms with more than 100 acres in operation (Type IV) and even smaller farms that resemble hobby enterprises (Type V). Off-farm employment served as a means of staying on the farm among hard-pressed operations in Types II and III, whereas a large number of the Type IVs were hoping that they would have an opportunity to get out of farming.

For most farm families, off-farm employment entailed costs and benefits. The costs of women's employment involved an increase in time pressure and stress, less shared time as a couple and family, and the loss of farm work. A good many of these women spoke of the radical decline of a valued life-style. The benefits were economic and social, and depended in part on the quality of the employment itself and the economic returns.

Off-farm employment gave some women a chance to develop their personal and occupational skills, especially in management and the professions, though a good many jobs were both menial and low-paying. Marital ties appear to have survived these stresses in most cases, but we do find evidence that marital relations are less than fully satisfying for women who are managing the diverse worlds of home, farm, and off-farm employment. A good many women with farming roots longed for the time when they were on the farm and worked with their husbands.

The painfulness of a lost farm is still a reality for a large number of men in displaced farm families, and they typically recall a period of emotional depression or anxiety in the 1980s. They remain more invested in the loss than their wives who tend to look to the future and a better life for their children. For many men the dream of a place of their own that they could farm has faded, even though they continue to hope that they might someday be able to farm. Wives who have experienced economic success after the farm loss were least sympathetic to this aspiration.

Rural children across the farm crisis era were most at risk in displaced farm families, as we have noted in Chapter 4. These Iowa children, however, were not merely or primarily victims of the farm crisis. They had responsibilities to perform, both in the household and on the farm, responsibilities that had much to do with the problems and challenges faced by families. We turn now to the roles they actually played in Iowa households, businesses and farms.

NOTES

1. This rate of off-farm employment is higher than that reported on the basis of polls of farmers. Lasley's Iowa Poll for 1984–1987 indicates that 56% of the farm households surveyed reported no off-farm employment. Age of farmer may be a factor. Lasley's sample of men is significantly older than our sample of farmers.

2. Mother reporting on her own materialism is the simple average of three items (importance that a family is well off financially; importance of having a great deal of money; and importance of having a well-paying job). The scale ranges from 1, low materialism, to 5, high materialism, and has an alpha of .58. The second scale has the mother reporting on the target. This scale is the simple average of three items (never seems to be happy with the amount of money we have; never satisfied with things we buy; and seems to think money grows on trees). The scale ranges from 1, low materialism, to 5, high materialism, and has an alpha of .70.

3. The passage of time since the farm loss appears to make no difference in attachment to the farm and its way of life or on the extent of depressed feelings. Also, men's age or life stage in the farm crisis made surprisingly little difference in attitudes and mood. Men's age does matter, however, when we take into account the job they entered after farming. The younger men, below the age of 40, were most attached to the lost farm if they held a job in the working class, and least attached if employed in a white collar job ($\overline{X}_s$ = 3.9, white collar, and 3.7, blue collar). The two occupational groups of younger men seem to represent different views of the future—the blue collar group signifies status loss whereas the white collar workers have experienced a transition to career opportunities. Reports of depressed feelings do not follow this pattern; only blue collar employment is linked to this state.

Chapter 6

Children in the Household Economy

Glen H. Elder, Jr., E. Michael Foster, and Monika Ardelt

Always there was work to do and always it came first.
—Son of midwestern farmer, from H. Kohn, *The Last Farmer*

Children's productive roles in the family economies of rural Iowa are elements of two adaptive strategies amidst scarce resources. As noted in Chapter 4, one strategy lowers demand, while the other includes ways of increasing the supply. Under intense economic pressures, families can reduce the need for a certain level of income by lowering expenditures, and also attempt to generate more income through additional earners or sales. In practice, Iowa families have lowered expenditures by putting off purchases and canceling others, from medical care to new furniture; and they have also done so by replacing the purchase of services with family labor, including child care by older youth. The earnings of wives and children, as well as additional hours and an extra job among men, are common ways of increasing total family income.

The work roles of children and adolescents generally imply paid employment, though we favor a broader definition that spans productive activities within and outside the household. Chores in the family are thus work responsibilities even when they are not coupled with an allowance or payment. This perspective is consistent with Hall's interpretation of work as "effort or activity . . . performed for the purpose of providing goods or services of value to others" (1986, p. 13). From the vantage point of the household economy, we assume that children's involvement in productive activity, when resources are scarce, makes children's contributions to the family economy even more valuable.

If children's roles are involved in family adaptations to economic life, resource scarcities of important kinds should increase the likelihood of substantial earnings by children, their involvement in household chores, and their financial contributions to family welfare. Three types of resource scarcity are most relevant to the circumstances of Iowa families: (1) *labor scarcity*, as expressed in the culture of farm family life (Rhodes, 1989); (2) *time pressure*, as related to the employment histories of husbands and wives—time pressure increases as work time increases (Burenstam, 1970); and (3) *economic hardship*, as indexed by income level and efforts to cut back expenditures (Elder, 1974). All three types of scarcity are likely to converge in the households of farm families.

Each type of scarcity has different consequences for children's contribution to the household and family enterprise. The chronic labor shortage of the family farm gives the young a significant role to play, a situation in which tasks call for people instead of a situation in which people search for employment. These labor demands apply especially to the world of boys and to their involvement in physically demanding work. Time pressures within the household of employed parents assign priority to the services children can provide in child care, kitchen work, and house cleaning, activities that are traditionally linked to the female gender. Lastly, economic hardship places value on the earnings and services children can provide, a contribution that boys and girls could make.

As suggested by these expectations, children's household and economic activities are still gender specific to a considerable degree, especially in the male-oriented culture of farm life (Fink, 1986). Young sons are socialized to farming through its labor requirements and male incentives, whereas daughters are more involved in child care opportunities to earn money at a young age and typically seek fulfillment in a more urban environment. With these distinctions in mind, we expect the Iowa boys to be more involved in paid jobs of an agricultural nature than girls, and the latter to be more involved in household responsibilities. This is a relative difference since girls as well as boys in farm country participate in major economic ventures, such as the raising of livestock through Future Farmers of America and 4-H clubs.

No doubt most parents have thought about the costs and benefits of their children's productive roles, and some perhaps have theories about what these activities mean to their children's development. Responsibility is a popular belief about outcomes of children's experience in taking on jobs and chores and there is some evidence of this developmental gain in the beliefs of Iowa parents. For example, one mother was convinced that her children learned responsibility by caring for livestock. This is one reason, in fact, why so many parents who no longer live on a farm regretted the loss. They believe that their children lost something special by not living in the country.

Such beliefs and interpretations make sense, although empirical support is not compelling (Elder, 1974, chapter 4; Goodnow, 1988). Moreover, a good many studies even suggest that the productive work of children and youth actually increases their risk of problem behavior (Greenberger & Steinberg, 1986; Mortimer, Finch, Shanahan, & Ryu, 1991), especially when it is time-consuming. Some of this association may reflect the tendency for troubled adolescents to seek paid employment as a more rewarding alternative to school or school failure. But there is a larger issue that has to do with the meaningfulness and significance of work. Many years ago, a study of children in the Great Depression observed that

> there is a suggestive resemblance between the role of children in deprived families and farm households. Labor needs are real and meaningful on the family farm, the jobs are demanding and adult-like, and children seem to take their responsibilities seriously. (Elder, 1974, p. 71)

The meaningfulness of children's farm responsibilities reflects, we believe, their consequences for other family members. The family counts on them to carry their responsibilities and so do the animals. Both suffer the consequences when they are forgotten or poorly discharged. As a farmer's son recalled, his early morning activities before breakfast and school were substantial:

> to feed and water the livestock, the cows, the heifers, the bull, the pigs, the chickens. We had to squat on milk stools . . . dodging the cow's tail, which could slap you silly; and in winter we had to shovel out the manure trenches. (Kohn, 1988, pp. 114–115)

Such work is part of a collective enterprise that calls for "required helpfulness", the performance of difficult or challenging tasks "in response to social requirements. . . . Under the incentive of high social demands helpers often act more effectively and more persistently than at other times" (Rachman, 1979, p. 1). Farm work among boys in the Iowa study should, it seems, be associated with more prosocial qualities than the discretionary work and earnings of nonfarm youth. Similar differences may be observed among girls.

We begin with paid work experiences over 1988–1989, estimate earnings for this period, and then focus on the children who claim they had a paid job at the time of the field study, in the winter and early spring of 1989. We explore the kinds of jobs held by boys and girls, as well as the types of employers, and ask whether they felt they worked more or less than age-mates.

The issue of required helpfulness comes into play on the uses of earnings. How did the children actually use their earnings: on personal indulgence or in other ways? Did they give any of it to parents for basic expenses or for the payment of school fees? The experience of required helpfulness can also be inferred by the perceived behavioral qualities of boys and girls who are earners, as reported by farm and nonfarm parents. Theory suggests that economically active boys and girls will be viewed more positively by parents in farm than in nonfarm families. This follows from the value placed on work in farm families.

CHILDREN'S WORK ACTIVITIES AND EARNINGS

For the full sample of 451 families, most boys and girls reported some earnings for 1988–1989 when they were interviewed during the winter and early spring of 1989. Less than 5% had no income to report, though a good many were not gainfully employed at the time of the interview. Between 50 and 55% reported no paid job, and, not surprisingly, the sons and daughters of farmers were less apt to be working for pay than boys and girls in nonfarm households: 40 vs. 51%. The peak labor demands for farm youth on cultivated acreage extend from the planting season in the spring to harvest time in late summer and the fall months.

According to estimates, boys tended to earn far more than girls over the year ($321 vs. $207), whereas girls fared better from their allowance, a yearly sum of $115 vs. $98 for boys. When asked how they earned their money, two gender-differentiated activities were most frequently mentioned, farm-related work and child care (see Figure 6.1).

Sixty-two percent of the boys mentioned farm work of some kind, including the care and sale of animals, compared to one-third of the girls. Thus, in rural Iowa, even nonfarm boys are significantly involved in farm work. Virtually all of the girls listed care of children as a source of income across the year—a total of 88% in contrast to only 24% of the boys. Beyond these two major activities, boys tended to specialize in yard work and in the delivery of newspapers, whereas girls ranked slightly higher on household tasks of one kind or another. This familiar pattern of gendered activities has much in common with the experiences of American adolescents over a half-century ago in the San Francisco Bay region (Elder, 1974).

As noted earlier, three forms of resource scarcity bear upon the work activities of boys and girls in rural Iowa: (1) the labor demands most evident within farm operations, when contrasted to those of nonfarm families; (2) the time pressures associated with mother's employment and the corresponding need for household help; and (3) economic hardship and, in particular, the economic pressures expressed by parental decisions to delay or eliminate purchases of goods and services. In theo-

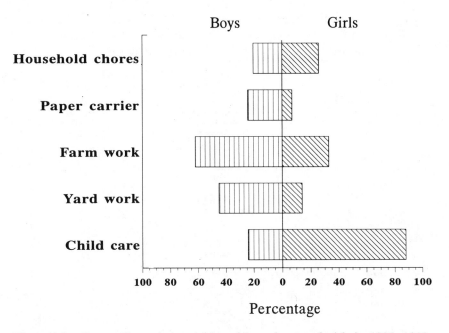

Figure 6.1. Reported earning activities of Iowa boys and girls in 1988–1989.

ry, each type of scarcity should increase children's incentives for a paid job.

We used the family types, mother's work hours, and economic adjustments to index the three forms of resource needs (see Table 6.1). Mean annual earnings and allowances were estimated for categories of these factors and then adjusted for their correlated effects and the influence of income level (as measured by per capita family income) in a multiple classification analysis.

Resource needs clearly make a difference in the estimated earnings and allowances of boys for 1988–1989. The sons of farmers rank well above all other subgroups on yearly earnings, an average of $554 for the year. This achievement is consistent with the wide range of economic opportunities on a family farm (Rhodes, 1989), especially among young boys when compared to their nonfarm classmates. Some of the boys also raised and sold their own stock, which was purchased from their fathers. A relatively small amount of their income came from parents in terms of an allowance. By comparison, boys from part-time farm operations rank at the bottom of the family types on earnings and allowance. These boys generally came from well-to-do families, but their comparative disadvantage on yearly income remains even with adjustments for income and

Table 6.1. Total Earnings and Allowance Last Year of Seventh-Grade Boys and Girls by Social and Economic Factors (Self-Report): Adjusted Means in Multiple Classification Analysis[a]

	\multicolumn{6}{c}{*Total annual figure adjusted for independent factors*}				
	\multicolumn{3}{c}{Report by boys}	\multicolumn{3}{c}{Report by girls}			
Social and economic factors	N	Average earnings ($)	Allowance ($)	N	Average earnings ($)	Allowance ($)
Family type[b]		$p=.00$	$p=.15$		$p=.57$	$p=.75$
Farm	42	554	82	48	203	92
Part-time farm	19	213	26	21	169	142
Displaced/lost farm	24	282	91	35	169	134
1st-generation nonfarm	76	251	107	72	250	119
2nd-generation nonfarm	54	294	128	60	188	106
Time pressures (mother's work)		$p=.15$	$p=.39$		$p=.59$	$p=.48$
No hours	42	237	63	59	199	85
<30 hours	48	359	98	64	200	108
30–39 hours	83	297	107	67	244	130
>39 hours	42	409	117	46	173	135
Economic adjustments		$p=.73$	$p=.20$		$p=.80$	$p=.69$
Low (0–4)	81	332	124	87	220	129
Moderate (5–8)	59	289	82	70	209	106
High (9–17)	74	335	83	79	190	107
Grand mean	215	321	98	236	207	115

[a] Statistical controls also include per capita income and family size.
[b] Only family type shows a statistically significant interaction effect by sex ($p = .00$). In particular, boys earn much more than girls on farms than in nonfarm settings.

economic adjustments. The apprenticeship system of the family farm may well be the critical factor here in addition to the demands for labor on midwestern stock and grain farms.

Work on the farm would have special meaning to boys who still think they have a future in farming, despite continuing troubles in the farm-belt. Is the effect of farm labor needs and opportunities, as well as the impact of economic pressures, more prominent among the older brothers of these seventh-graders? Slightly more than 100 of the boys had older brothers, and we compared their earnings for 1989–1990 on all factors shown in Table 6.1. The overall pattern is very much the same, but even more striking in relation to the importance of membership in a farm family and its economic well-being or disadvantage. The older brothers were approximately 2 years older and their earnings for the year were nearly double the figure of their younger sibling, $908. Their average earnings at $1,534 far exceeded the $800 reported by all other older brothers ($\beta = .26$, $p < .05$). In addition, the older brothers from disadvantaged families (on economic adjustments) ranked much higher on earnings than boys from less pressured households ($\beta = .24$, $p < .05$). The younger boys, by contrast, show no association between their earnings and economic disadvantage or mother's employment. Only the family farm seems to make a difference.

Girls on family farms appear disadvantaged in a number of economic respects when compared to their male counterparts. The future for them is typically one of leaving the farm for marriage and nonfarm employment, or higher education and working in paid employment along with marriage. Though some are involved in farm work of one kind or another, including the raising of animals, most depend upon child care for income. Child care away from home requires transportation by car, and the girls were still a couple of years away from a driver's license. However, they did not do any worse than nonfarm girls on yearly earnings, although they did fare more poorly on an allowance for the year. Both earnings and an allowance place farm girls at a disadvantage in relation to farm boys, and this does not change when we take full- and part-time farm operations into account.

The single most important determinant of the earning experience of our Iowa seventh-graders is membership in a farm family. Boys in farm families earned more than boys in other families and far more than girls. The difference is especially striking when only full-time farm families are compared to part-time farm operations and other families. With these findings in mind, we asked whether other family businesses might create an employment situation that resembles the experience of farm boys. Unfortunately, the number of family businesses not in farming was too small to permit exploration of this possibility.

Time Pressures and Adolescent Work

We have argued that time pressures in the family bear most directly upon the domestic chores or responsibilities of boys or girls, not on paid employment outside the family, and the data in Table 6.1 support this expectation in part. Earnings show very little association with the weekly hours of mothers' employment, but the picture changes when we turn to household chores. Approximately 52% of the boys and girls claimed that they had spent more time over the past year doing chores around the house because of their mother's or father's work. Child care was explicitly included under chores.

To obtain a more precise picture of these activities from the vantage point of parents, we asked the mothers whether their study children had taken a job to help meet expenses last year, and whether they had increased their household and other responsibilities so that the parents could work more hours. The fathers were asked a similar set of questions. Approximately one-fifth of the mothers reported the addition of a job by their son or daughter, and about two-fifths reported the addition of responsibilities as well.

As might be expected, the addition of a paid job is strongly correlated only with level of economic pressure, whereas economic, labor, and time pressures all made a difference in whether a mother's son or daughter assumed additional responsibilities (Table 6.2). Though boys and girls did not *earn* more in economically pressed families, their mothers and fathers were more likely than other parents to report that they had done more over the past year on paid work and household responsibilities. The increase is most noticeable among girls in the reports of both parents. By comparison, labor pressures on the family farm are most evident in the additional responsibilities of boys. This is the only family type that shows any effect on children's roles in the household economy.

Time and labor pressures are especially linked to the work hours of mother and to the size of the household. Both factors increased the size of household responsibilities, to which young daughters appear to be more responsive than sons. Larger households were most likely to have young girls involved in more domestic tasks over the past year, an increase that is more pronounced than among boys of similar age. Working mothers on paid jobs tended to report additional help over the past year from sons and daughters, and the prevalence of such help increased by the length of mother's work week. If we think of mother's employment and economic adjustments (cutting back on consumption, etc.) as key elements of family adaptation strategy, from generating income to reducing demand or outgo, these young Iowans are very much a part of the survival effort.

Timing and Context in Work Experience

Our portrait of work experience up to this point comes from a summation of earning activities and outcomes over an entire year. The annual cycle of rural life shows variation in the work activities of young and old from season to season (cf. McHale, Bartko, & Crouter, 1991), but a full account of this change is beyond the scope of our inquiry. We did, however, explore the work experience of boys and girls during the survey week of winter and early spring of 1989. At this time, approximately one

Table 6.2. Mothers' Report on Children's Required Helpfulness by Social and Economic Factors: Adjusted Percentages in Multiple Classification Analysis

Social and economic factors	Total N		Taken on additional job		Assumed more responsibilities	
	Boys	Girls	Boys (adj. %)	Girls (adj. %)	Boys (adj. %)	Girls (adj. %)
Family type			p=.71; β=.10	p=.68; β=.09	p=.01; β=.24	p=.49; β=.11
Farm	42	48	18	16	63	40
Part-time farm	19	21	8	24	33	40
Displaced/lost farm	24	35	12	23	31	46
1st-generation, nonfarm	76	72	17	26	34	38
2nd-generation, nonfarm	54	60	21	21	37	51
Time pressures mother's work			p=.84; β=.06	p=.12; β=.15	p=.07; β=.17	p=.00; β=.25
No hours	42	59	18	15	25	24
<30 hours	48	64	14	30	39	43
30–39 hours	83	67	21	28	40	47
>39 hours	42	46	16	19	48	56
Economic adjustments			p=.01; β=.23	p=.00; β=.36	p=.00; β=.29	p=.00; β=.25
Low	81	87	10	7	22	31
Moderate	60	70	12	18	48	39
High	74	79	29	42	53	60
Household size			p=.65; β=.03	p=.45; β=.05	p=.30; β=.06	p=.00; β=.22
5 or less	167	186	18	21	38	37
6 or more	48	50	15	26	46	64
Grand mean			17	22	40	43

of two claimed they had a paid job, a figure well below the number who reported earnings for the entire year.

In this wintry time of the year, girls were just as likely to have a job as boys, but, as during the year, their earning activities followed sex-specific lines. Two out of three girls were engaged in the care of young children, and another 16% mentioned doing household chores. Nearly one-fifth of the girls reported two jobs—usually child care and something else. Among the boys, one-third reported work in the operation of a farm, another one-third claimed to have a paper route, and the remainder did yard work or general chores. Not surprisingly, farm work was less common at this time of the year than over the entire year. Resource needs and pressures made a difference in how much time the seventh-graders spent on the job, but not in whether they had a paid job or not. None of the factors we have considered were useful in differentiating between the workers and nonemployed.

Missing from this account of work experience are the employers and other adolescents, their tasks and earnings. The employers of these seventh-graders were typically either parents or relatives, or a combination of the two. Over 9 out of 10 of the employed boys and girls reported one of these working arrangements. In a pattern reminiscent of Katz and Davey's (1978) stage of "semi-autonomous adolescence," where young adolescents of the mid-19th century lived and worked in another household (often a relative's), we find that the most common employers are relatives. About two-thirds of the adolescents reported that they only worked for relatives.

Working for Family and Self

The challenging labor needs of the family farm and the scarcity of adult time (owing to mother's employment and larger families) represent two examples of situational imperatives on helpfulness from children in our Iowa families. The evidence suggests that a good many of these children stepped into situations of family need and were helpful in ways that benefited the entire household. However, the sheer number of work hours and earnings does not tell us anything about required helpfulness. Indeed all of the money earned might have been spent on items of personal indulgence. The use of earned money, then, has the potential to tell us whether the boys and girls were working only for self or also for family.

Did they spend their money on discretionary items, such as personal entertainment, or was at least some of the money used to cover school expenses and more basic family needs? Were they, in fact, part of the family's economy? Contrary to our findings up to this point, how children use their earnings should be especially responsive to the economic needs of the family itself. Young adolescents may not have earned more in disadvantaged families, but they may have given more of their earnings to family needs. Conditions of economic hardship strengthen the ethic that personal earnings are at least partly for the family as a whole. Individualism flourishes when family welfare is not at stake.

The adolescents were presented with a checklist of uses for money, and they were asked to check any that apply. Four of the uses seemed most relevant to family welfare: paid for school necessities, gave some money to parents, used money for clothes and shoes, and put some money in savings. Money for school expenses and for parents most directly indicate a contribution to the family welfare, and a substantial number of boys and girls cited both of these uses. Two out of five girls said they used their money for school expenses and more than one-quarter said they gave some money directly to their parents. Approximately one-fourth of the boys listed these two uses. Money for clothes and savings are not necessarily a contribution to the family, though both can reduce expenses for the family unit.

We summed all Yes responses to the four uses to produce an index with values that range from 0 to 4. Girls ranked slightly higher than boys on uses of their money for family-related needs, =2.26 versus 2.00. When we take all three types of family scarcities into account (labor, time, and economic), the economic factor looms large in determining the uses of money, but labor considerations also play an important role. The effect of economic pressures is especially noteworthy among girls. Between 40 and 50% of the girls in high-pressure families reported that they gave money to parents and used some money for school expenses. These figures drop as much as 27% on money for parents among girls in the most privileged economic situation, a difference that is statistically significant ($p < .02$).

Beyond the consumption reductions of economic adjustments, we find additional evidence of economic pressures at work in families that lost farms. These families have endured a substantial period of economic hardship, an imprint that appears especially among the boys in these families after we make adjustments for economic cutbacks over 1988–1989. Boys in displaced farm families were significantly more likely ($p < .08$) than other boys to contribute directly to meeting family economic needs.

These findings may reflect the interaction between the unique collective culture of farm life, in which family members pull together under the common challenge of a family farm, and intense economic pressure. With origins in this farm culture, displaced farm families experienced the wrenching deprivations and dislocations of a way of life and mode of livelihood. Shared experience of this kind is known to foster solidarity and a willingness to contribute to the welfare of all.

This argument would be more compelling if farm youth were more likely than other adolescents to give some of their money to family-relevant causes. Except for children from displaced families, the data generally show this tendency to be more pronounced among farm boys especially, though not among girls from farm families. As a group, farm families in our study compare very favorably with the better off nonfarm families, and yet farm boys and those from displaced families rank at the top of family uses of personal money. If the collective norms of farm family culture are relevant to this finding, contributions to family needs should be strongest among boys in which father does not work off the farm and mother is not highly involved in such employment, and weakest among farm families in which most of the income is derived from off-farm employment.

We identified these groups from the farm family typology (see Chapter 4). Type 1 indicates full-time farming, Type 2 indicates substantial off-farm employment by the wife (husband still works mainly on farm), and our third category includes Types 3 (both husband and wife work off the farm) and 4 (husband does not think of self as farmer—most income comes from nonfarm employment, though farm acreage is still above 100). The mean scores conform to our expectations across the three groups, from 2.50 to 2.22 and 1.67, ($p = .02$). Some of this variation is economic, but it remains statistically significant even with adjustments for per capita income, household size, and economic adjustment ($p = .04$). The collective norms of farm culture may be a factor in these results, although farm girls fail to conform to this pattern. They are not more likely to use their earnings or money on family causes, unless their family is under heavy economic pressure.

Overall the work and financial experience of farm boys differs in significant ways from that of other boys. On average, they earn far more from their jobs, and this is especially true for the sons of fathers in full-time farming. The latter are also most likely to contribute their money to family-relevant causes. We interpret some of the difference in terms of the solidarity norms of farm culture and the roles boys play in this enterprise. Girls are less central to this culture, and we find little evidence of the distinctiveness of life in a farm family among their productive roles. However, girls are clearly responsive to the time pressures of households in terms of assuming domestic responsibilities, and the uses of their earnings are far more responsive to economic disadvantage than are the uses among boys.

Parental Views of Working Youth, Farm and Nonfarm

A good many of the Iowa youth were working in part for the welfare of their family since they devoted some of their earnings to family needs. To be sure, this behavior is not unique to farm communities, although the requirements of family life on the farm suggest that it is more valued in this setting than in urban places. The solidarity culture of life on the family farm also suggests that children's earnings would be highly valued by farm parents, particularly when the effort is part of an apprenticeship for farming, as it is for a number of the boys.

The valuing of such behavior brings us back once again to the concept of required helpfulness. As a rule, helpful behavior is valued by family members, but the more conventional view of adolescent earners does not depict helpful behavior. Indeed, most of the literature suggests that adolescents in paid jobs are likely to possess very different characteristics, from academic difficulty to involvement with drugs, alcohol, and theft (Greenberger & Steinberg, 1986). A paid job may, of course, provide a rewarding option to adolescents who are failing in school and derive little support or affection at home. Work may also develop a sense of competence, reliability, and persistence when it is meaningful, as in the completion of assignments that are counted on by significant others. Farm chores or tasks are meaningful in this manner.

Consistent with both the developmental and problem behavior perspectives on work experience among the young, Mortimer et al. (1991) reveal a more complex set of behavioral outcomes from the work of adolescents, both positive and negative, but this important longitudinal study and related studies are based on urban samples. What about the work experience of rural children and their older brothers and sisters? We have suggested that the socioeconomic world of farm families establishes an imperative of required helpfulness and productive labor for the young that favors constructive qualities, especially among males.

But what about life in small towns of 6,500 or less? Is it that different from life on a farm? Indeed, we know that a number of small-town adolescents have jobs on local farms. What, then, is the important difference? We believe that a key feature of farm life that clearly matters is the extent to which farm youth are part of a collective effort that makes their activities essential to the welfare of others. The effort extends beyond the self and assigns general value and significance to personal actions. The work of nonfarm adolescents, by contrast, is more likely to express individualistic sentiments. These sentiments would lead some youth to a job and, in other cases, they may actually result from the independence that employment provides (cf. Elder, 1974, chapter 4). With data at only one point in time, we are unable to distinguish between these different effects, between what youth bring to work and how work influences them. However we can determine whether certain behavioral qualities are associated with earnings and the use of money.

To explore such correlates, we selected 12 statements about sons and daughters that were answered on 5-point scales by mothers and fathers in 1989. These items were then correlated with the earnings and money use of boys and girls from farm and nonfarm settings. Table 6.3 shows correlation coefficients for the two subgroups of parents and their sons along with significance levels for differences between the coefficients.

Consistent with our findings to date, economically active boys in farm families are generally ascribed positive qualities by their mothers and fathers, when compared to boys who report little or no earnings. They are more likely than other parents to claim that they have enjoyed being a parent to their son. In their view, he is a hard worker who does well in school. They consider him more helpful and trustworthy when compared to the judgments of other parents. Economically successful farm boys are not viewed by parents as uncooperative or involved with drugs, alcohol, or tobacco.

In nonfarm communities, the dominant impression of boys who did particularly well on earnings is more negative than positive, although the results are not especially clear-cut. That is, earnings by themselves tell us very little about the nonfarm boy as portrayed by parents, unlike the results obtained on farm boys. Nevertheless, the accomplished earner among young adolescent boys has very different status in the two communities, farm and nonfarm. To bring out this difference more clearly, we divided the farm and nonfarm groups into three categories of equal size on sons' earnings and then computed percentages on key items.

Eighty-five percent of the farm fathers of sons in the most successful group of earners strongly agreed with the statement that being a parent to the study child was enjoyable. This compares to about two-thirds of the high earners in the nonfarm group. No differences between farm and nonfarm appear among sons with lower earnings for the year. Nearly two-thirds of farm fathers with successful earners reported that they totally agree with the statement "I trust my child," compared to two-fifths of the nonfarm fathers with boys in this earning group.

These and other variations generally reflect the greater work interdependence of farm boys. Half of the farm fathers with sons in the highest income category claimed that they were helped by the son on many an occasion. This compares to 30% of the nonfarm boys in this category. Across all three items, the farm-nonfarm difference is pronounced only among boys with the highest level of earnings.

The same contrasts appear on school performance and relations with

Table 6.3. Mothers' and Fathers' Descriptions of Sons by Their Earnings and Contribution to the Family Economy in Farm (N=42) and Nonfarm (N=173) Settings: Correlation Coefficients R

| | Mother's perceptions of sons | | | | | | Father's perceptions of sons | | | | | |
| | Earnings | | | Family contributions | | | Earnings | | | Family contributions | | |
	Farm N=42	Nonfarm N=173	Sig.	Farm N=42	Nonfarm N=173	Sig.	Farm N=42	Nonfarm N=173	Sig.	Farm N=42	Nonfarm N=173	Sig.
Positive assessments												
Enjoy being his parent	.27	-.14	**	.19	-.16	**	.27	-.03	**	-.00	-.06	
Trust my son	.11	-.07	**	-.13	-.05		.15	.01	*	-.10	.02	
He works hard	.33	.07	**	.01	-.07		.18	.02	*	-.13	.04	
He helps me do things important to me	.31	-.14	**	.08	-.11	**	.42	-.04	**	-.08	.02	
He is unselfish	.04	-.09		-.13	.00		.31	-.09	**	-.17	-.01	
He is a good student	.31	-.03	**	.20	-.07	**	.08	.06		.01	-.02	
Problem behavior												
He causes me a lot of problems	-.27	.00		.03	-.01		-.35	.04	**	-.10	.08	
He argues with me	-.21	.05	*	-.23	.08	**	-.24	-.05	*	-.16	-.02	
He refuses to take direction	-.28	.13	**	.05	.05		-.21	-.02	*	.23	.10	
He uses drugs	-.14	-.10		-.28	.07	**	-.07	-.07		-.09	-.01	
He uses alcohol	-.15	-.11		-.15	.01		.12	-.08		.05	-.03	
He uses tobacco	-.14	-.01		-.33	-.03	**	-.06	-.11		-.12	-.09	

* $p < .10$. ** $p < .05$. Nonfarm boys are defined in terms of membership in family types 4 and 5.

teachers. The mothers were asked about their sons' achievement in school. Eighty-five percent of the farm mothers with sons who rank in the top earning category reported an above average level of achievement. This compares to 45% of the farm mothers with sons who had relatively low earnings for the year and to one-third of the nonfarm mothers with sons in the highest earnings category. Positive relations with teachers follow the same pattern: the higher the earnings among farm boys, the greater the prospect of positive appraisal by parents. No such trend occurs among the working sons of nonfarm parents.

Among farm boys, in particular, our data suggest that the more ambitious were likely to work most industriously on earnings projects. Though most of the study boys on farms earned money, some were more successful than others in making money. Were the most successful boys also at the top on personal drive and persistence? The more ambitious may have been drawn to such endeavors in the first place and then experienced the reinforcing benefits of personal success with a farm project and sale. We compared the three categories of working adolescents on a measure of personal mastery (7 items, alpha $= .86$) that is based on questions the adolescents were asked concerning their sense of efficacy. A comparison of mean scores shows that earnings among farm boys are linked to a personal sense of mastery; the most successful earners were also likely to be the most efficacious ($r = .36, p < .05$), according to their own self-report. However, mastery is unrelated to the earnings of nonfarm adolescents ($r = .05, p = .41$).

On face value, the use of some earnings for the family welfare indicates rather directly a type of behavior that would be especially prized by parents, though it does not match earnings as a correlate of positive behavior among farm boys. This is particularly true among fathers and their judgments. Sons who score high on family uses of their earnings are generally more likely to be seen in a positive light by mothers when compared to sons with a more individualistic pattern of consumption. But we find no such outcome among fathers.

What do we find among girls in the two settings? Actual earnings for the past year could not be used in our analysis of the girls because they were so limited and skewed, particularly in the farm sector. In place of earnings, we relied upon our measure of the family uses of earnings. Overall, the pattern of correlations show little more than chance findings, although the strongest findings have much in common with our results for boys. Only one subgroup comparison of coefficients proved to be statistically significant on girls (using the judgments of mothers), in contrast to six statistically significant outcomes on boys. For earnings use, family-oriented girls were likely to be seen as trustworthy by mothers in the farm subgroup, though not in the nonfarm category (26 vs. 3%, $p <$

.05). They were also more likely to be described as a good student according to mothers' reports (29 vs. 5%, NS). No other correlations were statistically reliable among girls in farm families, or showed notable differences between the two settings. None of the perceptions by fathers were statistically reliable.

The pattern of correlations for Iowa boys and girls shows modest but provocative differences between ecological settings in the behavior of youth who are economically successful and use at least some of their income to help meet family needs. Among boys on farms, economic industry is highly valued and recruits the more competent, successful adolescents. An ethic of required helpfulness is reflected in the culture of farm life, and the behavior of economically successful farm boys generally conforms to this norm. Farm girls who use some of their money for family needs also tend to be characterized by mother in a positive way. Compared to this general pattern, children's earnings and the family uses of money do not correlate in a convincing manner with either positive or negative attributes among boys and girls in the nonfarm community.

SUMMING UP: HISTORICAL AND CONTEMPORARY ISSUES

The productive labor of children and adolescents offers three causal themes that bear upon the Iowa families and their children. The first involves the response of children and youth to socioeconomic needs, as in the household economy of working-class families during the 19th century (Haines, 1979). The family budget of these families frequently depended more heavily upon the earnings of young offspring than on the income of mothers. In contemporary Iowa, farm youth contribute through nonpaid and paid employment.

The second theme stresses the lure and constraints of the labor market, as during the Second World War. When young men left the labor market for active duty in the armed forces, their places were filled in part by women and older children. More often than not, women and children assumed responsibilities that heretofore had not been considered appropriate for them. School attendance in secondary school actually declined in the war years as young people flocked to the call of employment and good pay (Elder, 1980). In present-day Iowa, labor needs of the farm family economy are demanding and compete with other options among students in school.

The third theme features motivational dispositions and skills, and their role in explaining the work experiences of young people. Gainful employment among children and youth may express needs for mastery, social independence, and economic gain. In the hard-pressed 1930s, mounting economic pressures increased the appeal of paid jobs among teenagers—however meager the wage—and a substantial portion of deprived boys acquired jobs (Elder, 1974, chapter 4). In most cases, a portion of all earnings went to meet family needs. Staff observers in the study of depression-era families considered the employed to be more industrious and energetic than the nonemployed. They were also described as more efficacious than the nonworkers. A mother of one of these adolescent workers described him as having "one driving interest after another, usually a practical one" (Elder, 1974, p. 145). In rural Iowa today, we find evidence of this life pattern only among farm boys. The more economically successful described themselves in more efficacious terms.

These three perspectives—household economy, labor market, and individual needs—relate group and individual determinants of productive roles among children and youth. The household economy and labor market themes stress the imperatives of group life. A good many children in working-class families of early 20th century America obtained jobs in mills in order to help the family meet basic needs (Hareven, 1982). An ethic of required helpfulness typifies family life under the incessant pressures of making ends meet. Aspirations for personal economic gain and mastery may also have been involved. In the lives of contemporary rural youth in Iowa, group and individual forces also appear to shape their productive roles and responsibilities.

Within the downward trend of economic decline in the rural Midwest, resource scarcity exposed adolescents to the imperatives and ethics of required helpfulness. That is, the family situation itself prompted young adolescents to work, earn, and help out around the household. Labor scarcity refers especially to the labor-intensive demands of hard-pressed families and family farms, time scarcity in families results from mothers with long work weeks outside the household and a relatively large number of family members, and income scarcity is linked to low income and indications of expenditure cutbacks and postponements.

Well over 90% of the boys and girls reported work over the past year (1988–1989) that generated earnings. Boys specialized in field, animal, and yard work, whereas girls were most heavily involved in tasks of child care. Typically these young adolescents worked for their own parents and/or for relatives. The prevalence of employment by relatives brings to mind the social stage of semiautonomy in which young adolescents lived and worked in another household during the mid-19th century. The proximity of relatives to the Iowa youth gave them and their parents an appealing option along the age-graded pathway to social independence.

The imprint of labor needs and economic opportunities is most evident in the lives of farm boys. These adolescents rank well above farm girls and all adolescents in the total sum of their earnings. They are also more apt than nonfarm boys to think of themselves as working more than other youth, a judgment that most likely includes substantial nonpaid work. Economically successful boys from farm families were more likely to be described in positive ways by parents, both mother and father, when compared to such boys in nonfarm households.

Unlike a common picture of adolescent workers in urban settings, it is the farm boy with minimal earnings who is most likely to be described by parents as untrustworthy, argumentative, selfish, and unsuccessful in school. Farm parents most often depict the successful earner as helpful to them, enjoyable as a son, and a high achiever in school. By comparison, earnings tell us very little about the parent descriptions of the more economically successful boys in nonfarm communities. As for girls, a few strands of evidence show a similar contrast between the ascribed traits of girls who use their earnings for family needs in farm and nonfarm families, but the differences are too weak to warrant confidence.

Time pressures within the family make a substantial difference in the household responsibilities assumed by boys and especially girls, as reported by mother and father. Four out of five mothers held a paid job, and the higher the work hours per week, the more parents tended to report that the study child had assumed more responsibilities over the past year in order to help out at home. This report was more likely as well among parents with more than three children at home, in comparison to smaller households. Even with economic level controlled, the sons and daughters of working mothers were more likely to have a long work week, when compared with the employed adolescents of mothers who were not so employed.

Family economic pressures did not influence the level of earnings among boys and girls, but they did increase the prospects of taking a paid job or more work hours over the past year (1988–1989). As family cutbacks on consumption increased, boys and girls were more likely to be described as working more on paid jobs, according to mother and father. As expected, economic pressures also played an important role in determining how the adolescents used their earnings. Family uses were most often reported by boys and girls in displaced farm families and secondarily in farm households, when compared to other family types. The collective theme of farm family culture seemed to be more influential than economic hardship among boys.

Among girls, economic pressure played a more prominent role, both in relation to taking on added chores and using money for family needs. But apart from economic pressure, it is the daughter who generally contributed more of her earnings to family needs than the son. Consistent with the historical findings of Hareven (1982) and others, differences of this kind are reminiscent of historical American families where unmarried daughters played a critical role in the economic support of parents.

This chapter underscores the potential relevance of social ecologies for understanding children's work experience and its developmental implications, though we have barely made a dent in identifying factors that are consequential. Nevertheless, we find much similarity between the behavioral characteristics of depression-era boys who earned money and performed household chores under conditions of family hardship, and contemporary farm boys who excel among peers in earnings. And just as adolescent girls helped out their deprived families through household assistance and earnings, we find that girls in rural Iowa are playing similar roles under heavy economic pressure. The circumstances of depression-era and rural Iowa youth differ in many respects, but both groups are part of social systems that require helpful responses and the acceptance of adult life challenges and responsibilities.

PART III

Husbands and Wives

Chapter 7

Family Origins of Personal and Social Well-Being

Les B. Whitbeck, Frederick O. Lorenz,
Ronald L. Simons, and Shirley Huck

My deepest habit was assuming that differences between Rose and me were just on the surface . . . that somehow we were each other's real selves, together forever on this thousand acres. . . . But after all, she wasn't me . . . now. . . . I saw Daddy, and I also saw her.

—J. Smiley, *A Thousand Acres*

In earlier chapters we have considered the family and community economic trends that have placed many Iowans at risk for serious economic deprivation. We now examine the family histories of the Iowa parents and their resourceful or deprivational legacy in managing hard times. Using retrospective reports of early family experiences, we examine the effects of this experience: (1) on the quality of adult relations with aging parents, and (2) on personal self-confidence and positive interaction styles, qualities that promote healthy social relationships and the potential for coping successfully with stressful times.

EARLY AND LATER FAMILY EXPERIENCES

Early family relationships are thought to provide a blueprint for later life relationships, both within and outside the family. Caspi and Elder observe that "interactional styles established in the developmental history tend to operate in two ways: 1) by leading a person to select environments in which the pattern is readily enacted; and 2) by being projected onto ambiguous situations that can be structured to permit the pattern to be expressed" (1988, p. 231). Relationship styles learned in one situation are particularly likely to be evoked in other situations of similar struc-

149

ture. This may be particularly true for later life family interactions between adult children and their parents.

There is substantial evidence that interaction styles are learned in families. Patterson's social learning approach is especially informative in understanding this process (Patterson, 1982, 1986a; Patterson & Bank, 1987). Patterson has shown that coercive, aggressive parenting, characterized by harsh disciplinary techniques, elicits aggressive responses in children. The children's aggressive behavior, in turn, evokes negative reactions from parents, which generate "coercive chains" where one party attempts to control the other through aversive interactional techniques. These behavior patterns tend to generalize to other settings, from peers, to school, and to workplace.

Across four generations, Elder and his colleagues (1986) found that acquired personality dispositions established a link between behavior patterns in successive generations. Early family relationships shape personality dispositions, which, in turn, foster a reproduction of these interactional styles in the next generation. The study's findings indicate a cyclical pattern of intergenerational transmission in which parental instability manifested by irritable, explosive behavior increased the likelihood of erratic parent-child relationships. Such outcomes enhanced the developmental risk of similar personality traits and interaction styles in the next generation.

There is also evidence for a similar pattern of social reproduction of rejecting behaviors and depressed affect across generations. Whitbeck and his associates (1992) found that rejecting parenting by the grandparent generation increased the likelihood of depressed affect in the succeeding parent generation. Depressed affect among parents, in turn, made rejecting parenting behaviors more likely toward their adolescent offspring in the third generation, increasing the risk of depressed affect among boys and girls. Consistent with Elder's transmission model, the findings suggest that interactional styles are reproduced across generations through the development of personality traits that evoke such interaction styles.

Sroufe and Fleeson (1988) and others (see Bowlby, 1973, 1980, 1982) provide a complementary account of this process. They suggest that individuals develop images of themselves and others in relationships that are based on prior social experiences. These "represented relationships" are carried forward into novel situations and create expectations for interactions, which influence others as well as our perceptions of access to particular others. Thus, individuals are "selected, responded to, and influenced in directions compatible with previous relationship learning" (Sroufe & Fleeson, 1988, p. 29).

Building on these accounts, we hypothesized that the negative quality of early family interaction (behaviors and moods) experienced by the Iowa parents in their childhood would adversely affect their self-confidence and consequently diminish their success in establishing supportive social ties during the farm crisis of the 1980s. Second, we hypothesized that a positive interaction style also links childhood socialization with access to social support. The more negative the family environment of childhood, the less positive the parent's present interaction style, and consequently the lower the access to supportive relationships. Finally, we proposed that disrupted parent-child relations in the early years would lead to less satisfactory parent and adult-child interactions today, thus affecting available support across the parent and grandparent generations.

Several dimensions of poor parenting have been linked to decreased self-confidence and social competence in youth. Numerous measures of nonoptimal parenting, such as the absence of warm and supportive parenting (Gecas & Schwalbe, 1986; Whitbeck et al., 1991a), coercive parenting behaviors (Coopersmith, 1967; Rollins & Thomas, 1979), and harsh or abusive parenting behaviors (Oates & Peacock, 1985) are predictive of both low self-esteem and aversive or problematic interactions with others (Harter, 1983; Patterson, 1982). Likewise, a parents' depression or hostility is likely to have adverse effects on children's self-concepts and overall maladjustment (Conger et al., 1992; Conger, Conger et al., 1993).

Weissman and her colleagues (Weissman, Paykel, & Klerman, 1972), reporting on a sample of clinically depressed women, found them to be less involved in their children's daily lives, less affectionate, and less communicative than women in a nondepressed control group. In subsequent studies, depressed mothers have been found to be less consistent, more irritable, less spontaneous, and less involved with their children (Beardslee, Bemporad, Keller, & Klerman, 1983; Orvaschel, 1983). Billings and Moos (1983) also found less cohesiveness, more conflict, less expressiveness, and greater disorganization in families where either parent had been recently treated for depression. This combination of child-rearing characteristics provides the conceptual base that serves as the starting point for investigating the linkages between child-rearing histories of the IYFP parents, their current relations with their parents, and personality characteristics predictive of contemporary social relations.

The first model we consider (*the continuity model*) links indicators of early family experience (parent depressed affect, hostility, rejection of child, child monitoring) to reports of current relationship quality between adult children and their aging parents. This model suggests that early parenting practices may impair parent-child relations even into adulthood to the detriment of both generations. Thus, we expected to see continuity in the quality of parent-child relations from childhood and adolescence into the adult years for parents in the study.

The second model (*the mediational model*; Figure 7.1) views personal characteristics or dispositions as a link between early family experiences and reported levels of social support from friends and extended family. We reasoned, first, that self-confident adults are more likely to seek out social contacts than people with less confidence, and that they would consider themselves deserving of assistance from others. Second, we expected that a predisposition to a positive interaction style would be more attractive to others compared to colder, more critical, or irritable behaviors. In general, the mediational model proposes that a childhood history involving parental depression, hostility, and rejection will adversely affect the self-confidence and behavioral dispositions of IYFP parents, whereas a history of monitoring and involvement will promote personal and social competence.

The present analysis related to these two models is necessarily limited by its reliance on retrospective reports of childhood. However, retrospective reports of parental rejection appear to be relatively stable over time, correlating at about .5 over a 2-year period (Pearson, Cowan, & Cohn, 1991). This suggests that, whatever the degree of retrospective bias, it will tend to be long term rather than simply a reflection of transient mood states. Some research evidence also suggests that reliable recall is more likely around issues that carry more importance for the individual (Quinton & Rutter, 1988). We believe that treatment during childhood has great significance in the lives of adults (e.g., Whitbeck et al., 1992).

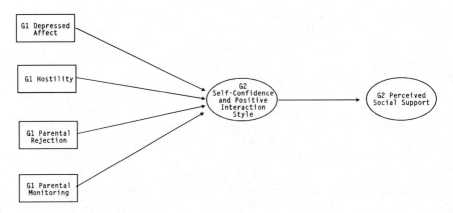

Figure 7.1.   The mediational model linking childhood history, personal characteristics, and perceived social support from friends and extended family.

THE GRANDPARENT GENERATION

For analyses related to the continuity model concerning the effects of early interactional history on contemporary adult child-parent relationships, the sample was limited to reports from study adults who had living parents. Four hundred and twenty-six of the possible 1,804 grandparents for the IYFP families were deceased. After losing additional subjects due to listwise deletion for missing data, the analysis for the continuity model was based on G2 adult children's reports regarding 1,350 members of the grandparent generation. Analyses for the other models were based on the complete sample using the retrospective reports for G2 study adults of their early family experiences, whether their parents were currently living or not.

Because of the relatively young age of (G2) study adults, the grandparent generation (G1) was mostly comprised of the young-old. The majority of grandparents, therefore, were still living, self-sufficient, and in good health. Thus, they had the capacity, in most instances, to provide significant social support to IYFP families experiencing high levels of economic stress. Seventy-six percent (1,378) of the possible 1,804 members of the grandparent generation (G1) of the study families were living. Their median age was 62 years. Only 4% of the men and 2% of the women of the grandparent generation were aged 80 years or older.

For the most part, members of the grandparent generation have remained in Iowa. Eighty-seven percent of the IYFP grandparents reside in the state and, therefore, live relatively close to their adult children. When those living in states immediately bordering Iowa were included, the number living about one day's drive or less from their children increased to 93%. The vast majority (97%) of the grandparent generation lived in their own homes. Three-fourths of the elderly parents still lived with their spouses. Most of the study adults reported that their parents' health was good to excellent (68%), with only a few at this stage of life (8%) indicating that their parents' health was poor or very poor.

Owing perhaps to the relatively young age and independence of the grandparent generation, adult children reported lower frequencies of contact with their parents than has been found in more representative samples of the elderly population (Harris, 1975; Shanas, 1977). Only about 5% of the adult children reported seeing their parents daily. Approximately half (48%) of the study adults reported seeing their parents once a week or more. Twenty-two percent reported seeing their parents about once a month. Almost one-third (30%) reported seeing parents less than once a month.

Although frequency of contact between generations was lower than expected, the quality of contemporary relationships between generations was very good. Forty-two percent of the adult children reported that their relationships with their parents were "excellent," and an additional 46% rated their relationships as "good." Only 12% indicated significant problems in their current relationships with their parents. Similarly, adult children's descriptions of their childhood were generally positive. Over one-third rated their early adolescent relationships with their parents as "very happy"; one-half rated the relationships as "fairly happy." The number of adult children who ranked their childhood relationships with their parents as only "fairly happy" may be indicating some discomfort associated with this period of development. Although any indication of less than excellent relationship quality may be indicative of discomfort in intimate relationships (see Glenn, 1990, on ratings of marital relationship quality), a substantial proportion of the adult children were content with the quality of both their current and childhood relationships with their aging parents.

The life stage of the Iowa parents helps to explain the relatively low levels of exchange between generations. Sussman has (1985) suggested a cyclical pattern of intergenerational support characterized by an early flow of support from parents to children when adult children are first married, a hiatus in support as adult children become independent, followed by a flow of support from adult children to parents as parents age. The study participants appear to be nearing the end of a plateau period of mutual generational independence. As the grandparent generation moves from young-old to middle- and old-old, the rates of exchange may be expected to increase. At the present time, very little monetary support flows between generations. Less than 2% of adult children reported giving monetary aid to parents and even in those cases, amounts were very low. Similarly, few adult children reported having had loans or monetary gifts from parents. Adult children were more likely to provide services such as transportation, housework, and meals, rather than material aid, for their elderly parents. About 20% of the IYFP parents reported they had provided some of these services; 6% reported they had provided such services extensively.

We also wanted to know the social backgrounds of these Iowa grandparents. How does their experience anticipate the current circumstances of their adult sons and daughters? Table 7.1 indicates that the modal occupation for men of the grandparent generation (G1), when IYFP parents were children, was farming (59.7% and 42.2% of the fathers for IYFP fathers and mothers, respectively). The majority of women of the grandparent generation worked in the home. Only about 10% of the grandfathers were professionals or managers. Median education for the men and women of the grandparent generation was 12 years of schooling. Over one-fourth of the men of the grandparent generation had an eighth-grade education or less, slightly more than 40% had graduated from high school. Women of the grandparent generation were somewhat more likely to have graduated from high school (about 50%) and were about as likely as the men to have graduated fromcollege. Less than 3% of the grandparent generation had earned college degrees. The data suggest, then, that the grandparents were primarily skilled workers, entrepreneurs, or housewives and that their occupational training came primarily from life experience rather than from advanced education.

Most of the Iowa parents (70%) recalled their families' financial status when they were growing up as about average when compared to other families in their area. Almost 20% reported that their families were below to far below the financial status of their neighbors. Eleven percent of the adult males and about 9% of females recalled that at some point when they were growing up their families had received some sort of public assistance such as county relief, AFDC, or food stamps. This proportion of serious disadvantage in their families of origin is comparable to the current level of stress in the IYFP families, 11% of whom were living below the poverty line (see Chapter 4).

Table 7.1. Occupations of the Grandparent Generation (G1) when IYFP Parents were Children

Occupational history	Reported by IYFP (G2) fathers (%)		Reported by IYFP (G2) mothers (%)	
	G1 fathers (N = 448)	G1 mothers (N = 449)	G1 fathers (N = 448)	G1 mothers (N = 451)
No paid employment	—	69.3	0.4[a]	53.2
Professionals, managers, owners, & officials	9.6	4.0	11.0	4.2
Clerical & kindred workers, salesworkers	4.2	12.7	5.1	16.8
Craftsmen & Foremen	10.7	0.4	19.6	1.8
Operatives & kindred workers	10.5	4.0	12.7	4.2
Operatives & private housework	1.6	7.3	3.3	16.9
Farmers & farm laborers	59.7	0.7	42.2	0.9
Other	4.7	1.6	5.6	2.0

[a] Disabled and retired

MEASUREMENT

Two measures were used to evaluate the parent-child relationship when the adult children were growing up: parental rejection and monitoring. *Parental rejection* was measured by the adult-children's (G2) reports about their relationships with their mother and father when they were "about the same age as their seventh-grader." The measure consisted of five items, which related to degrees of trust, care, fault-finding, dissatisfaction with the child, and blame projected on the child for the parents' problems. Response categories ranged from 1 (*strongly disagree*) to 5 (*strongly agree*). Cronbach's alphas for fathers' reports of parental rejection were .84 for their fathers and .81 for their mothers. The reliability coefficients for mothers' reports of parental rejection were .90 for their fathers and .87 for their mothers.

Parental monitoring was measured with six items, which concerned the degree of G1 involvement in, and awareness and control of, children's activities when the adult-children were growing up. These items reflect concern for the child and included questions such as how often the parent knew where the child was and whom he or she was with, how often the parent discussed things that were going on in the child's life, and how often the parent set times for bed on weekend nights. Response categories ranged from 1 (*always*) to 5 (*never*). This item was reverse-coded so that a high value indicated higher parental monitoring. Cronbach's alphas for parental monitoring were .92 for fathers' reports of their fathers and .85 for their mothers. Alphas for mothers were .92 for reports of their mothers and .82 for reports of their fathers.

In addition to measures of parent-child interaction, two measures of more general G1 characteristics during childhood were used to determine the effects of grandparent personality traits on the contemporary adult child-parent relationship and on adult children's personality characteristics of self-confidence and positive interaction style. The adult child's perception of their *G1 parents' level of depression* when they were growing up was measured by three items indicating whether the parent was often sad or depressed, was happy or high-spirited, and felt inferior to others. Response categories for these items ranged from 1 (*strongly disagree*) to 5 (*strongly agree*). A high value indicated greater parental depression. Cronbach's alphas for fathers' reports regarding their parents were .60 for their fathers and .60 for their mothers. Coefficients for mothers' reports of their parents were .59 for their fathers and .66 for their mothers.

Parental hostility pertained to the adult child's perceptions of the parent as an angry or hostile person during the time the adult child was growing up. The construct was measured with four items, which concerned the degree to which the G1 parent was viewed as (1) being angry at the way he or she was treated by others, (2) physically violent or abusive to others, (3) argumentative, and (4) frequently losing his or her temper. Response categories ranged from 1 (*strongly disagree*) to 5 (*strongly agree*); so that a high value for the scale indicated greater hostility on the part of the parent. Reliability coefficients for IYFP fathers' reports of their parents were .84 for their fathers and .81 for their mothers. Coefficients for IYFP mothers were .87 for their fathers and .81 for their mothers.

The quality of the current adult child-parent relationship was assessed with a single item, which asked the adult children to rate their current relationship with each of their parents from 1 (*excellent to*) 5 (*very poor*). The item was reverse-coded so that a higher score reflects higher quality. *Health* and *age* of the G1 parent were added to the first model, the continuity model, to control for their effects on current relationship quality. Health was measured by a single item, which asked the adult child to assess the overall health of each parent. Response categories ranged from 1 (*excellent to*) 5 (*very poor*). The item was reverse-coded so that a higher score reflects better health. Age refers to the chronological age of IYFP grandparents.

For the mediating model of social support (Figure 7.1), G2 *self-confidence* was assessed with three indicators: coping ability, mastery, and self-esteem. These measures and the underlying construct (self-confidence) they assess are described in Chapter 2. Confirmatory factor analysis for the construct also is reported in Chapter 2. Cronbach alpha for the individual indicators ranged from .74 (fathers' mastery) to .88 (mothers' self-esteem).

Regarding positive interaction style, G2 warmth and agreeableness in interactions with others was measured with five items from the NEO Personality Inventory (Costa & McCrae, 1985). These items assessed willingness to engage in social interaction and overall gregariousness. The measure included items such as "I really like most people I meet"; "I'm known as a warm and friendly person"; and "I really enjoy talking to people." Cronbach's alpha for the warmth and agreeable measure was .64 for mothers and .66 for fathers. The items were summed to create a single indicator for the positive interaction construct.

Finally, social support from friends and extended family was measured with three indices that derive from the Interpersonal Social Evaluation List (ISEL) developed by Cohen, Mermelstein, Kamarck, and Hoberman (1985). Chapter 2 describes the three indicators of support used here (appraisal, belonging, tangible support) and evaluates their psychometric adequacy. Analyses reported in Chapter 2 demonstrate that the social support measures are reliable and that they are discriminable from ongoing personality characteristics.

RESULTS

The Continuity Model in Parent-Child Relations

At the bivariate level the quality of the study adults' current relation-ship with parents was correlated with all of the measures of early parent-child interaction and parental characteristics. For example, the quality of the current relationship between adult sons and their fathers is strongly and negatively related ($r = -.53$) to sons' reports that they were rejected by their fathers when they were growing up. The same correlation for adult daughters and their fathers ($r = -.52$) generalizes the finding across both IYFP parents.

Ordinary least squares regression analyses (Table 7.2) showed that recalled parental rejection had the strongest and most consistent effects on the quality of adult children's contemporary relationships with their parents (standardized regression coefficients ranged from $-.397$ for adult daughters and their fathers to $-.236$ for adult daughters and their mothers). Recalled rejection by G1 parents negatively affected the quali-ty of the adult child-parent relationship regardless of sex of child or parent. Parental monitoring was positively associated with the quality of the current adult child-parent relationship only when parent and child were the same gender.

For parental depressed affect, three of the four possible paths were statistically significant and negatively related to current relationship quality. The effects for fathers reported by sons were very weak or non-significant. Recalled parental hostility adversely affected the quality of

Table 7.2. The Effects of Early Parental Characteristics on Current Relationship Quality with Parents: Regression Coefficients in Standard Form

G1 characteristics and behaviors	Reported by G2 adult sons		Reported by G2 adult daughters	
	G1 fathers	G1 mothers	G1 fathers	G1 mothers
Depressed affect	−.090	−.090*	−.177*	−.118*
Parent hostility	−.100	−.152*	.057	−.201*
Parent rejection	−.303*	−.353*	−.397*	−.236*
Parent monitoring	.238*	.056	.074	.108*
Parent health	.115*	.090*	.086*	−.006
Parent age	.044	.191*	.109*	.073*
R^2	.372	.400	.320	.314

* $p \leq .05$ (one-tailed).

later relationships between mothers and children, but not relationship quality between fathers and children. Age and health of elderly parents were generally positively associated with contemporary relationship quality. The continuity model explained between 31% ($R^2 = .314$, mothers and daughters) and 40% ($R^2 = .40$, mothers and sons) of the variance in contemporary adult child-parent relationship quality.

The Mediational Model From Family Origins to Social Support

For the mediational model (Figure 7.1), at the bivariate level, early parental rejection was negatively correlated with all of the measures of self-confidence and warm and agreeable interaction styles (e.g., $r = -.20$ for paternal rejection and adult sons' coping), and positively associated with measures of recalled parental depressed affect and hostility (e.g., $r = .50$ for G1 fathers' depression and rejection as reported by adult daughters). Parental hostility and depression were also negatively associated with measures of self-confidence and warmth and agreeableness at the bivariate level. Regardless of the gender of the adult child, parental monitoring was strongly and negatively associated with parental depression, hostility, and rejection. Parental monitoring had weak or no association with measures of self-confidence for women, but moderate positive association with self-confidence for men. Parental monitoring was positively associated with warmth and agreeableness for both men and women.

Analyses for self-confidence. Latent variable structural equation modeling was used to evaluate the mediating model of social support. We first estimated the model for self-confidence as a mediator. Table 7.3 provides results of the analysis for the measurement model. Because each of the grandparent characteristics was measured with a single indicator, all of the factor loadings for these constructs (e.g., G1 depressed factor) equal one. Indicators for the self-confidence and social support constructs also had satisfactory factor loadings, ranging from .574 (appraisal for adult daughters and G1 fathers) to .862 (belonging for adult sons and G1 fathers).

The results for estimates of the structural model for self-confidence (Table 7.4) indicated that early recalled parental rejection and recalled parental depressed affect were consistently and negatively associated with self-confidence among G2 offspring (e.g., the standardized path coefficient equals $-.218$ for G1 father depressed affect and G2 father self-confidence). The only variation in this pattern was among G2 males, where, in addition to parental rejection and depressed affect, parental monitoring by mother was positively associated with self-confidence. Re-

Table 7.3. Factor Loadings for Latent Constructs for the Self-
Confidence Model

Study variables	G2 adult sons		G2 adult daughters	
	G1 fathers	G1 mothers	G1 fathers	G1 mothers
G1 parental characteristics and behaviors				
1. Report of parent depressed affect	1.000	1.000	1.000	1.000
2. Report of parent hostility	1.000	1.000	1.000	1.000
3. Report of parent rejection	1.000	1.000	1.000	1.000
4. Report of parent monitoring	1.000	1.000	1.000	1.000
G2 self-confidence indicators				
5. Self-report of coping behaviors	.792	.792	.792	.798
6. Self-report of mastery behaviors	.763	.763	.696	.699
7. Self-report of self esteem	.804	.797	.866	.856
G2 social support indicators				
6. Self-report of appraisal	.583	.593	.574	.576
7. Self-report of belonging	.862	.861	.802	.801
8. Self-report of tangible support	.700	.704	.763	.763

called maternal hostility actually had a significant positive relationship
with sons' self-confidence. There was a consistent and strong positive
relationship between G2 self-confidence and G2 adults' ability to establish satisfactory and supportive social relationships across all four models
(e.g., adult daughters' self-confidence had a path coefficient of .498 to
social support in the model for G1 fathers).

As shown in Table 7.4, the self-confidence mediational model explained between 6 and 7% of the variance in G2 self-confidence for
women and between 11 and 12% for men. Over 20% of the variance in
G2 social support was explained by the model. Moreover, with only one
exception (mother monitoring for G2 fathers), none of the G1 characteristics were significantly related to social support, consistent with the
mediational form of the model. The chi-squareds for the models were
well within acceptable limits. The goodness-of-fit indices were all .98 or
higher (Joreskog & Sorbom, 1989).

Analyses for positive interaction style. The results for the warmth and
agreeableness model were similar to those for the self-confidence model.
Table 7.5 provides the results for the measurement model analyses. Because single indicators were used for the parent characteristic and interaction constructs, all of these factor loadings equal 1. The factor loadings

Table 7.4. Standardized Path Coefficients for the Self-Confidence Model

Study variables	G2 adult sons		G2 adult daughters	
	G1 fathers	G1 mothers	G1 fathers	G1 mothers
Structural (path) coefficients				
1. Parent depressed affect to self-confidence	−.218*	−.201*	−.112*	−.134*
2. Parent hostility to self-confidence	.082	.118*	−.029	.034
3. Parent rejection to self-confidence	−.248*	−.154*	−.147*	−.227*
4. Parent monitoring to self-confidence	−.033	.148*	−.018	−.077
5. Self-confidence to social support	.426*	.401*	.498*	.492*
Explained variance				
Model R^2	.133	.130	.060	.075
Self-confidence R^2	.119	.107	.056	.068
Social support R^2	.218	.221	.253	.260
Tests for model fit				
χ^2 (df = 10)	37.65 (p=.038)	23.57 (p=.486)	38.13 (p=.034)	30.78 (p=.160)
Goodness-of-fit index	.983	.990	.983	.987
Adjusted goodness-of-fit index	.961	.977	.962	.970

* $p \leq .05$ (one-tailed).

Table 7.5.   Factors Loadings for Latent Constructs for the Warmth and Agreeableness Model

Study variables	G2 adult sons		G2 adult daughters	
	G1 fathers	G1 mothers	G1 fathers	G1 mothers
G1 parental characteristics and behaviors				
1. Report of parent depressed affect	1.000	1.000	1.000	1.000
2. Report of parent hostility	1.000	1.000	1.000	1.000
3. Report of parent rejection	1.000	1.000	1.000	1.000
4. Report of parent monitoring	1.000	1.000	1.000	1.000
G2 positive interaction style				
5. Warmth and agreeableness	1.000	1.000	1.000	1.000
G2 social support indicators				
6. Self-report of appraisal	.614	.617	.573	.573
7. Self-report of belonging	.834	.837	.779	.780
8. Self-report of tangible support	.708	.712	.788	.788

for social support were acceptable, consistent with the self-confidence model.

Turning to the structural model (Table 7.6), early parental rejection was consistently negatively associated with G2 warmth and agreeableness (e.g., the standardized path coefficient equals −.228 between G1 mothers' rejection and G2 sons' warmth and agreeableness). The effects were weakest for the influence of recalled rejection by fathers on warmth and agreeableness among G2 women. There was a weak positive association between recalled parental monitoring by fathers and warmth and agreeableness among women. Unlike results for the self-confidence model, G1 parent depressed affect was not related to interaction style (warmth/agreeableness) for either adult sons or daughters. Finally, characteristics of warmth and agreeableness were consistently and positively related to G2's supportive relationships outside the family.

Three of the G1 measures were significantly related to social support; however, the mediational model fit the data quite well even with this small number of direct effects. The goodness-of-fit index was .98 and above for all of the mediational models. Moreover, family relationship histories explained between 5 and 6% of the variance for G2 warmth and

Table 7.6. Standaridzed Path Coefficients for the Warmth and Agreeableness Model

Study variables	G2 adult sons		G2 adult daughters	
	G1 fathers	G1 mothers	G1 fathers	G1 mothers
Structural (path) coefficients				
1. Parent depressed affect to warmth and agreeableness	-.028	-.054	-.047	-.058
2. Parent hostility to warmth and agreeableness	.009	-.022	.000	.050
3. Parent rejection to warmth and agreeableness	-.213*	-.228*	-.111*	-.220*
4. Parent monitoring to warmth and agreeableness	.055	.071	.102*	.056
5. Warmth and agreeableness to social support	.335*	.323*	.243*	.229*
Explained variance				
Model R^2	.092	.132	.055	.081
Warm/agreeable R^2	.064	.095	.045	.063
Social support R^2	.162	.171	.074	.082
Tests for Model Fit				
χ^2 (df = 10)	17.25 (p=.069)	12.02 (p=.284)	11.44 (p=.324)	8.96 (p=.536)
Goodness-of-fit index	.990	.993	.994	.995
Adjusted goodness-of-fit index	.965	.976	.977	.982

* $p \leq .05$ (one-tailed).

agreeableness for women and between 6 and 10% for men. The models explained between 7 and 8% of the variance for G2 social support for women and between 16 and 17% for men.

DISCUSSION AND CONCLUSIONS

These findings provide evidence that early family relationships set the stage for styles of interaction later in life both within and outside the family. Recalled early relationships with parents were related to the quality of contemporary relationships between aging parents and their adult children at midlife, thus influencing a primary source of support in times of trouble. Relationship histories contribute to persistent patterns of family interaction that profoundly influence the propensity and ability of lineage systems to respond efficiently in times of distress. Families who have never learned to communicate effectively or who have established dysfunctional communication patterns are less likely to be able to maintain high-quality relationships later in life and, therefore, are less likely to be able to successfully establish patterns of support and mutual exchange (Whitbeck, Simons, & Conger, 1991).

Similarly, early parent-child relationships were related to developmental outcomes that affected the degree to which offspring were able to establish and maintain supportive social relationships outside the family later in life. A history of rejecting parenting decreased adults' self-confidence, which in turn decreased the likelihood of establishing supportive relationships outside the family. A history of rejecting parenting also decreased the likelihood of positive, warm, and agreeable interaction styles among the study adults. This served to reduce the likelihood of a supportive network of friends and extended family to which they could turn in times of trouble.

Although early family relationships may not explain a great deal of the variance of later relationship patterns, relationship histories provide an important element in understanding coping behaviors in times of stress. Styles of interaction affect the availability of support or the extensiveness of one's support network as well as one's ability to ask for and negotiate the terms of assistance with members of the support network. These findings were particularly consistent regarding the detrimental effects of family relationship histories characterized by parental rejection. This corroborates other research that indicates that nonoptimal parenting has persistent effects for offspring into midlife (Caspi & Elder, 1988; Simons et al., 1991b; Whitbeck et al., 1991) Early family interaction patterns are likely to be repeated in situations involving similar role enactments, making later life negotiations surrounding mutual support difficult for family members with a past history of relationship problems.

Early family experiences generalize to support systems outside the family as well. Feelings of low self-worth may result in lowered expectations regarding the availability and likelihood of support within existing social networks, resulting in a less extensive and effective support system. Similarly, negative early relationship learning within the family diminishes the likelihood of developing warm and agreeable interaction styles. This, in turn, decreases one's social attractiveness and reduces the potential for extensive, supportive social networks.

Because this analysis relies on retrospective data concerning relationship history, it provides a weaker test of the effects of early relationships than would prospective models of these phenomena. However, the similarities between the prospective models presented in subsequent chapters and the retrospective models discussed here give some credence to the findings. The impact of early relationship experience within the family may have lifelong consequences for expectations about relationships and one's ability to perceive and acquire social support in times of need. We next consider how the results of these early experiences affected the ability of IYFP parents to cope with contemporary economic stress.

Chapter 8

Doing Worse and Feeling Worse: Psychological Consequences of Economic Hardship

Frederick O. Lorenz, Rand D. Conger, and Ruth Montague

I felt I was a bomb about ready to go off. . . . I felt so stressed and hassled.
—Iowa wife, displaced farm family, 1987

The emotional distress of this Iowa farm wife occurred in response to the bitter loss of a 1,000-acre farm. Previous studies have linked economic conditions to individual psychological well-being, especially depression and demoralization (Horwitz, 1984; Kessler et al., 1988). We now extend these findings to rural families by testing hypotheses about the effects of economic conditions on the depressive symptoms of husbands and wives, and by examining the mediating effects of family and extrafamilial social support. Our basic models are derived from those discussed in Chapter 1 (Figures 1.1 and 1.2). We elaborate them by adding dimensions of social support that, we propose, should affect and be influenced by the economic stress process. As indicated in Chapter 7, the availability of social support rests, at least in part, on the developmental history of Iowa parents and its influence on their sense of self and dispositions toward others.

ECONOMIC HARDSHIP AND EMOTIONAL DISTRESS

In this chapter we are particularly interested in linking economic hardship to the psychological state of parents in the study. Based on earlier discussion and analysis (Chapters 1 and 4), the exogenous variables for the following analyses are represented on the left side of Figure 8.1

under the general heading of family economic hardship. As noted in Chapter 1, our conceptualization of economic hardship derives from several research traditions including work on poverty (per capita income), rural economic stress (debt-to-asset ratio), reduced levels of living (income loss), and job disruptions (unstable work). These related but nonequivalent indicators of economic circumstances are used as a group to represent a family's current financial situation.

The domains of economic hardship included in Figure 8.1 were discussed in Chapters 1 and 4. Briefly, per capita family income represents aspects of both socioeconomic status and vulnerability to economic strain (McLeod & Kessler, 1990; Pearlin, 1989). Income loss, which reflects a downward trend in material resources, has been found to have a pronounced effect on family functioning and subsequent personal attitudes and behaviors when it is severe and lasting, as in the Great Depression (Bakke, 1940; Elder, 1974). Debt-to-asset ratio captures not only relative wealth; for many rural families, it also reflects the changing fortunes and redistribution of resources that occurred during the mid-1980s (Murdock & Leistritz, 1988). Unstable work refers to the patterns of interrupted employment that create uneven income flows and that often place psychological strains on individuals experiencing such events

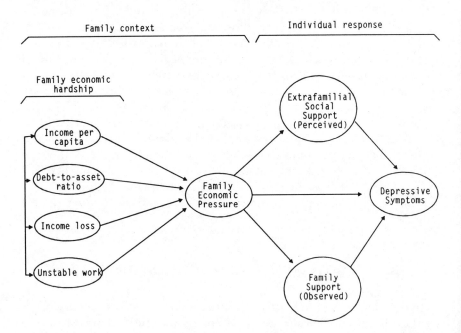

Figure 8.1. Theoretical model for the relationship between economic hardship and depression in husbands and wives.

(Pearlin, 1983; Perrucci & Targ, 1988; Robertson, Elder, Skinner, & Conger, 1991; Thoits, 1983).

Figure 8.1 states that economic hardship affects an individual's emotional distress, operationalized here as depressive symptoms, indirectly through economic pressure. As described in Chapters 1 and 4, and elsewhere (Conger et al., 1990, 1992; Conger, Conger, et al., 1993; Elder et al., 1992), our index of economic pressure involves an assessment by both husband and wife that their family cannot maintain an adequate standard of living, that they are having difficulty paying bills, and that they have had to cut back on expenses to make ends meet.

The model in Figure 8.1 proposes that it is the impact of economic hardship on painful adjustments in daily living (as measured by the economic pressure construct), and not hardship per se, that directly affects depressive symptoms.

The Role of Social Support

The model in Figure 8.1 elaborates the theoretical arguments in Chapter 1, however, by specifically addressing the role of social support in the economic stress process. In Chapter 7, we showed that child-rearing histories affect contemporary social ties by shaping personality characteristics associated with social competence. We now consider how supportive social relations might affect adaptation to economic stress. Research on generalized stress processes has underscored the importance of supportive relationships, both within and beyond the immediate family, for health-related outcomes (Caplan, 1974; Cassel, 1974; Cobb, 1976). This paradigm has grown into a major research endeavor, with scholars periodically reviewing its accomplishments and continued potential (Coyne & Downey, 1991; House, Umberson, & Landis, 1988; Kessler et al., 1985; Vaux, 1988).

Critics have argued that most research on social support has not clearly distinguished between support, social networks and social ties, nor has it clarified the mechanisms through which friendships become a resource to counteract stressful life events or situations (Ritter, 1988; Hobfoll and Stokes, 1988). These critics and others have proposed that, for knowledge to advance, greater attention must be paid to (1) the distinction between structural and functional aspects of support (Cohen and Syme, 1985; House et al., 1988; Ritter, 1988), (2) the distinction between perceived and received support (Eckenrode and Wethington, 1990; Wethington and Kessler, 1986), (3) the relative importance of family compared to friends (Reis, 1990; Wills, 1990), (4) the processes whereby support is garnered (Cutrona, Suhr, & MacFarlane, 1990; Hobfoll & Stokes, 1988), (5) differences between men and women in the mediating role of support (Ensel, 1986; Thoits, 1987), and (6) the match between type of support and the stressors experienced (Cutrona, 1990; Cutrona & Russell, 1990).

Social support outside the nuclear family.   The model in Figure 8.1 addresses several of these issues by differentiating between supportive interactions with family members and the functional support received from outside the nuclear family. The classical, mediating effect of friendship is represented by the paths linking extrafamilial social support to depressive symptoms, and economic pressure to social support. Consistent with this literature, we hypothesize that a significant negative path links social support to depressive symptoms.

Husbands or wives who acknowledge the presence of strong supportive friendships are expected to report fewer symptoms of depression when compared to others facing the same level of economic pressure but perceiving themselves to be without support from friends. The path linking economic pressure to social support may be either positive or negative. A positive path represents evidence for an additive buffering effect (Wheaton 1985), implying that people, when faced with stressful situations, reach out to their friends to garner the support they need. Conversely, a negative path between social support and economic pressure suggests that, with greater levels of economic pressure, individuals feel singled out or isolated—perhaps even abandoned—by their friends.

For these rural families, we expect that traditions of self-reliance and the maintenance of appearances should lead to decreased social support as parents withdraw from social networks to conceal their economic problems and feelings of failure (Davidson, 1990; Smiley, 1992). That is, we propose a negative association between economic pressure and extrafamilial social support. We expected that these mediating processes were more likely than moderating or buffering effects of social support (Kessler et al., 1985).

Social support from outside the family could be measured in several ways. Extrafamilial social support is measured in this study by perceived social support rather than by descriptors of the social network from which support is received. This approach follows from the contention that the experience of support is information that leads one to believe that he or she is cared for, esteemed and valued, and belongs to a network of mutual obligations (Cobb, 1976). Although this implies that social support exists only to the extent that the recipient believes it exists, perceived support does appear to be a more sensitive indicator of social influences than the objective existence of that resource (Cohen, Mermelstein, Kamarck, & Hoberman, 1985; Hobfoll & Stokes, 1988). For example, perceived social support predicts psychological well-being over and above the actual support received from one's network of friends (Wethington and Kessler, 1986).

From a methodological perspective, perceived social support has been found to be related, although weakly, to actual descriptions of friendship network size and centrality, and to objective indicators of support received (Cutrona, 1989; Hobfoll & Stokes, 1988; Wethington & Kessler, 1986). However, by its very subjectivity, perceptions of support may be part of a larger, overarching construct or cognitive structure that relates to depression (Watson & Clark, 1984). Lakely and Cassidy, for example, argue that low perceived social support may be an aspect of a more general negative worldview in which "interrelated negative beliefs about the self, the world, and the future are organized into depressive schemas that lead to negatively biased information processing and subsequent depression" (1990, p. 337).

Fincham and Bradbury (1990) report experimental research that demonstrates that perceptions of supportive behaviors are sensitive to the mood of the recipient. If negative affectivity does, in fact, tie together the distinctive concepts of emotional distress (e.g., symptoms of anxiety, hostility, or depression) and perceived social support, then one is confronted with the confounding hypothesis that this overarching construct is simultaneously affecting both perceptions of social support and reports of depressive symptoms, and that both perceived social support and depressive symptoms are spuriously related.

Family support. From a more substantive perspective, extrafamilial social support may pale against the more salient and immediate support fostered by close family relationships. Reis (1990) has observed that, more than anything else, people express a desire for, and life satisfaction depends upon, close intimate relationships. Fincham and Bradbury (1990) note that marriage itself is often viewed as an index of social support, and that marital satisfaction and social support are empirically related. Yet the conceptual relationship between marriage, close family ties, and social support has been recognized only recently.

Drawing on a review by Gottlieb (1985), Hobfoll and Stokes note that social support was originally thought of as an environmental resource closely connected with social interactions. Whereas extrafamilial social support appears important in providing the "weak ties" that are necessary in garnering a wide array of tangible resources, close relationships are immediately salient because from them "one is likely to receive actual provision of resources when they are required, and one is likely to make the attribution that the aid signifies love or deep caring" (Hobfoll & Stokes, 1988, p. 503). Family members provide both the immediate informational support, advice, and guidance in problem solving that can only come with intimate knowledge of the recipient's needs, resources and personal situations, and also the esteem support that lets the recipient know that he or she is valued and admired (Reis 1990; Wills 1990). Conversely, close but troubled relationships are likely to provoke strong negative attributions, creating an atmosphere of "duplicity, manipulation, and cruelty" that can exacerbate rather than ameliorate stressful situations such as economic hardship (Reis, 1990, p. 26).

We hypothesize the existence of the same general pattern of relationships linking family support to both depressive symptoms and to economic pressure as we did for perceived extrafamilial social support. Again, we expect that the rural tradition of self-reliance leads to embarrassment and a sense of failure when parents cannot maintain a desired level of living. These emotions, we expect, should produce tension and withdrawal in family relations as indicated by a negative association between economic pressure and family support (Figure 8.1). Although our data do not allow us to separate the confounding issue of support perceived or received from the issue of the relative salience of family versus friends, we can make progress by distinguishing between individual perceptions of social support and certain behavioral aspects of immediate family support. Our behaviorally oriented measures of family support are consistent with Hobfoll and Stoke's (1988) argument that supportive relationships require both a minimal level of social integration plus observable supportive interactions.

Differences Between Husbands and Wives

One of the most consistent epidemiological findings over the recent past is that depressive symptoms are approximately twice as prevalent among females as males (Ensel, 1986). Although the complexity of gender roles makes it difficult to separate sources of the differences between men and women, one theme that emerges from the literature is that women are more active participants in social interactions and receive more support, especially emotional support, from their friendships than do men. However, men may be more involved in the economic aspects of daily life, and may draw more on the instrumental aspects of social relations.

There is some evidence that men benefit more than women from a large network of acquaintances, though women appear to be more self-disclosing and benefit more from close, intimate relationships (Hobfoll & Stokes, 1988; House, Umberson, & Landis, 1988). These generalizations are insightful in describing gender differences, but it is not clear that they translate to differences in the relationships among concepts in the proposed theoretical model. We speculate that the model in Figure 8.1

will hold for both husbands and wives, with perhaps stronger coefficients linking economic variables to other variables for husbands while wives may have stronger coefficients linking support to depression.

MEASUREMENT

Economic Hardship and Economic Pressure

The measures of economic hardship and the concept of economic pressure are family-level variables. Variables measuring dimensions of economic hardship were obtained from a financial questionnaire that was filled out either by husbands and wives together or by the spouse who usually took care of financial and tax matters. The concept of economic hardship is incorporated into the model in Figure 8.1 through four exogenous variables: per capita income, debt-to-asset ratio, income loss and unstable work history. *Per capita income* was measured by dividing total family income by family size. This measure correlates .98 with the income-to-needs ratio described in Chapter 4. Thus, both measures adjust level of income for any economies of scale created by a larger number of family members. The measures for *debt-to-asset ratio* and *unstable work* were described in Chapter 4 and details regarding their computation can be found there.

Income loss was calculated by subtracting a report of family earnings in 1987 from reported family earnings in 1988. Earnings were based on the joint or collective earnings of both husband and wife. For farmers, the calculations included total farm receipts minus total operating expenses. Approximately 12% of the families reported lower income in 1988 than in 1987, while the median change in income was between a 5 and 10% increase.

Three indices are used to measure the concept of *economic pressure*. Details regarding the three indicators for the construct can be found in Chapter 4. The indicators include economic adjustments or cutbacks, the inability to make ends meet (general felt constraints), and not having enough money for necessities (specific felt constraints).

Perceived Social Support and Family Support

The two concepts mediating the relationship between economic pressure and mental health (depressive symptoms), perceived social support and family support, were both measured with multiple indices from a single source. *Perceived social support* was measured using the ISEL developed by Cohen et al. (1985). All items were revised so that respondents indicated sources of support outside the nuclear family. Based on factor analyses of data from an earlier study of 74 rural families (Conger et al., 1990), 12 of 40 items from the ISEL were selected to be included in our questionnaires to tap three dimensions of social support: appraisal, belonging, and tangible support. This social support measure is described in Chapter 2 and its psychometric characteristics are also evaluated there.

The concept of *family support* was defined as the extent to which immediate family members behave in a generally supportive way toward the husband or the wife. The important distinction between the measure of family and nonfamily support involves the source of information. Family supportiveness was assessed using ratings by trained project observers and thus eliminates method variance confounds in estimated relationships between study constructs (e.g., between support and depressed mood).

Family supportiveness toward the husband was measured by combining observational ratings from videotaped family interactions (see Chapter 2) on three categories. The first category, *warmth/supportiveness*, was defined as observed expressions of interest, care, concern, support, encouragement, and responsiveness by one family member toward another. When directed toward the husband/father, it was measured by combining the observational ratings of warm/supportive behaviors toward him by his wife in Tasks 2 and 4, by the target child in Tasks 1 and 2, and the sibling in the study in Tasks 1 and 2. An index for the wife/mother was similarly constructed. The observer ratings within each task ranged from 1 to 5, so that potential scores for the index ranged from 6 to 30. The actual median score was 12 for both husbands and wives, with approximately one-half of the scores between 10 and 14.

The second category was *transactional positive*, defined as the extent to which two people, as they interact, initiate and reciprocate warmth, endearments, or physical affection. This measure indicates the degree to which family members reciprocate one another's positive behaviors. Again, coders rated each dyad in a task for expressions of positive transactions, and an index of family members' positive transactions with the wife/mother were obtained by summing the ratings assigned to the wife and husband in Tasks 2 and 4, the mother and target child in Tasks 1 and 2, and the mother and target's sibling in Tasks 1 and 2. An index for the husband/father was similarly constructed. The median scores were 13 and 14 for husbands and wives, respectively.

The last category, *relationship quality*, was the coder's subjective evaluation of the quality of the relationship between two people. This score evaluated, all things considered, how emotionally close each family member was to each other member. Using the same tasks, family relationship quality for each of the two parents was obtained by combining the individual scores from interactions with spouse, target, and sibling. The median score was 19 for both husbands and wives, with approximately half of the scores between 16 and 22.

Depressive Symptoms

We triangulated on the concept of depression by using measures of depressive symptoms from three sources: self, spouse, and observer. The index of *self-reported* depression was measured using the depression subscale from the Symptom Check List-90-Revised (SCL-90-R; Derogatis, 1983). In the SCL-90-R, respondents are presented with a list of symptoms and asked how much discomfort each has caused "in the past week including today." Although the response categories ranged from *not at all* (1), to *extremely* (5), for nearly all items, the responses were clearly skewed in the direction of *not at all,* and were therefore dichotomized to capture whether or not the symptom was present, and then summed. The actual items emphasized symptoms of low energy and feelings of despondency, and were identified in factor analyses as distinctive from other related SCL-90-R dimensions such as anxiety, hostility, and somatization. Examples include "loss of sexual interest or pleasure," "feeling low in energy and slowed down," and "feeling no interest in things." The resulting scores ranged from 0 to 12 symptoms, with about one-third of the husbands and one-fourth of the wives reporting no symptoms.

Spouse report of depression was obtained by asking a respondent, on a 5-point Likert scale, whether his or her spouse was "a happy person," and whether he or she is "always sad or depressed." Responses to the two items were scored to reflect greater distress and summed, with a median score of 4 for both husbands and wives on a scale with a range from 2 to 10. An *observer rating* of depression was obtained from a single interaction rating scale in Task 4. The rating scale, labeled "internalized negative," represented the observer's assessment of the extent to which the husband or wife expressed emotional distress as dysphoria (unhappiness, sadness) or anxiety (worry, fear). For both husbands and wives, scores ranged from 1 to 5, with a median of 3.

RESULTS

The analysis was conducted by evaluating both the measurement models and the proposed theoretical model, and by comparing alternative models that would have provided competing interpretations of the underlying processes. At an early stage of the analysis, we also examined the data for evidence of moderator effects. For clarity of presentation, this largely interactive process is presented as a series of discrete activities.

Measurement Model

The model in Figure 8.1 was evaluated by first examining the relationship of indicators to their concepts, and then estimating the strength of relationships among the concepts. The measurement model, presented in Figure 8.2, shows how specific indicators are hypothesized to relate to the four endogenous concepts.

Economic pressure is reflected by its three indicators, as noted by arrows leading from economic pressure to economic adjustments (ADJ), general felt constraints (FLT1), and specific felt constraints (FLT2). The

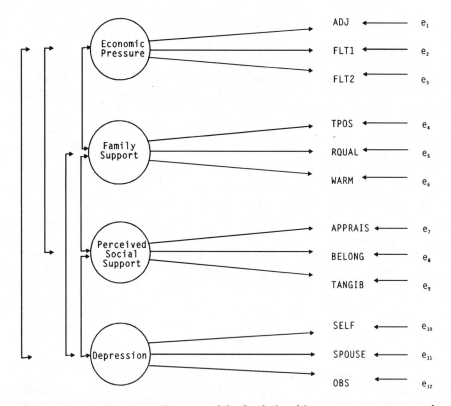

Figure 8.2. Confirmatory factor model of relationships among concepts and between concepts and their indicators.

absence of arrows linking economic pressure to other indicators means we assume that each indicator of a concept represents only that one concept.

Similar assumptions are implied in the arrows linking family support to positive transactions (TPOS), relationship quality (RQUAL), and warmth/supportiveness (WARM); perceived social support to its dimensions (APPRAISal, BELONGing and TANGIBle); and depression to its three sources of reports (SELF, SPOUSE, and OBServer). The arrows between each pair of concepts mean that we assume that all the concepts are correlated, while the *lack* of arrows linking the residuals (e_i) to one another implies that all error terms are assumed to be uncorrelated. The exogenous concepts of income per capita, debt-to-asset ratio, income loss and unstable work are not included in the model because we have only one indicator of each. For these indicators (see Chapter 2) we assume that each is measured without error and that there is a perfect correspondence between the concepts and their indicators.

The results in Table 8.1 provide general support for the proposed confirmatory factor model. All of the coefficients shown for both husbands and wives were significant, and the magnitude of most of the coefficients was reasonably large. For husbands, the coefficient of .78 linking ADJ to economic pressure means that about 61% of the variance in family adjustments was explained by the economic pressure construct. The weakest coefficients were those linking husband's depression to his own self-report (.41) and to the observer's report (.43). The overall chi-squared statistic of 72, with 48 degrees of freedom for the husband's measurement model, could not be substantially improved without considerable loss of parsimony.

For wives, the model yielded similar results, but with two complications. Fitting the proposed model from Figure 8.2 to the data produced a chi-squared of 95.5, with additional evidence that significant improvements could be realized by allowing the husband's report of her depression to align itself as an indictor of economic pressure, and by allowing specific felt constraints (FLT2) to align with family support (see Table 8.1). After several additional experiments in releasing constraints and realigning indicators with concepts, these two alterations in the original model provided significant improvements in the fit of the model to the data [$\chi^2(46) = 69$]. In the revised model, the coefficient of $-.36$ linking husband's report of his wife's depression to economic pressure may reflect an inability on his part to separate the economic conditions under which they live from his assessment of her depression.

The correlations among the concepts (see Table 8.2) indicate that, for husbands, depression was significantly related to economic pressure (.51), family support ($-.29$) and perceived social support ($-.21$), but

Table 8.1. Results of Fitting the Confirmatory Factor Analysis Model
to Data for Husbands and Wives (*N* = 426)

	Factor loadings	
Concepts and indicators	Husbands	Wives
Economic pressure		
Adjustments (ADJ)	.78	.78
Felt constraints-general (FLT1)	.92	.92
Felt constraints-specific (FLT2)	.80	.79
Spouse report of depression (SPOUSE)		−.36
Family support		
Transactional positive (TPOS)	.86	.80
Relationship quality (RQUAL)	.62	.65
Warmth/supportiveness (WARM)	.79	.82
Felt constraints specific (FLT2)[a]		−.11
Perceived social support		
Appraisal (APPRAIS)	.59	.59
Belonging (BELONG)	.82	.78
Tangible (TANGIB)	.71	.79
Depression		
Self-report (SELF)	.41	.51
Spouse report (SPOUSE)	.66	.71
Observer report (OBS)	.43	.46
Chi-squared (degrees of freedom)	72 (48)	69 (46)

[a] Variables introduced to improve the fit of the measurement model for wives.

these latter three concepts were not significantly related to each other. These correlations suggest that social support, observed or self-reported, is negatively related to depressed mood.

The coefficients reported in Table 8.2 indicate that the correlations between wives' depression and economic pressure (.64), family support (−.36), and perceived social support (−.36) were all significant, and all slightly stronger than those observed for husbands. Again, observed support was equally predictive of depressed mood as perceived support, suggesting little method variance bias in the self-report measure.

Model Evaluation

Because our measures of economic hardship and economic pressure are family-level variables that incorporate the responses of both husbands and wives, estimates of the relationship between them were the same for both spouses. As shown in Table 8.3, economic pressure had a strong inverse relationship with income per capita (−.40), followed by debt-to-

Table 8.2. Correlations Among Endogenous Concepts

Constructs	Husbands (1)	(2)	(3)	Wives (1)	(2)	(3)
1. Economic pressure	—			—		
2. Family support	−.11	—		−.13	—	
3. Perceived social support	.06	−.06	—	.04	−.12	—
4. Depression	.51	−.29	−.21	.64	−.36	−.36

asset ratio (.33), income loss (.14), and unstable work history (.11). Overall, the four exogenous variables explained 39% of the variance in economic pressure. The four exogenous variables were only modestly intercorrelated, reinforcing our view that they represent different, largely independent domains of economic hardship or well-being rather than being highly correlated indicators of a single theoretical construct.

Our data provided evidence consistent with the argument that economic hardship affects individual family members only indirectly, through economic pressure. Although the paths linking the exogenous variables and economic pressure were relatively strong, the direct effects of economic pressure on perceived social support from outside the nuclear family were modest for both husbands (−.06) and wives (−.12). These

Table 8.3. Standardized Regression Coefficients for the Hypothesized Model Linking Economic Hardship and Depression in Husbands and Wives ($N = 426$)

Dependent concepts predicted by explanatory concepts	Coefficients (with t-value)* Husbands	Wives
Economic pressure predicted by:		
Income per capita	−.40 (−8.6)	−.40 (−8.6)
Debt-to-asset ratio	.33 (7.3)	.33 (7.3)
Income loss	.14 (3.4)	.14 (3.3)
Unstable work	.11 (2.7)	.11 (2.6)
Perceived social support predicted by:		
Economic pressure	−.06 (−1.1)	−.12 (−2.0)
Family support predicted by:		
Economic pressure	−.12 (−2.2)	−.14 (−2.4)
Depression predicted by:		
Economic pressure	.47 (4.9)	.45 (5.7)
Perceived social support	−.17 (−2.3)	−.34 (−4.2)
Family support	−.23 (−3.0)	−.31 (−4.1)
R^2	.33	.49

* For $t \geq 2.00$, $p < .05$

results are consistent with the proposed theoretical model for wives only. Economic pressure, however, was significantly and negatively related to family support for both husbands (−.12) and wives (−.14), consistent with the theoretical model.

When models not shown in tabular form were estimated that included direct paths from the exogenous variables to social support and family support, the results provided little evidence of any direct or indirect effects of measures of economic hardship on either perceived social support or observed family support. Only the indirect effects of income and debt-to-asset ratio on husbands' and wives' family support were statistically significant, and then only modestly. There were no significant indirect effects linking the exogenous variables to perceived social support.

The coefficients for the regression of depression on economic pressure, perceived social support, and observed family support were all significant in the predicted directions. For husbands, level of depression was strongly predicted by economic pressure (.47) as we hypothesized, but social support (−.17) and family support (−.23) also contributed significantly to the explanation of husband's depressive symptoms. Essentially, the same pattern was found for wives, with some evidence of even stronger effects linking depression to social support (−.34) and family support (−.31).

Overall, the explanatory constructs explained 33% of the variance in husbands' depression, and 49% of the variance in wives' depression. Applying procedures outlined by Sobel (1987), all four of the exogenous variables in Figure 8.1 had significant indirect effects on both husbands' and wives' depression.

Model Comparison

The causal ordering of variables in the theoretically specified model in Figure 8.1 was justified a priori. However, our confidence in this model relative to other hierarchically related competing models was strengthened through a series of model comparisons that followed the strategy outlined by Anderson and Gerbing (1988) and elaborated in Chapter 2. This strategy led to the following observations: First, the overall chi-squared goodness-of-fit statistics for the theoretical model in Figure 8.1 were 127.9 for husbands and 156.6 for wives, both with 93 degrees of freedom. Although further improvements in the summary statistics were realized by correlating selected measurement error residuals, the improvements resulted in no substantive changes in the interpretation of the model and, in fact, detracted from the essential parsimony of the original model.

Second, we estimated fully recursive models that linked the four exogenous variables to all of the subsequent endogenous concepts. A comparison of this "saturated" model with our theoretically derived model resulted in no statistically significant improvement, as evaluated by the degree of change in the overall chi-squared statistic, in either the husbands' or the wives' results. None of the 12 possible direct paths linking measures of economic hardship to husbands' social support and family support were significant in the predicted direction, nor were any of the parallel paths for wives.

Finally, we compared our theoretical model with the most restrictive but theoretically interesting alternative possible, represented by the situation where economic pressure is predicted by the four exogenous variables, but all of the paths linking the endogenous concepts are set equal to zero. For this model, the chi-squared increases significantly to 208 for husbands and 257.3 for wives, both with 98 degrees of freedom. The difference in chi-squared between these two models, with 5 degrees of freedom, is a significant 80.1 for husbands and 100.7 for wives. A further examination of several other intermediate models all led us to the conclusion that our theoretical model was the most appropriate alternative model.

Evidence of Moderating Effects

The theoretically derived model in Figure 8.1 was estimated after careful attention to the possible implications of moderator effects that may have caused the relationships between any two concepts to be conditional upon the relative presence or absence of a third concept. For the models above, we found little evidence that interaction effects invalidated the substance of our argument, yet some of the results from our investigation of interactions are suggestive enough to merit additional comment.

In the classical regression model, interaction effects are introduced by creating the multiplicative products of two or more variables. But as discussed in Chapter 2, the preferred approach when estimating models with multiple indicators is to divide the data into two (or more) groups based on the distribution of values on one of the concepts, and then compare coefficients between the two groups for all remaining relevant concepts in the model. Although standardized coefficients are being reported, all comparisons were based on covariance matrices, which is the appropriate procedure when comparing across subgroups (Bollen, 1989).

Three models were examined for both husbands and wives. In the first model, we compared the relationships between economic pressure, family support, and depressive symptoms for those who reported high and low perceived social support from outside the nuclear family. In the second model, we compared the relationships between economic pressure, perceived social support, and depression for those who were high and low on family support. These two models evaluated whether social support might buffer or reduce the effect of economic stress on depressive symptoms in a multiplicative fashion beyond the additive effects already shown. For these first two models, the results demonstrated no significant differences between subgroups for the hypothesized model for either husbands or wives.

Because economic stress has been shown to have differential effects depending on family social status (Liker & Elder, 1983), in a third model, we compared the coefficients relating economic pressure to family support, perceived social support and economic pressure for those families with low and high per capita family income. This third model, when applied to wives, produced differences between low- and high-income families that were startling enough to merit further comment. First, for both the high- and low-income families, neither family support nor perceived social support was significantly related to economic pressure (see Table 8.4). Second, economic pressure was significantly related to depression for wives in both low-income (.48) and high-income (.50) families, but the difference was not significant between the two groups.

However, there were pronounced differences between wives from relatively low- and high-income families in the effects of social and family support on depression. As shown in Table 8.4, for wives from low-income families, family support was significantly related to depression (−.55), but perceived social support was not (−.20). For wives from high-income families, family support was not significant (−.13), but social support from outside the family was (−.51). From data not presented in tabular form, we observed that a somewhat greater proportion of wives from low-income families did not work outside the home (21.5% compared to 16% of the wives in high-income families), and those that did have outside employment were more likely to be working part-time.

For wives who did work outside the home in 1988, the average annual wages and salaries for wives from low-income families was $6,100, compared to $11,600 for wives from higher-income families. The wives of lower-income families were less well-educated: 58% had 12 years of school or less and only 11% had 16 years of school or more; in contrast, only 33% of the women from higher-income families had 12 years of school or less and 26% had 16 years of education or more. These work and educational differences translate into indicators of community involvement: wives from lower-income families belong to fewer community organizations (25% belong to none), and they are less likely than

Table 8.4.   Standardized Regression Coefficients for Model Linking
Economic Pressure and Depression in Low ($N = 210$) and High
($N = 216$) Income Wives

Dependent concepts predicted by explanatory concepts	Coefficients (with t-value)*	
	Low income	*High income*
Perceived social support predicted by:		
Economic pressure	−.02(−0.3)	−.14(−1.9)
Family support predicted by:		
Economic pressure	−.05(−0.6)	−.10(−1.4)
Depression predicted by:		
Economic pressure	.48(3.6)	.50(4.9)
Social support	−.20(−1.8)	−.51(−4.0)
Family support	−.55(−3.9)	−.13(−1.2)
R2	60	47

* For $t \geq 2.00$, $p < .05$.

wives from higher-income families to actively participate in meetings and
hold office in community organizations.

The scenario this suggests is that wives from low-income families focus
proportionately more of their efforts and resources on their family, and
if their family does not provide a supportive atmosphere, they are more
likely to feel depressed. In contrast, wives from higher-income families
are more likely to be in occupations or involved in community activities
that are rewarding and provide larger networks of friendships. In this
situation, the confiding and supportive quality of these extrafamilial
friendships appear to be a relatively more important factor in determining whether or not they will feel depressed.

DISCUSSION

In this chapter we drew on earlier theoretical and empirical analyses
from Chapters 1 and 4 to evaluate a model of rural economic stress. An
elaborated theoretical model was proposed in Figure 8.1, and the match
between the theoretical model and data from our sample of rural families provide evidence for several important conclusions.

First, the finding that several domains of family economic hardship or
well-being affected depression in individual family members only indirectly through economic pressure is important because it establishes the
primacy of daily experience and the adaptive process in dealing with
economic conditions. For our sample, depressive symptoms were more

prevalent among husbands and wives with (1) lower incomes, (2) incomes that were declining relative to previous years, (3) higher debt-to-asset ratios, and (4) unstable work patterns. But the relationship between these exogenous predictors and depressive symptoms disappeared once the family's awareness of economic difficulties and behavioral adjustments to these economic conditions were taken into account.

This result is consistent with previous studies relating the farm crisis to depressive symptoms among farm operators (Armstrong & Schulman, 1990; Belyea & Lobao, 1990), and with our previous pilot study of a smaller sample of rural families ($N = 74$), which examined the effects of economic stress on marital quality and instability and on child development (Conger et al., 1990; Elder et al., 1992; Lorenz et al., 1991). By including measures of daily experience and adaptive processes, our model elaborates previous findings that have linked specific economic conditions to individual well-being (Horwitz, 1984; House et al., 1988; Kessler et al., 1988).

Second, our theoretical model included family and extrafamilial social support as mediating variables, continuing a contemporary research theme that began with Cassel (1974) and Cobb (1976). In this theme, social support can have either an additive (mediating) or a multiplicative (moderating) buffering effect on the relationship between economic pressure and, depressive symptoms (Wheaton, 1985).

Our data provide some evidence for support mediation but no evidence for a social support/stress buffering effect. According to the additive model, social support helps alleviate the negative consequences of economic pressure on depression when individuals rally family and friends to their plight, a process that would be empirically substantiated by a positive relationship between economic pressure and our various indicators of support.

For our data, the relationships between economic pressure and subsequent family and perceived social support are both negative, although weak, so that any cumulative indirect effects of economic pressure through social support serve to exacerbate rather than alleviate symptoms of depression. These relationships were predicted in that we expected that rural parents, who live in an environment promotive of individual self-reliance, would tend to withdraw from social relationships because of the stigma they attach to economic failure.

According to the multiplicative model, social support ameliorates the effects of economic pressure on depressive symptoms by reducing the strength of the relationship between these two variables; but again, for our sample of husbands and wives, the relationships between economic pressure and depressive symptoms were essentially the same, regardless of whether their perceived social support or observed family support were high or low.

Our data do provide evidence of significant direct effects of social and family support on depressive symptoms for both husbands and wives. But the relationship is complex. Consistent with numerous previous studies that suggest that women are more actively involved in social interactions and receive more support from them than do men (House et al., 1988; Hobfoll & Stokes, 1988), one can note in Table 8.3 that the relationship between both perceived social support and family support is stronger for women than for men. But even that relationship is not so simple. As witnessed by our results in Table 8.4, where that support comes from may well depend on status-related variables.

The women in our sample with relatively low incomes were less likely than women from higher-income families to hold jobs outside the home or off the farm, and they belonged to fewer community organizations. Their world appears to revolve around their family. If that family actually provides significant support, then the depressive consequences of hard economic times are greatly reduced, but if that family withholds support, then reports of depressive symptoms multiply.

In contrast, women from relatively high-income families average higher levels of education, are more likely to work outside the home, and belong and actively participate in more community organizations. Their membership and participation in these organizations is significantly related to their perceived social support, so much so that the image one gets is that of independent and worldly women whose existence is only partially defined by their relationships with their husbands and families, but who are nevertheless vulnerable to depression. For these women, the relative effects of perceived social support on depressive symptoms are about as strong as the direct effects of family economic pressure.

Finally, this study is one of the first to use direct observation of family interactions as a basis for making judgments about family support. The results are encouraging. Following arguments by numerous authors, we expected the effects of family support on depressive symptoms to be greater than the effects of extrafamilial social support; family support is supposedly more intimate, consistent, and immediate. The resulting coefficients between depressive symptoms and both types of support, however, were roughly equal (see Table 8.3). Our data, though, contain an important mismatch: Family support was observed directly from videotapes of family interactions, while extrafamilial social support was based on the respondent's self-reports.

From previous studies, we know that coefficients linking two concepts that are both obtained from a single reporting agent tend to be inflated relative to coefficients obtained from two different agents (Lorenz et al., 1991). Even though the confirmatory factor analysis we reported in Chapter 2 established that respondents were able to conceptually distinguish perceived social support and depressive symptoms, the correlations between the two concepts are presumed to be higher than if reports of that support were obtained from a third person.

The fact that the coefficients linking depressive symptoms to family support and to perceived social support are about the same suggests, however indirectly, that actual family support may have a stronger influence on psychological distress than actual extrafamilial social support. Indeed, earlier analyses in which husbands and wives provided self-reports of spousal support and own emotional affect produced associations between constructs that were about twice the size of those reported here for observed family support and depressive symptoms (Lorenz et al., 1991).

The present findings suggest that self-report measures of social support that are significantly related to depressive symptoms are probably not a method variance artifact in that observed social support produces similar evidence for such empirical relationships. Moreover, nuclear family support is probably more predictive than outside support of negative mood in that self-reported family support would likely be much more strongly correlated with distress than the observed family support reported here. Because these observational measures of family support do not contain a method variance bias that is likely to increase the magnitude of estimates of main effects, these results are quite conservative compared to findings based on reports by a single family member.

These findings provide important support for the first stages of our theoretical model discussed in Chapter 1 (see Figures 1.1 and 1.2). We now consider the next step in the model: from economic pressure and emotional distress to marital conflict and disruption.

Chapter 9

Economic Stress and Marital Relations

Rand D. Conger, Xiao-Jia Ge, and Frederick O. Lorenz

You just yell at me if I spend money.[wife] You yell if I spend money.[husband]
—Exchange between spouses in an economically
distressed rural family

In Chapter 1 we developed a theoretical model proposing that economic pressures lead to emotional distress and demoralization for adults. Analyses in the previous chapter supported this proposition. Moreover, the results showed that, although social support reduces somewhat the negative psychological effects of financial problems, economic pressure has a strong and persistent influence on the psychological status of these Iowa parents.

This chapter examines the next step in the postulated process from economic and emotional distress to disruptions in marital relations. The quotation that begins this chapter comes from a financially stressed couple in our sample whose interaction during the videotaped marital task illustrates the reciprocated financial conflicts we expected would be exacerbated by economic troubles. In the following analyses, we focus on hardship-induced marital hostility and its consequences.

In developing a conceptual model of how economic problems might affect marriage, we were influenced both by earlier theory and research and by our observations of rural spouses. During the videotaped interactions, a continuing theme in their remarks was the sense that dealing with financial difficulties took their attention away from their marital relationships, oftentimes leading to time for only brief interchanges between them and to significant pessimism about their lives and futures. For example, one financially stressed Iowa father told us,

187

Times are hard. I can remember when I was the only one working, and
we had money left over. Now, I work two jobs. My wife works full-time and
we still have trouble making ends meet.

Adjustments such as these involving increased work hours and as yet
unresolved financial hardships can produce both depressed and angry
feelings. Indeed, one mother told us, while talking to her husband during a videotaped discussion, that she felt so overwhelmed by their inability to solve their economic problems that she no longer turned to him for
solace or direction. Instead, she now ignored her husband and sought
advice from her father regarding plans for the future. These feelings
also were expressed by another wife who told us

I . . . highly resent my husband's debt and selfishness. I would like a
better home and to be able to be rewarded for my hard work instead of
being limited by his failures and debts. I'm tired of his bills always being a
pressure.

Another husband told us that, because of economic strains, both he
and his wife were continually sad and depressed and pessimistic about
their future. He noted that they constantly argued about finances as a
result of their inability to find any mutually acceptable solutions to their
problems. These themes of time pressures, demoralization, and conflict
are pervasive in the interviews with economically stressed Iowa couples.
They also characterize reports from other studies of disadvantaged rural
families (Rosenblatt, 1990). We place them within the context of previous research and theory to develop a testable model of economic stress
and marital relations.

ECONOMIC STRESS AND MARITAL RELATIONS

Research conducted across several decades of the 20th century has
demonstrated the potentially adverse impact of economic stress on family relations (Bakke, 1940; Conger et al., 1984; Dooley & Catalano, 1988;
Elder, 1974; Heffernan & Heffernan, 1986; Kaduschin & Martin, 1981;
Lasley & Conger, 1986; Rosenblatt 1990; Straus, Gelles, & Steinmetz,
1980; Voydanoff & Donnelly, 1988). For two-parent families with children, the marital dyad is a critical point of entry for adverse economic
influences that eventually affect child and adolescent development. This
approach to the study of family economic hardship, which emphasizes
the importance of family relationships in response to financial difficulties, is consonant with a more general perspective on psychosocial stress

processes recently proposed by Coyne and Downey (1991). They argue that the impact of chronic strains and acute stresses on individual development can best be understood within the context of one's closest social ties. They note that troubled relationships may mediate or moderate the adverse effects of stressful events or conditions as well as act as significant stressors in their own right. Studies of economic influence on family life fit well with this general theoretical framework.

Mounting economic pressures generally bring budgetary matters to the fore, enhancing preoccupation with financial issues that, in many families, generate frustration, anger, and general demoralization (Conger et al., 1990, 1991, 1992; Dooley & Catalano, 1988; Elder & Caspi, 1988; Liker & Elder, 1983). These strong emotional responses to serious financial difficulties are consonant with findings from a rich history of social psychological research that demonstrates the unfortunate consequences of negative events and conditions for human health and behavior (Berkowitz, 1989). The impact of the aversive experience of economic stress on individual well-being is further exacerbated by its indirect effects through the responses of other family members.

Despite the considerable evidence that economic factors play an important role in the dynamics of family relationships, empirical findings are not entirely consistent across studies. For example, some investigators report a positive relationship between socioeconomic status and marital quality (perceptions of happiness or satisfaction with the marriage), while others observe no significant association between the two. When supportive evidence is reported, the correlations are generally modest in size (Piotrkowski, Rapoport, & Rapoport, 1987). Analyses involving both objective and subjective measures of economic circumstances also show a mix of findings. For example, Atkinson, Liem, and Liem (1986) found a significant inverse relationship between duration of unemployment and marital quality for white-collar but not blue-collar respondents. Larson (1984) found mean differences between groups of employed and unemployed spouses for total dyadic adjustment, but not for the satisfaction, affection, or cohesion subscales of the Dyadic Adjustment Scale. In a study of 75 laid-off workers, Perrucci and Targ (1988) obtained no significant correlations between economic strain (feelings that resources are inadequate to meet one's needs) and marital happiness nor between marital happiness and change in employment status.

Conger et al. (1990) proposed that the inconsistencies in earlier findings regarding economic stress and marital relations may have resulted at least in part from the absence in most previous research of information about the quality of marital interactions. They hypothesized that the quality of behavioral exchange between couples would link economic difficulties to satisfaction or happiness in the relationship. The results from their study of 76 rural and small-town couples were consistent with this hypothesis. They found that several dimensions of economic hardship (low income, income loss, and unstable work) were positively associated with hostility and negatively related to emotional support in marriage and that these relationships were indirect through the daily financial strains and pressures experienced by economically stressed couples.

Marital warmth and supportiveness played a secondary role in these processes. Hostility had the dominant impact on marital quality and we focus on this dimension of marital interaction in the present analyses of the over 400 couples who participated in the IYFP. These investigators also found that economic hardship had a more adverse influence on the behaviors of husbands than wives. The end result of the process from hardship to disrupted marital interactions was lower marital satisfaction and greater marital instability for couples exposed to serious financial difficulties.

This earlier study made headway in charting the ties between economic hardship and family processes, but the constraints of a small sample limited the generalizability of the findings. Moreover, the earlier sample was relatively middle-class, including only one family with a level of living below the poverty line. Thus, in the present analyses we extend the earlier work by utilizing a larger sample that is more heterogeneous in terms of economic well-being. In addition to these methodological extensions, we also elaborate the conceptual framework employed in the earlier study. Specifically, in those analyses the theoretical model did not include an intervening psychological mechanism to account for the association between economic strain and overt behavior. Here we add dysphoric mood to the analytic framework to examine the role that negative feelings may play in exacerbating irritable behaviors in marriage. The resulting theoretical model for economic hardship and marital relations that guides the following analyses is derived from the overall perspective on family economic stress described in Chapter 1.

THE THEORETICAL MODEL

Figure 9.1 provides an outline of the theoretical model guiding the present analyses. As noted, it extends the earlier model proposed by Conger et al. (1990) by separating negative emotional affect into two component parts: depressed mood and overt hostility toward spouse.

The elaboration of the model helps to clarify the emotional substrate that underlies the behavioral dimensions of marital response to economic stress. The theoretical framework begins with relatively objective economic circumstances that, taken together, represent various dimensions of economic hardship or well-being found in several research traditions. For these analyses we used four different indicators of financial status described earlier in this volume: per capita family income, debt-to-asset ratio, unstable work, and income loss (see Chapters 4 and 8).

Although there is some evidence that either chronic or acute economic stress may have a direct impact on individual well-being and family relationships (McLoyd, 1989), following from our discussion in Chapter 1, we postulated that adverse financial circumstances would affect depressed mood and the quality of marital interactions primarily through each spouse's perception of difficulties in meeting material and economic needs (economic pressure). That is, we expected that difficulties in financial circumstances should have an influence on individual distress once they begin to disrupt daily living by reducing the family's ability to purchase necessities or by forcing serious cutbacks in expenditures. Economic pressures also demoralize by focusing attention on meeting financial needs to the neglect of other desired activities. Thus, in the proposed model, hardship conditions are expected to be linked to spousal depression and hostile interactions only indirectly through their association with perceived economic pressure. Moreover, we expected that de-

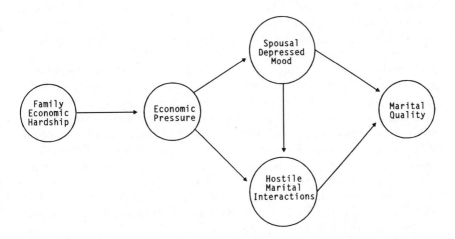

Figure 9.1. The theoretical model linking economic hardship to marital relations.

pressed mood would partially mediate the relation between pressure and marital conflict.

The elaboration of our earlier model of these phenomena (Conger et al., 1990) to include depressed mood as a mediating variable between economic pressure and marital conflict derives from the growing empirical evidence for such a process. As noted, earlier findings clearly link economic stress to emotional distress such as anxiety and depression. In addition, both experimental and naturalistic studies of depressed affect demonstrate its association with irritable or hostile behavior toward intimates (Berkowitz, 1989; Downey & Coyne, 1990; Patterson, 1982). Thus, in Figure 9.1 we propose that economic pressure will be both directly related to hostility as well as indirectly related through its influence on negative mood. The direct path from economic pressure to hostility remains in the model because there may well be other psychological mediators, as yet unidentified, in addition to depression that are important linking variables in this process.

The direct path in the model from economic pressure to hostile marital interactions is derived primarily from research on families during the hard economic times of the 1930s. Liker and Elder (1983) report that income loss during the early 1930s was positively associated with marital tension or hostility later in the decade. Chronic economic hardship (an index composed of unemployment, receiving public assistance, and remaining at a low income level) was even more strongly related to marital tension, both concurrently and prospectively. Marital tension also was associated with higher rates of marital instability (separation or divorce), a result that is consistent with other reports linking economic hardship to marital dissolution (Teachman, Polonko, & Scanzoni, 1987). Liker and Elder's findings suggest that economic hardship influences marital quality (measured in their study by a rater's judgment of the degree of tension and conflict in the marriage) in large part through the disagreement over finances that it promotes between spouses and through the tense, explosive, irritable behavior it elicits from men.

These findings led us to expect that one important mechanism through which economic disadvantage affects spousal perceptions of marital quality is its impact on negative marital interactions. Liker and Elder (1983) did not have a self-report measure of marital quality; thus they were not able to test directly this hypothesized process. Their measure of marital tension was primarily an indicator of the quality of spousal interactions rather than of feelings about the marriage because its highest category ("highly volatile") included a rater's judgment that there was chronic tension and extreme conflict between spouses.

These results regarding conflict over finances, men's explosiveness and irritability, and generalized marital tension and conflict suggest that economic stress should have a significant influence on marital quality through its effect on irritable or conflictual behaviors within the marital dyad. The model in Figure 9.1 illustrates this process. Contemporary research on the behavioral correlates of marital distress and satisfaction also supports the predicted negative association between hostility and marital quality (Conger et al., 1990; Noller & Fitzpatrick, 1990).

This brings us to the last path in the model, from depressed mood to marital quality. We include this relation in the model under the assumption that a depressed spouse is generally more difficult to live with, more withdrawn, and less helpful than a less distressed partner (Downey & Coyne, 1990). These qualities in a spouse have been shown to be negatively related to marital quality (Glenn, 1990; Gottman, 1979; Margolin & Wampold, 1981; Noller & Fitzpatrick, 1990).

In this investigation we test the empirical validity of the proposed theoretical model. Observed differences found between husbands and wives in their response to economic stress in an earlier study (Conger et al., 1990) led us to test the general model separately for each spouse. The first analysis assesses the extent to which economic stress is associated with the husband's negative mood and hostile behaviors toward spouse and, in turn, wife's marital quality. We expected that the influence of economic problems on wives' marital quality would be entirely indirect through husbands' depressed mood and hostile behavior. The second analysis examined the same process regarding the combined influence of economic stress and wife's depressed affect and hostile behavior on the husband's marital quality.

MEASUREMENT

The following description of measures begins with the exogenous economic constructs that relate to economic hardship in the model presented in Figure 9.1, and then moves to indicators for endogenous constructs working from left to right in the theoretical model. To minimize the biases in estimates of path coefficients produced by single sources of information (Bank et al. 1990; Lorenz et al. 1991), we follow the advice of Bank and his colleagues (1990) and, to the extent possible, include multiple reporting agents for each construct. As will be shown later, this procedure at times involved the inclusion of method factors to reduce biases in parameter estimation (see Chapter 2).

Family economic hardship was assessed using the measures described in Chapter 8 (per capita income, debt-to-asset ratio, unstable work, income loss). The indicators for *economic pressure* also are described in Chapter 8, as are the measures for depressed mood.

Each spouse's *hostility* was assessed using three informants: self, spouse, and observer. On a 5-point scale from low to high evidence of hostile behavior, both problem-solving (Task 2) and marital (Task 4) task observers rated the extent to which an observed individual was hostile (e.g., derogating, demeaning) toward his or her spouse. Importantly, these scales were derived from two independent coders (i.e., each task was rated by a separate observer). These two ratings were summed and averaged to create a single *observer rating of hostility* as one indicator for the construct. Interobserver reliability was acceptable (.73, Task 2, husbands; .88, Task 2, wives; .79, Task 4, husbands; .78, Task 4, wives).

Both spouses responded to four items that asked how distressed they had been during the past week [1 (*not at all*) to 5 (*extremely*)] by their own temper outbursts, argumentativeness, shouting or throwing things, or conflicts with family and co-workers. These items were summed to produce a *self-report hostility* indicator for each spouse. The internal consistency was .67 for husbands, .68 for wives. *Spouse-reported hostility* was assessed by asking each person how often (1 = *always*, 7 = *never*) during the past month their partner had engaged in each of nine different hostile behaviors when the couple spent time together. The items included acts such as shouting or yelling, arguing, and getting angry. The alpha was .91 for wife's rating of husband and .90 for husband's rating of wife. All hostility indicators were coded such that a higher score indicates greater hostility.

The measures of *marital quality* also involved multiple informants. Each spouse reported his or her degree of happiness with the marriage on a 6-point scale from 0 (*extremely unhappy*) to 5 (*extremely happy*). Following the rationale elaborated by Fincham and Bradbury (1987), this item was used as a *self-report* indicator for a global construct of marital quality. These couples also were asked the same question with the same response categories with reference to their partner's marital happiness. This item was used as a *spouse-report* indicator of marital quality. Finally, the Task 4 observers were asked to provide a subjective rating from 1 (*low quality*) to 5 (*high quality*) of the overall quality of the marriage (interobserver reliability = .77). This rating was used as an *observer report* indicator for the marital quality construct. In making this rating, observers were instructed to provide their subjective impression of the overall happiness or satisfaction with the relationship that each spouse expressed during Task 4. Later analyses show that these three indicators of marital quality are highly intercorrelated and appear to tap a common dimension of happiness and satisfaction with the relationship.

RESULTS

Correlations, Means, and Standard Deviations

Table 9.1 provides the means, standard deviations, and correlations for all study variables in the theoretical model. Correlations for the analyses involving husband's mood and behavior and wife's marital quality (Model 1) are above the diagonal; the correlations for the analyses predicting husband's marital quality are below the diagonal (Model 2). Because all of the economic measures are the same for both sets of analyses, their intercorrelations, means, and standard deviations are the same as well. In most instances the exogenous economic variables (per capita income, unstable work, debt-to-asset ratio, income loss) were significantly correlated, ranging from $r = .01$ (income loss and debt-to-asset ratio) to $r = -.22$ (per capita income and debt-to-asset ratio). The modest magnitude of these intercorrelations supports the use of these measures as indicators of separate constructs rather than as indicators of a single dimension of family economic hardship.

On average, these rural Iowa couples report a great deal of happiness in their marriages. The mean scores for self-reported happiness (3.84 for wives, 3.80 for husbands) indicate that most spouses rate themselves on the positive end of the marital quality continuum (between happy and very happy). The results also show, however, a great deal of variability in perceptions of satisfaction with the marriage ($SD = .97$, wives; $SD = 1.03$, husbands), suggesting that many of these couples are unhappy with their marital situation. Interestingly, spouse reports of partner's happiness indicate lower marital quality than self-reports ($M = 3.65$ for husband report of wife's happiness; $M = 3.55$ for wife report regarding husband happiness). Again the variability in these reports (reflected in the standard deviations) suggests a great deal of unhappiness in marriage for many of these couples. The important question in the following analyses is whether economic hardship and the postulated mediating processes help to explain the significant variation in marital quality observed among these couples. The zero-order correlations provide initial information regarding the hypothesized processes.

Consistent with the conceptual model, per capita income, unstable work, income loss and debt-to-asset ratio were all significantly related to indicators of economic pressure, e.g., $r = -.44$ for per capita income and unmet material needs and $r = .35$ for debt-to-asset ratio and economic adjustments. Also consistent with the model, correlations among the exogenous economic variables and indicators of depressed mood, mari-

Table 9.1. Correlations, Means, and Standard Deviations for All Study Variables[a]

Study variables	Means		SD		Study variables					
	Model 1	Model 2	Model 1	Model 2	(1)	(2)	(3)	(4)	(5)	(6)
1. Per capita income	8,103	8,103	5,747	5,747	—	-22	-13	-14	-37	-44
2. D/A ratio	0.42	0.42	0.28	0.28	-22	—	18	01	35	37
3. Unstable work	0.31	0.31	0.53	0.53	-13	18	—	06	20	18
4. Income loss	3.51	3.51	1.35	1.35	-14	01	06	—	18	17
5. Economic adjustments	6.40	6.40	4.16	4.16	-37	35	20	18	71	71
6. Material needs	17.67	17.67	4.83	4.83	-44	37	18	17	71	72
7. Ends meet	0.02	0.02	2.35	2.35	-49	34	20	16	62	72
8. O. depression	3.15	3.23	0.94	0.90	-08	10	06	03	26	30
9. Self-depression	1.46	1.61	0.43	0.50	-11	09	01	05	23	30
10. Spouse depression	3.95	4.02	1.26	1.13	05	06	01	-06	05	08
11. O. hostility	3.36	3.78	1.20	1.38	-05	-04	-03	02	06	12
12. Self-hostility	5.73	5.91	1.52	1.72	-12	08	02	08	21	25
13. Spouse hostility	19.02	20.05	7.35	7.08	-04	05	08	07	12	18
14. O. marital quality	3.35	3.35	0.88	0.88	06	-09	-04	-05	-10	-17
15. Self-marital quality	3.84	3.80	0.97	1.03	02	-05	-02	02	-09	-15
16. Spouse marital quality	3.65	3.55	1.01	1.03	00	01	-03	-06	-09	-14

(continued)

Table 9.1. (Continued)

Study variables	(7)	(8)	(9)	(10)	(11)	(12)	(13)	(14)	(15)	(16)
1. Per capita income	-49	-12	-10	-13	-03	-08	-05	06	04	-02
2. D/A ratio	34	10	07	08	12	13	07	-09	-04	-01
3. Unstable work	20	05	08	08	06	04	06	-04	00	-05
4. Income loss	16	05	07	13	-03	08	04	-05	-05	01
5. Economic adjustments	62	16	16	23	12	12	21	-10	-13	-06
6. Material needs	72	21	23	30	12	16	25	-17	-19	-14
7. Ends meet	—	17	19	28	05	10	18	-13	-19	-14
8. O. depression	28	—	16	28	14	09	15	-18	-16	-16
9. Self-depression	32	20	—	28	03	66	19	-04	-10	-26
10. Spouse depression	10	22	27	—	18	20	45	-22	-45	-27
11. O. hostility	10	27	10	21	—	15	34	-41	-22	-17
12. Self-hostility	28	14	62	23	21	—	36	-14	-13	-25
13. Spouse hostility	11	11	22	42	28	28	—	-33	-63	-50
14. O. marital quality	-13	-29	-08	-22	-46	-16	-27	—	-39	28
15. Self-marital quality	-17	-13	-16	-47	-26	-17	-52	32	—	47
16. Spouse marital quality	-13	-20	-35	-34	-35	-30	-42	35	47	—

[a] Correlations for the husband depression/hostility and wife marital quality model, model 1, above the diagonal; for the wife depression/hostility and husband marital quality model, model 2, below the diagonal.

Note: Decimal points omitted for correlations coefficients. For $r \geq .10$, $p < .05$, two-tailed test. O, observer report; self, self-report; spouse, spouse report, where shown for each measure. Because measures (1) through (7) are family members, the means and standard deviations are the same for both models.

tal interactions and marital quality were quite modest and statistically significant in only a few cases (e.g., r = −.11 between income and wife's self-reported depression, $p < .05$). These correlations suggest that family economic status may play a role in the marital relationship only to the extent that economic disadvantage creates financial pressures or strains, as was found in the previous evaluation of the model (Conger et al. 1990).

The intercorrelations among the separate indicators of economic pressure were quite robust, as high as .72 between spousal perceptions of unmet material needs and the family's inability to make ends meet. As expected, most correlations among the economic pressure measures and the mood and marital hostility variables were statistically significant and in the predicted directions (e.g., $r = .26$ between economic adjustments and the observer rating of wife's depression). Indicators for the economic pressure construct also were significantly correlated with most of the marital quality indicators (e.g., $r = −.19$ between unmet material needs and wife's self-report of marital quality). The coefficients reported in Table 9.1 also show a large number of significant correlations among indicators of hostility and depressed mood (e.g., $r = .22$ between wife's self-reported depression and her husband's rating of her hostility). Likewise, most indicators of depression and hostility were significantly related to measures of marital quality (e.g., $r = −.26$ between husband's self-report of marital happiness and the observer report of wife hostility). Finally, the results reported in Table 9.1 show that correlations among indicators within constructs are, in most instances, of reasonable magnitude (e.g., $r = .47$ between wife's self-reported marital happiness and husband's report of her happiness).

Evaluation of the Theoretical Model

For all of the following analyses standardized parameter estimates were made first by controlling for age and education for each spouse and then without these controls. Because the inclusion of these variables had no significant impact on the findings, they are omitted in this report. Figure 9.2 provides the results for the first model involving family economic conditions, family economic pressure, husband's depressed mood, husband's hostility, and wife's marital quality. The regression coefficients were estimated using methods of maximum likelihood (Bollen, 1989; Joreskog & Sorbom, 1989).

Working from left to right in the model, the strongest predictor of economic pressure was per capita income (−.41) followed by debt-to-asset ratio (.31), income loss (.14), and then unstable work (.11). Each coefficient was statistically significant and, as a set, they explained 39% of

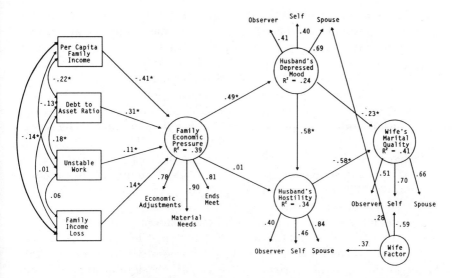

Figure 9.2. Maximum likelihood estimation of the theoretical model for husband's mood and behavior. Significant correlations for same reporters across constructs (not shown) are included in the estimated model. For starred coefficients, $p < .05$. $\chi^2_{(87)} = 101.98$, $GFI = .972$, $CN = 473.5$.

the variance in economic pressure. As expected, economic pressure was positively and significantly related to husband's depressed mood (.49); however, even though the zero-order correlations reflected a significant and positive relationship between economic pressure and hostility for both spouses (see Table 9.1), there was no direct path from pressure to hostility, only an indirect relation through depressed mood. Depressed mood was strongly associated with greater hostility (.58).

Consistent with the proposed model and earlier findings (Conger et al., 1990), both depressed mood (−.23) and hostility (−.58) were negatively related to wife's marital quality. The model also was tested including a direct path from economic pressure to wife's marital quality. This procedure produced no significant change in chi-squared; thus, pressure was only indirectly related to marital quality through husband's mood and behavior. The model accounted for 41% of the variance in wife's marital quality.

To reduce the method bias inherent in having wife's report as an indicator for husband's mood, behavior, and own marital quality, a method factor also was included in the model. Loadings on the wife method factor were .37 (wife's report of husband's hostility), .28 (wife's report of husband's depressed mood), and −.59 (wife's report of own marital quality). The estimation of the method construct helps to control for the unique dispositions of the informant that may systematically affect reports of different phenomena, thus artificially inflating correlations among constructs (Bank et al. 1990). For example, a relatively more depressed individual may be inclined to evaluate more negatively the quality of relations with others, their moods, and their behaviors (see Chapter 2). Thus, correlations will be high among these variables because of this underlying predisposition rather than because of the actual state of affairs. For the same reason, indicators based on reports from the same agent were allowed to correlate across constructs when associations were statistically significant (see also Lavee, McCubbin, & Olson, 1987; Thomson & Williams, 1984). To simplify the presentation, these correlations are not shown in either Figure 9.2 or 9.3.

Several analyses attest to the fit of the mediational model (Figure 9.2) including a critical N greater than 200 (Hoelter, 1983) and a goodness-of-fit index greater than .90 (Joreskog & Sorbom, 1989). Moreover, the factor loadings on all constructs were statistically significant and .40 or greater (e.g., the loading for husband's self-reported hostility = .46). These findings replicate well the results from the earlier test of the model (Conger et al., 1990) and demonstrate the importance of elaborating the earlier conceptual framework by adding the mood construct.

Turning to Figure 9.3, which provides the results of the analyses for the mediational model linking economic stress to husband's marital quality, the findings again show that economic conditions were significantly related to economic pressure. As before, the strongest predictor of economic pressure was per capita income followed by debt-to-asset ratio, income loss, and unstable work. The results reported in Figure 9.3 also demonstrate that the wives in this study were just as likely as men to become depressed, and through their depression to become more hostile toward their spouses. The structural coefficients from economic pressure to wife's depression (.46), and from depression to hostility (.76) were both statistically significant and in the expected directions.

As with the husband model, economic pressure was not directly related to wife's hostility. In contrast with the husband's findings, wife's depression was not directly related to husband's marital quality. Despite that fact, the model accounted for 68% of the variance in husband's happiness with the relationship. Again, evaluation of a change in chi-squared demonstrated no direct association between economic pressure and marital quality. And, as before, the fit indices and the factor loadings of indicators on constructs suggest that the proposed mediational model fits the data reasonably well. The method factor for husbands was included in the model to reduce method variance confounds in the prediction of marital quality.

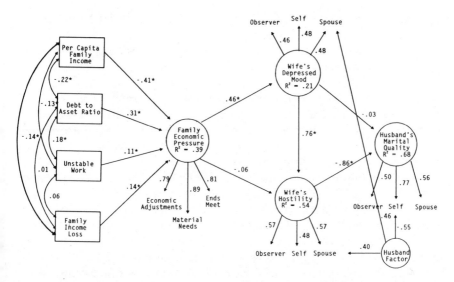

Figure 9.3. Maximum likelihood estimation of the theoretical model for wife's mood and behavior. Significant correlations for same reporters across constructs (not shown) are included in the estimated model. For starred coefficients, $p < .05$. $\chi^2_{(85)} = 152.44$, $GFI = .961$, $CN = 309.5$.

DISCUSSION

These findings trace a process whereby the economic stresses and strains experienced by these rural families generated adverse consequences for marital happiness and well-being. Consonant with the overall theoretical perspective presented in Chapter 1, and the more specific hypotheses considered here, we see that economic pressures have a negative impact on partners' emotions, which in turn have direct and indirect effects on marital quality through the hostile exchanges they exacerbate between spouses. Thus, the transition of many of these families from acute economic dislocation during the 1980s to chronic economic problems as they enter the 1990s appears to have a continuing legacy in terms of marital strain.

To recapitulate, the analyses in this chapter were designed to achieve three primary objectives aimed at increasing understanding of the consequences of continuing economic stress for these rural couples. First, we were interested in conducting a more adequate empirical evaluation of a mediational model of economic stress and marital quality than had been possible in an earlier study with a much smaller sample (Conger et al., 1990). In each variation of the model tested here, the fit between model and data was quite good. Thus, we have increased confidence regarding the empirical validity of the earlier findings.

As a second objective we were interested in elaborating the model examined in the earlier analyses by including depressed mood as a psychological mediator between economic pressure and hostile behaviors toward spouse. The results presented here demonstrate the importance of examining this process in greater detail. Specifically, these results demonstrate that economic pressure has a significant, direct effect only on feelings of depression or dysphoria, which in turn exacerbate an irritable style of interaction with spouse.

Especially important, it appears that depressed mood brings wives directly into the economic stress process. Earlier research has clearly shown that men become more irritable under economic pressures, but results have been inconclusive regarding women's response to hardship (Conger et al., 1990; Liker & Elder, 1983). The present results suggest that depressed mood, an emotional problem more typical of women than men (Downey & Coyne, 1990), links hardship to wives' as well as husbands' irritability and clarifies their role in marital response to economic stress.

Also important, these results replicate the earlier findings for economic influences on husbands' behaviors and their relationship with wife's marital happiness and satisfaction. Family economic hardship was positively related to economic pressure for men, which in turn was associated with increased hostility, through depressed mood, toward their wives. These findings also replicated those of Liker and Elder (1983) who showed that husbands who experienced the hard times of the 1930s became hostile and irritable in response to economic problems. Wife's marital quality was negatively affected both by husband's hostility and depressed mood.

Another significant extension of the earlier work was the present finding that the proposed theoretical model works almost exactly the same when wife's behaviors are predicted by economic stress. The only substantive difference was the failure of wife's depression to predict husband's marital quality. The results suggest that both husbands and wives suffer reduced happiness in marriage when their partners are more hostile. Interestingly, this relation is especially pronounced for men who apparently are less tolerant of their wives' irritability than the reverse. This difference may be the result of social norms that are more accepting of male than female aggressiveness. Wives, on the other hand, are more likely than men to be unhappy in marriage when the husband is depressed. This, too, may result from the generally accepted view that men should be confident and self-assertive. Failure to meet this standard may more seriously violate women's than men's expectations for the marital relationship.

   In addition to the importance of adding depressed mood to the model, we expect that the differences in findings for wives in this study compared to our earlier test of this model (Conger et al., 1990) also reside in the greater economic stress of the present group of couples. Husbands and wives in the present study were ten times more likely to be living in poverty than those in the earlier research. Thus, our third objective of testing the model with a more economically heterogeneous sample proved to be worthwhile. These findings suggest that there may be a threshold effect such that, when economic stress gets high enough, women as well as men are brought directly into the stress process. It is also likely that these contemporary women were more directly influenced by economic stress than those living during the depression years (Liker & Elder, 1983) because of their greater responsibilities in family economic life.

   Despite their obvious limitations such as the cross-sectional nature of the data and homogeneity of family structure and location, the present findings add to the growing evidence that economic stress may exact a heavy toll in marriage. We expect that the adversity experienced by the rural Iowa couples extends to others facing hardship in different times and different places (e.g., Liker & Elder, 1983; Voydanoff & Donnelly, 1988). Moreover, the present results suggest that, to understand these processes, one must consider both the daily consequences of economic disadvantage (e.g., felt economic pressure) and also the behavioral interactions between spouses that link stressful events and conditions to problematic interpersonal relations. A next obvious step in the program of work described here is to identify characteristics of individual spouses, relationships, and social context that mitigate or exacerbate such processes. Research of this type will help to identify possible targets for prevention or intervention that will help couples successfully cope with economic hardships that come and go during the marital life cycle (Duncan, 1984).

   Another important question regards the linkage between marriage and adolescent development. As noted in Chapter 1, we hypothesized that marital response to economic stress should play an important role in developmental outcomes for the rural children and adolescents in this study. In the next chapter, we turn our attention to this dimension of our theoretical model.

PART IV

Adolescent Development

Chapter 10

Economic Pressure and Harsh Parenting

Ronald L. Simons, Les B. Whitbeck,
Janet N. Melby, and Chyi-In Wu

I suppose if ya had more money . . . yes, . . . things would probably change. But you
don't have it and they argue with ya. They want it and you don't have it and you
holler at them more.
— Financially distressed farmer describing conflicts
about money with his sons, 1988

Following from the conceptual model developed in Chapter 1, we have
seen that economic pressures in the lives of these Iowa families are
associated with high levels of psychological distress and conflict in marriage. The proposed theoretical framework next asks, Will these difficulties experienced by spouses affect their competence as parents? And
how will the quality of the marital bond influence the relationship between economic pressure and parental behavior? In this chapter we examine these stress-mediating and -moderating processes.

It has only been within the past decade that researchers have begun to
devote significant attention to identifying factors that account for variations in parenting practices. In the research that has been completed on
this issue, family economic hardship has emerged as an important determinant. Using data collected during the Great Depression, Elder (1979,
Caspi & Elder, 1988) found that fathers who had experienced significant
economic loss tended to employ irritable, arbitrary disciplinary practices.
Recent studies with more contemporary samples have found an association between economic pressure and inept parenting for mothers as well
as fathers (Conger et al., 1984; Galambos & Silbereisen, 1987; Lempers,
Clark-Lempers, & Simons, 1989; Patterson et al., 1989; Simons, Lorenz,
Conger, & Wu, 1992a; Simons, Whitbeck, Conger, & Melby, 1990). In
contrast to the 1930s, the majority of women now work outside the home
and hence share responsibility with the husband for financial support of

207

the family. As a result of these changes, it appears that economic strain may now operate to disrupt the parenting of both mothers and fathers.

While these studies provide evidence of a link between economic pressure and inept parenting, a few investigators have reported what might be interpreted as discrepant findings. Perrucci, Targ, Perrucci, and Targ (1987) and Thomas, McCabe, and Berry (1980) found that parents rarely reported deteriorations in parent-child relationships following job loss. It should be noted, however, that in both of these studies unemployed workers either received relatively generous economic assistance or were middle-class with substantial financial assets. As noted in previous chapters, it is not job loss, or even level of income per se, that primarily disrupts family processes. Rather it is economic pressure that disrupts family relationships. It does not appear that severe economic strain was prevalent to a very large degree among the samples employed in the Perrucci et al. and Thomas et al. studies.

The relationship between economic pressure and disrupted parenting is to be expected given recent findings from studies of the consequences of aversive events and conditions. Evidence from both laboratory and survey research indicates that unpleasant events or conditions promote hostility, negative thoughts and memories, psychomotor tension, and a tendency to behave aggressively toward others (Berkowitz, 1989). Thus, in general, the frustration produced by economic hardship should foster an irritable, aggressive psychological state that operates to decrease warmth and increase hostility displayed toward others. Consistent with this contention, the findings reported in Chapter 9 indicated that economic pressure increases depressed mood as well as hostility expressed toward the marital partner. In the present chapter we examine a similar hypothesized process for parent-child interaction. Economic pressure is expected to increase the probability of harsh, explosive discipline, with feelings of hostility and irritability serving to mediate this relationship.

Whereas economic pressure is thought to disrupt parenting, spouse support is usually assumed to be a coping resource that serves to foster competent parenting. In emotionally close marital relationships, the spouse is a source of advice, assistance, and emotional support. Such a relationship should foster psychological well-being, reduce hostile feelings and psychological distress, and decrease the probability of harsh, explosive parenting. A tense, conflictual relationship, on the other hand, would be expected to function as an aversive event, serving to increase harsh, explosive behavior toward children.

Consistent with this view, a variety of studies have reported a significant association between quality of the marital relationship and quality of parenting such that high marital satisfaction promotes competent parenting (Belsky, Gilstrap, & Rovine, 1984; Engfer, 1988; Easterbrooks &

Emde, 1988; Feldman, Nash, & Aschenbrenner, 1983; Meyer, 1988; Pederson, 1982). This relationship has been shown to hold for both mothers and fathers, in various countries, and for parents of infants, toddlers, and preschoolers (Belsky, 1990). A recent study by Cox, Owen, Lewis, and Henderson (1989) reported that the influence of marital quality upon parenting remains after controlling for the effects of parents' psychological characteristics.

Whereas these studies suggest that parenting behavior is influenced by close ties in marriage, other research (Conger et al., 1990; Liker & Elder, 1983), as well as the findings reported in Chapter 9, indicates that economic pressure often creates marital tensions. These findings suggest that, in addition to any disruptive influence upon parenting produced by psychological distress such as hostile feelings, economic hardship is likely to elicit explosive discipline through its deleterious impact upon marital interaction. This pattern of effects is illustrated in Figure 10.1.

The theoretical model shown in Figure 10.1 extends the conceptualizations of economic stress and family relations provided in earlier chapters. For example, in Chapter 9 we found that economic pressure exacerbates depressive symptoms and that these negative feelings, in turn, affect the quality of marital interactions. To simplify the presentation, in Figure 10.1 we indicate direct paths (A and D) from economic pressure to supportiveness from partner and hostility toward spouse. A complete depiction of the general theoretical model (see Chapter 1) would include emotional distress as a psychological mediating variable between economic pressure and marital supportiveness and between economic pressure and hostility. By omitting this mediating variable, however, we are able to more clearly present processes that occur beyond initial distress and to analyze statistical interactions that are important in understanding the role of marital support in the processes of interest. To complete the discussion of Figure 10.1, spouse support is depicted as having a direct effect upon harsh parenting (path F) and an indirect effect through hostility (paths E and B). Economic pressure is shown as influencing harsh parenting (operationalized in later analyses as explosive discipline) through its effect upon hostility toward spouse (paths A and B) and through its negative impact upon the marital relationship (path D).

Although much of the effect of economic pressure upon harsh parenting is expected to be expressed indirectly through increased hostility and decreased marital support, it seems unlikely that all of the effects of financial pressures upon parenting are channeled through these two factors. Parents who are under high economic strain are liable to be preoccupied and minimally involved in the parenting role. As a consequence, they are apt to respond to child demands in an inconsistent

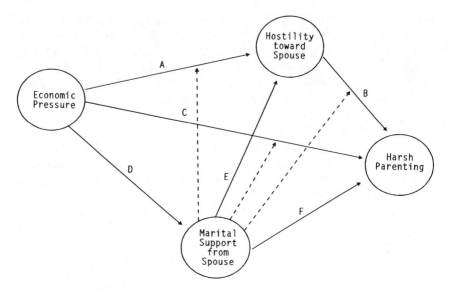

Figure 10.1. The conceptual model.

fashion. Also, their response may often be explosive as immersion in financial difficulties diverts attention from parenting until serious or flagrant child misbehavior jars them into action. Thus, path C indicates that economic pressure is expected to have a direct effect upon parents' disciplinary practices in addition to its indirect effects through hostility and spouse support.

In addition to testing for the direct and indirect effects depicted in Figure 10.1, we examined the extent to which spouse support moderates the impact of economic pressure upon parental behavior. Although researchers often posit that marital support is a coping resource that reduces the damaging influence of life stress upon parenting (Belsky & Vondra, 1989; Cicchetti & Rizley, 1981), few studies have actually examined whether spouse support serves this function. There is some evidence, however, that a supportive marital relationship reduces the disruptive influence of economic pressure upon parental behavior. Elder, Liker, and Cross (1984) found this buffering effect for fathers in their study of families of the Great Depression, whereas Simons, Beaman, Conger, and Wu (1992) found this result for mothers using IYFP data.

If spouse support has a buffering effect, it may be produced in any of three ways. These three avenues are depicted by dashed lines in Figure 10.1. The figure indicates that spouse support may moderate the damaging influence of economic pressure upon parenting by reducing the relationship between economic pressure and hostility (path A), by diminishing the association between hostility and parental behavior (path B), or by lessening the relationship between economic pressure and harsh parenting (path C). Thus, in addition to testing for a buffering effect, we are concerned with providing some understanding of the point in the economic stress process where such an effect occurs.

MEASURES

Economic pressure. The three self-report indicators used to measure economic pressure were described in Chapters 4 and 8.

Support. As noted in Chapter 4, because of method variance biases, measures of social support are often criticized for relying exclusively upon self-report instruments. In an attempt to reduce this problem, a composite measure of spouse support was formed by combining scores on a self-report instrument with those from an observational scale.

The self-report instrument consisted of 20 items focusing on various behaviors that spouses sometimes display during interaction with each other. Respondents were asked to think about times during the prior month when they had spent time talking or doing things with their spouse and to indicate how often during these occasions their mate had engaged in the actions described in each item. The response format ranged from 1 (*always*) to 7 (*never*), with a middle category of 4 (*about half of the time*). Eight of the items involved supportive behaviors (e.g., helping you with something important to you, showing support and understanding, acting loving and affectionate) and they were summed to form a supportive interaction scale. Responses were coded so that a high score indicates greater support. The other 12 items focused upon coercive actions contrary to expressions of support (e.g., criticize you, ignore you, try to make you feel guilty). These items were summed to form a coercive interaction scale (the higher the score, the greater the coerciveness). The correlation between these two scales was −.52 for mothers and −.63 for fathers. The two scales were standardized, and a measure of spouse support was formed by subtracting the standardized coercive interaction scale from the standardized supportive interaction scale.

It was important to include both positive and negative items in the spouse support measure as some persons may be inconsistent in their behavior, sometimes showing support but at other times engaging in criticism and attack. Clearly, such a person is a less dependable source of support than a mate who is consistently helpful and affectionate. Thus, respondents obtained a high score on the self-report scale if their spouse displayed high levels of warmth, encouragement, and assistance while manifesting few coercive behaviors.

The observational scale of supportiveness was constructed from the warmth/support and hostility observational ratings of spousal interaction from Task 4 (the marital interaction task). Each scale is rated from 1 (*no evidence of the behavior*) to 5 (*extreme evidence of the behavior*). The warmth/support scale focuses upon the extent to which a person shows interest and concern for his or her spouse. Coders cue to nonverbal communication (e.g., physical gestures, eye contact), emotional expression (e.g., smiling, laughing), supportiveness (e.g., showing concern for the other's welfare, offering encouragement), and responsiveness (e.g., asking questions to show interest, head nods). The hostility scale focuses upon the extent to which an individual displays hostile, angry, critical, or rejecting behavior toward his or her spouse.

The interobserver reliability coefficient for the warmth/support scale was .72 for both fathers and mothers, while for the hostility scale the coefficients were .79 and .78 for fathers and mothers, respectively. The correlation between the warmth/support scale and the hostility scale was −.46 for mothers and −.45 for fathers. As with the self-report measure, an observational measure of spouse support was formed for both mothers and fathers by subtracting the hostility scale from the warmth/support scale. Thus persons who scored high on the observational indicator of spouse support were individuals whose partners were displaying high levels of affection and encouragement coupled with little anger and criticism, i.e., they were a dependable source of support.

The correlation between the self-report and observational measures of spouse support was .34 for mothers and .30 for fathers. A composite measure of spouse support was formed for each of the parents by standardizing and then summing their self-report and observation scores. As will become clear in the following analyses, a composite measure was constructed, rather than utilizing the measures as two separate indicators of a latent construct, to facilitate testing for the moderating influence of spouse support.

When multiple regression procedures are employed, moderator effects are investigated by testing the significance of interaction terms formed by multiplying the potential moderator by the explanatory variable it is thought to moderate. Such interaction terms are problematic, however, when SEM is employed to investigate the effect of explanatory variables consisting of latent constructs constituted by multiple indicators, as is the case with economic pressure in the present analysis. The recommended approach in such situations is to divide the sample into two groups (e.g., at the median) that are high and low on the moderator construct and to examine differences in the effect of the explanatory variable between the two groups (Bollen, 1989; Joreskog & Sorbom, 1989). Albeit, if the moderator construct is to be divided at the median, it is necessary that it be represented by a single indicator. For this reason, the self-report and observational indicators were summed to form a single composite measure.

Hostility toward spouse. Self-report, spouse-report, and observational ratings were used to measure hostility toward spouse. Indicators for this construct are described in Chapter 9.

Explosive discipline. As our measure of harsh parenting (see Figure 10.1), we examined the disciplinary practices of the IYFP mothers and fathers. Explosive discipline involves the use of harsh and inconsistent disciplinary practices to control or influence child conduct. This construct was measured through three indices: a parent self-report scale, a child-report scale, and an observational ratings scale. For each of these indicators, a measure of parental consistency was subtracted from a measure of parental hostility and coercion. Thus respondents scoring high on any one of the indicators were harsh and inconsistent in their approach to discipline whereas those with low scores showed little hostility and were quite consistent in their disciplinary practices.

The self-report measure of harsh discipline consisted of four items concerned with the extent to which the parent yells, spanks, slaps, or hits with an object when disciplining the adolescent (Simons et al., 1991). The response format for the scale ranged from 1 (*never*) to 5 (*always*). Coefficient alpha was .54 for fathers and .58 for mothers. The self-report measure of consistent discipline consisted of four items focusing upon the extent to which the parent is consistent in applying sanctions, allows the child to talk his or her way out of a punishment, follows through on threats, and the parent's emotional state dictates response to misbehavior. The consistent discipline scale used the same 5-point response format as the harsh discipline scale. Coefficient alpha was .68 for fathers and .63 for mothers. The consistent discipline scale was subtracted from the harsh discipline scale to form a self-report measure of explosive parenting.

The child-report measures consisted of the same items as those employed in the parent self-report instruments except that they were reworded so that the child reported about the parenting practices of his or her parents. Coefficient alpha was .74 and .70 for the harsh discipline of fathers and mothers, respectively, and .53 and .45 for the consistent discipline of fathers and mothers, respectively. As was done with parent reports, the consistent discipline scale was subtracted from the harsh discipline scale to form a child-report measure of harsh parenting.

An observational measure of explosive discipline was formed by combining the scores from four observational rating scales. The observing rating of harsh discipline evaluates parents' use of punitive or severe disciplinary techniques such as belittling, shaming, yelling, threatening, or hitting in response to misbehavior. The hostile parenting scale focuses upon the extent to which the parent shows irritability, rejection, hostile criticism, anger, or contempt toward the child. The angry/coercion scale evaluates the extent to which the parent attempts to influence the child through tactics such as stubbornness, angry whining, verbal threats, sarcastic affect, or hostile commands. Finally, the consistent discipline scale assesses the extent to which children appear to have clear expectations for what will happen if they violate rules and the degree to which the parent follows through with an expected consequence when misbehavior occurs. The observational measure of explosive discipline was defined as the sum of the harsh discipline, hostility, and angry/coercion scales minus the consistent discipline scale. Coefficient alpha for this index was .60 and .62 for the parenting of fathers and mothers, respectively.

The four rating scales used to construct the observational measure of explosive discipline were taken from Task 1. As noted earlier, the observational measure of spouse support was based upon ratings from Task 4 and the observational measure of hostility was derived from ratings from Tasks 2 and 4. Hence, the coders who provided the ratings of explosive discipline were different persons from those who rated hostility or spouse support, thereby reducing the problem of method variance bias for the observational measures.

RESULTS

The correlation matrices for the measures used in the study are presented in Table 10.1. The coefficients above the diagonal are for mothers, those below the diagonal are for fathers, and the associations on the diagonal represent correlations between mother and father scores. The pattern of correlations is similar for both parents. The measures of economic pressure are related to the measures of hostility and harsh parenting. The single indicator for spouse support shows moderate negative associations with the measures of hostility and modest negative relationships with the measures of harsh parenting. Although the magnitude of the correlations is variable, the various measures of hostility are positively related to harsh parenting.

The LISREL 7 statistical program was used to assess the relationships between the latent constructs (Joreskog & Sorbom, 1989). The bivariate

Table 10.1. Correlation Matrix for All Study Variables

Study variables	Economic pressure				Hostility			Explosive discipline		
	(1)	(2)	(3)	(4)	(5)	(6)	(7)	(8)	(9)	(10)
1. Ends meet	—	73*	72*	-12	24*	17*	13*	18*	20*	26*
2. Material needs	73*	—	62*	-07	25*	11*	10	16*	16*	27*
3. Economic adjustment	72*	62*	—	-04	21*	13*	06	14*	20*	21*
4. Spouse support	-18*	-11	-07	58*	-15*	-23*	-49*	-13*	-18*	-24*
5. Hostility, self-report	16*	10	11	-17*	07	29*	21*	38*	27*	26*
6. Hostility, spouse-report	25*	20*	24*	-34*	24*	48*	30*	10	20*	24*
7. Hostility, observer-report	12	06	12	-44*	21*	32*	54*	17*	20*	23*
8. Harsh Parenting, self-report	23*	25*	16*	-14*	28*	14*	11	30*	34*	39*
9. Harsh Parenting, child-report	21*	20*	21*	-15*	10	26*	18*	22*	63*	30*
10. Harsh Parenting, observer-report	21*	27*	18*	-17*	13*	22*	21*	31*	30*	77*

Note: Decimal points omitted. Coefficients above the diagonal are for mothers, coefficients below the diagonal are for fathers, and coefficients on the diagonal represent correlations between mother and father scores.

* $p \leq .01$

association between the latent constructs for economic pressure and explosive discipline was .40 for mothers and .47 for fathers. Both coefficients are significant at the .01 level. The model presented in Figure 10.1 posits that spouse support and hostility serve to mediate this association. The results from fitting the data to the proposed model are shown separately for mothers and fathers in Figures 10.2 and 10.3, respectively. The models presented in these figures were obtained over several iterations as insignificant paths were deleted one at a time.

Figure 10.2 shows that for mothers the findings are largely consistent with the hypothesized model. Economic pressure has a small direct effect upon explosive discipline as well as an indirect effect through mother's hostility in the marriage. Further, economic pressure shows a negative association with father's support for mother which, in turn, is negatively related to mother's hostility. The findings depart from the hypothesized model in that spouse support shows no direct effect upon explosive discipline. The path between spouse support and explosive discipline did not approach statistical significance and deleting it from the model pro-

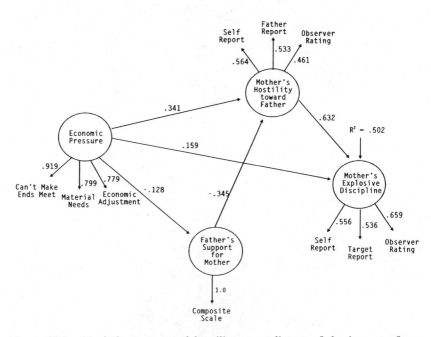

Figure 10.2. Marital support and hostility as mediators of the impact of economic pressure upon the explosive parenting of mothers. All path coefficients are statistically significant, $p < .05$. $\chi^2_9 = 43.44$, $P = .041$, $GFI = .981$, $CN = 416.45$.

duced a significant reduction in chi-squared. The goodness-of-fit test (.981) and critical N (416.45) indicate that the final, trimmed model is quite consistent with empirical findings.

Figure 10.3 shows the same pattern of findings for fathers. Economic pressure demonstrates a direct effect upon explosive discipline and an indirect effect through hostility. Economic pressure also decreases mother's supportiveness, which influences explosive discipline indirectly by increasing father's hostility toward her. The summary statistics (chi-squared, GFI, and CN) suggest a good fit between the theoretical model and the data.

In order to test for the buffering effect of spouse support, both mothers and fathers were divided into two groups, depending on whether they were above or below the median on spouse support. The associations between economic pressure, hostility, and explosive discipline were then compared for parents high and low on spouse support using the multiple groups comparison option of LISREL 7.

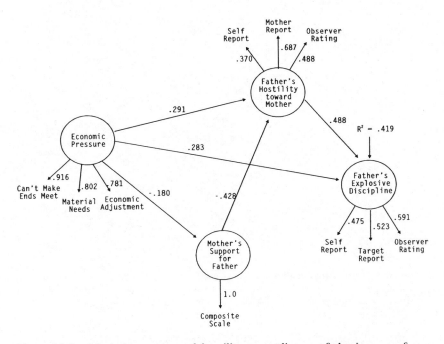

Figure 10.3. Marital support and hostility as mediators of the impact of economic pressure upon the explosive parenting of fathers. All path coefficients are statistically significant, $p < .05$. $\chi^2_9 = 41.90, P = .057, GFI = .981, CN = 433.90$.

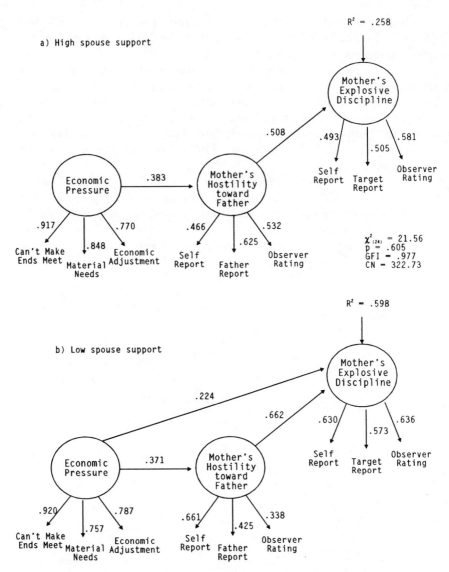

Figure 10.4. The impact of economic pressure and hostility upon the parenting of mothers (a) high (b) low on spouse support. All path coefficients are statistically significant, $p < .05$. $\chi^2_3 = 29.43$, $P = .167$, $GFI = .973$, $CN = 278.44$.

Figure 10.4 presents the findings for mothers. Model B shows a significant association between economic pressure and explosive discipline (.224) for women low on spouse support, whereas there is no significant association between these two constructs in Model A for those high on spouse support. Further, the coefficient between hostility and explosive discipline is larger in Model B than in Model A (.662 versus .508, respectively). Both of these findings are consistent with the contention that spouse support moderates the impact of stressful events upon parenting. The summary statistics showed a good fit for both the high and low support models.

To test the significance of these differences, the models were estimated with all of the corresponding parameters in the two models constrained to be equal, and then reestimated allowing either the path between economic pressure and explosive discipline, or the path between hostility and explosive discipline to differ between the two models (Bollen, 1989; Joreskog & Sorbom, 1989). Freeing the path between economic pressure and explosive discipline reduced chi-squared for the models from 65.39 to 59.89, a change of 5.50 with 1 degree of freedom; freeing the path between hostility and explosive discipline reduced chi-squared from 65.39 to 60.71, a change of 4.68 with 1 degree of freedom. Both of these changes in chi-squared are significant at the .05 level. Thus the results indicate that, for mothers, spouse support moderates the disruptive influence of economic pressure upon parenting in two ways: It diminishes or eliminates the direct effect of economic pressure upon parenting and it reduces the association between hostility and parenting. Other analyses showed that wife support did not moderate (i.e., reduce) the adverse impact of economic pressure or father hostility to spouse on father's harsh parenting.

DISCUSSION

Results from the present study largely supported the hypothesized model and suggest that economic pressure increases the probability of harsh, explosive parenting through various avenues. First, consistent with research regarding the consequences of aversive events (Berkowitz, 1989) and with the findings reported in Chapter 9, economic pressure fostered hostility between spouses that appears to "spill over" into explosive disciplinary practices. As Berkowitz notes, stimuli that elicit anger and strong emotions in one context, such as the marriage, create feelings that may lead to similar responses in other contexts, such as the parent-child relationship. Second, while high spouse support served to lower hostility, economic pressure operated to undermine the marital relationship and diminish access to spouse support. Finally, economic pressure had a direct effect upon harsh parenting independent of its indirect influences through spouse support and hostility.

The latter finding is consistent with the contention that parents who are under high economic strain are liable to be preoccupied and mini-

mally involved in the parenting role until serious or flagrant child misbehavior jars them into action. Such transgressions are likely to demand
a harsh response, so that the pattern of parenting displayed is inconsistent and explosive, vacillating between noninvolvement and harsh reactions. Economic strain would be expected to evoke this pattern of harsh
parenting regardless of level of hostility. We have shown elsewhere, for
example, that economic pressure has a direct influence on conflicts over
finances with adolescents, and thus a direct impact on explosive exchanges in parent-child relations (Conger et al., in press).

In addition, past research has linked supportiveness in the marital
relationship to quality of parenting (Belsky et al., 1984; Cox et al., 1989;
Engfer, 1988; Easterbrooks & Emde, 1988; Feldman et al., 1983; Meyer,
1988; Pederson, 1982). In the present study, spouse support was expected to exert both an indirect and direct effect upon harsh parenting.
A supportive spouse should foster emotional well-being and decrease
hostility, whereas a tense, conflictual relationship should function as an
aversive event, serving to increase hostility above and beyond that fostered by financial problems. Thus, spouse support was posited to have an
indirect effect upon harsh parenting through its impact upon hostility.
This indirect effect was supported by the findings.

We also postulated that there would be a direct effect from spouse
support to explosive discipline as a supportive spouse is a source of
advice and assistance in the parenting role. Such advice and assistance
might be expected to foster positive parenting, regardless of the parent's
level of hostility in marriage. The results failed to corroborate this hypothesis. For both mothers and fathers, the effects of spouse support
upon parenting were mediated by conflicts with spouse. Recently, Belsky
and Vondra (1989) have suggested that the influence of marital support
upon parenting may be indirect through its effect upon the parent's
psychological well-being. This contention would seem to be supported by
the finding in the present study that spouse support influences explosive
discipline by reducing hostile feelings and behaviors toward one's spouse
that are likely to carry over into relations with children.

Thus, spouse support has a direct impact on marital hostility, which
counteracts, to some degree, the adverse influence of economic pressure.
We also hypothesized that a supportive spouse would buffer the effect of
economic pressure on marital hostility and harsh parenting. The findings showed that support by husbands served to moderate the association
between economic pressure and mother's explosive discipline, and between mother's hostility and her explosive discipline. Husband's support
did not modify the relation between economic pressure and mother's
hostility toward him. These findings suggest that supportive husbands
lower the probability that economic pressure will cause mothers to be-

come explosive, inconsistent, and distracted in their parenting; and, rather than diminishing their wives' hostility in response to economic pressure, supportive husbands reduce the likelihood that this hostility will spill over into their parenting practices.

Whereas supportive husbands served to moderate the impact of economic pressure and hostility upon the parenting of wives, supportive wives did not produce similar moderator effects for their husbands. This finding is consistent with the findings of Simons, Lorenz, Conger, and Wu (1992), who found that spouse support operated to buffer the impact of economic pressure upon the supportive, involved parenting of mothers, but not fathers. These researchers speculated that this difference may be related to the oft-reported finding that the psychological well-being of women is more strongly affected by the quality of the marital relationship than is the case for men (Campbell, Converse, & Rogers, 1976; Glenn & Weaver, 1981; Lee 1978). Thus the buffering effect that spouse support provides for women may result from the fact that a supportive husband buoys his wife's self-esteem and life satisfaction, thereby countering the threat to emotional well-being presented by aversive events such as economic strain. The parenting of husbands, on the other hand, is not buffered by the support of their wives because their psychological well-being is more strongly influenced by factors other than by the quality of their marriage.

This explanation would suggest that husband support produces a buffering effect by reducing the wife's emotional response to aversive events. But, as just noted, although husband support was found to moderate the impact of both economic strain and hostility upon parenting, there was no indication that it functioned to temper the relationship between economic strain and hostility toward spouse.

Rather than being rooted in emotional responses to the marital relationship, gender differences in the moderating effects of spouse support may be a function of dissimilarities between mothers and fathers regarding the role of parent. Most couples continue to view parenting as fundamentally the domain of the wife (LaRossa, 1986; Simons, Beaman, Conger, & Wu, 1992). Men are usually much less involved than their wives in the daily care and supervision of the children (Belsky, Gilstrap, & Rovine, 1984; Clarke-Stewart, 1980; Ehrensaft, 1983; Lamb, 1977; Parke, 1981). Thus, most of the burdens of child care fall to the mother, who is expected to discharge her parenting responsibilities regardless of the stressors or emotional distractions that may be operating in her life.

Given this situation, it seems likely that a supportive husband might reduce the probability that life stress will influence the quality of the wife's parenting. A supportive husband is sensitive to his wife's emotional state and is likely to provide increased assistance with parenting during times of stress. This assistance might be expected to lessen the probability that the wife's emotional state will impact her parenting.

Whereas the wife's involvement in parenting is normatively obligated, the husband's level of participation is more a matter of choice. To the extent that fathers are involved in parenting, their behavior tends to center upon playing with the child and enforcing discipline (Simons, Beaman, Conger, & Wu, 1992). Fathers who are experiencing stress and hostility are likely to play with their children less and perform the role of disciplinarian more harshly. Whereas the supportive husband may relieve his wife of parenting duties, thereby reducing the impact of emotional distress upon her parenting, it seems unlikely that wife support would exert this moderating effect upon husband's parenting. Husband involvement in parenting tends to be low and largely voluntary. Thus the supportive wife is not in a position to relieve him of burdensome parenting duties. And, although parenting is largely the domain of the wife, discipline is often considered a legitimate activity for the father. Thus, the husband is likely to discipline in a fashion that he sees as appropriate, regardless of the wife's level of support.

In order to test the validity of these contentions, future research needs to focus upon the avenues through which economic strain and marital support exert their influence upon parenting. Studies need to investigate the processes through which stressors and spouse support influence parenting, rather than limiting concern to the associations that exist between stress, marital relationships, and parenting. Family interaction is shaped by culturally prescribed roles and responsibilities and hence the mediating mechanisms may differ by gender of parent.

Thus far we have found a great deal of support for the overall theoretical processes outlined in Chapter 1. For these Iowa families, economic pressure has had a demoralizing influence on parents. Support from other family members helps to reduce psychological distress; nevertheless, for many of these mothers and fathers financial problems created increased depression and dysphoria that exacerbated conflict and hostility in marriage. As shown in the present chapter, these hostile emotions and behaviors spill over into harsh and irritable parenting. We now turn to an examination of how disrupted parenting affects emotional well-being in the younger generation.

Chapter 11

Resilient and Vulnerable Adolescents

Ronald L. Simons, Les B. Whitbeck, and Chyi-In Wu

The life stories of . . . resilient youngsters now grown into adulthood teach us that competence, confidence, and caring can flourish, even under adverse circumstances, if children encounter persons who provide them with the secure basis for the development of trust, autonomy, and initiative.
— E. E. Werner and R. S. Smith, *Overcoming the Odds*

Consistent with previous studies, the theoretical model proposed in Chapter 1 indicated that children living in families experiencing significant economic hardship tend to show a number of adjustment problems, and that these developmental difficulties are largely in response to the changing moods and behaviors of their parents. Earlier chapters have shown that mothers and fathers in our Iowa families became more depressed, irritable, and harsh in response to hardship conditions. In the present chapter we examine the extent to which these changes in parental behavior *mediate* the impact of economic strain on adolescent adjustment. In addition to testing for this mediating effect, we test the degree to which the impact of economic hardship on adolescent adjustment is *moderated* by social ties to peers and adults outside the nuclear family.

ECONOMIC STRESS AND ADOLESCENT DEVELOPMENT

Compared to those from more prosperous households, youth from families experiencing economic hardship are likely to have less spending money, wear worn or inexpensive clothing, participate in fewer social and recreational activities, and live in a more humble dwelling. As a consequence, they often cannot meet middle-class standards regarding dress and social involvements, and may be spurned by more affluent peers. Thus family economic hardship is apt to be a frustrating and dispiriting condition that increases an adolescent's risk for developmental problems. Earlier research (e.g., Conger et al., 1992) and the model proposed in Chapter 1 suggest that such frustrations may not have a direct effect on adolescent adjustment so long as parents are not too distressed by economic problems. A direct link between financial hardships and adolescent development is a reasonable alternative to the proposed model, however, and we test for such a direct effect in later analyses.

In addition to this possible direct effect on adjustment, economic pressure is likely to influence adolescent development indirectly through its impact on quality of parenting. The hypothesis that the effect of economic strain upon child adjustment is mediated by inept parenting was advanced by Elder in his research on depression-era families (Elder, 1974, Elder, Caspi, & Downey, 1986). Two recent studies have examined the extent to which the influence of economic strain upon adolescent adjustment is mediated by family processes. Silbereisen and Sabinewalter (1988) found that although family integration was reduced by financial hardship and, in turn, diminished adolescent adjustment, economic strain also had a strong direct effect upon an adolescent's well-being.

Using IYFP data, but somewhat different measures of constructs from those employed in the present chapter, Whitbeck et al. (1991a) found that most of the impact of economic pressure upon adolescent adjustment was mediated by parental behavior. Only a small association remained between economic strain and adolescent self-esteem once the effects of parenting had been removed. The present chapter extends these studies by examining the degree to which support from peers or adults outside the nuclear family serves to moderate the effect of economic pressure and parenting practices upon the adjustment of adolescents.

ECONOMIC STRESS AND ADOLESCENT RESILIENCE

During the past decade, researchers have gone beyond investigating the influence of risk factors (e.g., poverty, family structure) upon child developmental outcomes and have begun to search for protective factors that reduce the deleterious effects of potentially hazardous events and circumstances (Garmezy, 1983; Rutter, 1985, 1990). Concern with protective factors has been stimulated by recognition of the fact that many children appear to be stress-resistant. They manifest positive developmental outcomes even though they have been exposed to adverse environmental conditions. Such children are often labeled *resilient*.

External Systems of Social Support

Research on resilient children suggests that three broad sets of variables operate as protective factors: (1) personality characteristics such as high self-esteem, (2) positive family environment, and (3) availability of support systems external to the nuclear family (Garmezy, 1983; Garmezy & Rutter, 1985; Masten & Garmezy, 1985). The present chapter focuses upon the latter set of factors: external support systems. Most of the research to date has focused upon the first two sets of variables. Although there is strong evidence that children are more resistant to adverse environmental conditions when they possess positive self-esteem or a warm, cohesive family environment (Garmezy, 1983; Garmezy & Rutter, 1985; Masten & Garmezy, 1985), research concerned with the protection afforded by support systems not involving the nuclear family (parents and siblings) is rather sparse.

Research on the protective function of children's external social support systems is important for two reasons: First, situations that put children at risk for negative developmental outcomes also undermine the personal characteristics of the child and the child's family that are associated with effective coping. Economic hardship, for example, tends to reduce perceptions of self-efficacy (McLoyd, 1989) and to disrupt the parent-child relationship. Access to social support outside the family, on the other hand, is less apt to be influenced by stressful events and circumstances unique to the family and its members.

Second, it is probably easier for human service organizations and school personnel to increase a child's level of external social support than to modify either his or her personal characteristics or family environment. Community or school-based programs concerned with enhancing social support for children might be formulated with minimal cooperation from children and families. Hence, of the three classes of variables identified as potential protective factors, access to external support offers the most promise for designing interventions to assist children identified as being at risk.

Protective Influences of Social Support

Scores of studies have investigated the extent to which social support serves to buffer adults against the threat of stressful events and circumstances. Many of these studies have found social support to be a significant coping resource that reduces or moderates the impact of adverse conditions on adult psychological and physical distress (Cohen & Wills, 1985; Kessler et al., 1985; House et al., 1988). In contrast, little research has focused upon the protective function of social support for children (Wolchik, Sandler, & Braver, 1987). Thus, the present study provides important new information about these processes. Specifically, we consider two types of extrafamilial social support: support from adults outside the nuclear family and support from peers. Most studies limit their concern to the main effects of such support. Generally, these studies find that support provided by adults outside the family is associated with positive child adjustment, whereas nonsignificant relationships are found between peer support and adjustment (Wolchik et al., 1987).

A few studies have examined the issue of whether external support operates as a protective mechanism for children. Werner and Smith (1982), for example, found that resilient youth sought and received help with problems from peers and older relatives. Dubow and Tisak (1989) reported inconsistent findings regarding the stress-buffering effect of teacher and peer support. Results from a study by Zelkowitz (1981) indicated that children whose families were living under highly stressful conditions but who received high levels of support from adults outside the family were significantly less aggressive than children who experienced high levels of stress coupled with low levels of support.

The present study examines the protective role of support from outside the nuclear family for seventh-grade adolescents living in families that vary in terms of economic stress. An important innovation in the research reported here is the use of different indicators of adjustment for boys and girls. Past studies have established that, following puberty, girls are three times more likely than boys to experience internalizing problems such as depression, whereas boys are three times more likely than girls to manifest externalizing problems such as aggression or delinquency (Ebata, Petersen, & Conger, 1990; Graham, 1979). While adolescent females tend to respond to stress with perceptions of helplessness, low self-esteem, and depression, males tend to react with hostility and conduct problems (Aneshensel, Rutter, & Lachenbruch, 1991). When boys do exhibit symptoms of depression, they are often preceded by hostile, antisocial behavior, and are not usually associated with the self-castigation that accompanies the dysphoria of girls (Block & Gjerde, 1990). Therefore, in an effort to investigate the form of maladjustment typically exhibited by each of the sexes, different indicators of adjustment are used for girls and boys. The indicators for girls are concerned with psychological well-being and focus on feelings of low worth and helplessness, whereas those for boys involve conduct problems and concentrate on aggressive and delinquent behavior.

MEASURES

Economic pressure. The three father and mother self-report indicators used to measure economic pressure were described in Chapters 4 and 8.

Harsh parenting. The three indicators of harsh, explosive, inconsistent parenting were described in Chapter 10. They include a parent self-report scale, a child-report scale, and an observer rating scale.

Psychological well-being. Two scales were used as indicators of girls' psychological well-being. *Rosenberg's self-esteem scale* (1965) was employed as a measure of perceptions of self-worth. Cronbach's alpha for this 10-item scale was .85. *Pearlin's mastery scale* (Pearlin et al., 1981) was utilized as a measure of perceived mastery or control. Coefficient alpha for this 7-item scale was .71.

Antisocial behavior. Two instruments were used as indicators of boys' antisocial behavior. The first was a self-report *delinquency checklist* adapted from the National Youth Survey (Elliott, Huizinga, & Ageton, 1985; Elliott, Huizinga, & Menard, 1989). Respondents were asked to indicate how often during the preceding year [0 (*never*), 4 (*6 or more times*)] they had engaged in each of 23 delinquent activities. The acts varied from relatively minor offenses such as skipping school to more serious offenses such as attacking someone with a weapon or stealing something worth over $25.

The second measure consisted of the *hostility subscale of the SCL-90-R* (Derogatis, 1983). Past research has established the reliability and validity of this instrument (Derogatis, 1983). The subscale contains six items that ask respondents to rate how much [1 (*not at all*), 5 (*extremely*)] they have been bothered by various hostile feelings and behaviors during the preceding week (e.g., feeling easily annoyed or irritated, shouting, or throwing things). Coefficient alpha was .78.

Peer support. Social support from peers was measured by a three-item self-report scale. The target seventh- graders were asked to indicate the extent to which they agreed or disagreed with the following statements concerning their closest friends:

1. I can depend on these friends for help or advice when I need it.
2. These are the kind of people I like to spend time with.
3. These friends care about me.

The response format ranged from 1 (*strongly disagree*) to 5 (*strongly agree*). Respondents who indicated that they had no close friends were coded as 1 on all three statements. Responses to the three items were summed to form a peer support scale. Coefficient alpha was .76 for boys and .77 for girls.

Adult support. Target seventh-graders were asked: "Do you have any relatives, such as grandparents, aunts, uncles or cousins who you can talk to about your problems and worries?" Those who answered Yes to this question were asked to indicate how frequently they have contact with this relative or relatives, with potential responses ranging from 1 (*never*) to 5 (*more than once a week*). Individuals who responded with a No to the first question were coded as a 1 (*never*) on the frequency question. The adolescents were also asked: "Are there any adults who are not your relatives who you can talk to about your problems and worries?" Again, respondents who answered Yes were asked to indicate how frequently they have contact with this person, while those who stated that they did not have access to such an adult received a 1 (*never*) for frequency of contact. A measure of adult support was constructed by summing responses to the two frequency of contact questions.

RESULTS

Figure 11.1 presents the main-effects model for girls. LISREL VII was used to perform the analysis. The figure shows that peer support is associated with psychological well-being (.269) but adult support is not. Economic pressure has a direct effect on psychological well-being (−.182), as well as an indirect effect through harsh parenting. The factor loadings for all constructs were statistically significant and ranged from .563 (target report of harsh parenting) to .898 (felt constraints 1 for economic pressure). The model fit the data well (e.g., GFI = .986).

Figure 11.2 presents the main-effects model for boys. As was the case for girls, economic pressure has a direct effect on adjustment (.189), as well as an indirect effect through harsh parenting. It is adult support rather than peer support, however, that is related to antisocial behavior. As for the girls' model, factor loadings on constructs were substantial and the model achieved a good fit with the data (GFI = .959).

Figures 11.1 and 11.2 considered the main effects of economic pressure, harsh parenting, and the two support constructs on adolescent adjustment. The next set of analyses examined the extent to which the two types of support serve to moderate the impact of economic pressure or harsh parenting on the psychological well-being of girls or the antisocial behavior of boys.

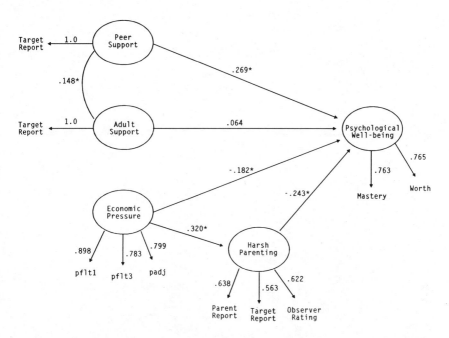

Figure 11.1. Main-effects model for girls. $\chi^2_9 = 15.61$, $P = .980$, $GFI = .986$.

The distribution of scores on adult support tended to cluster around the median. Thus, in order to obtain subgroups high and low on support from adults, both girls and boys were divided into the lowest, middle, and highest third regarding scores on the adult support measure. The middle group was deleted from the analysis. Table 11.1 presents maximum likelihood estimates of the impact of economic pressure (β_{31}) and harsh parenting (β_{32}) upon adjustment for girls and boys high and low on adult support.

Table 11.1 shows that the association between economic pressure and psychological well-being (β_{31}) is $-.402$ for girls low on adult support and .06 for those high on adult support. This pattern is consistent with a moderator effect. There was a change in chi-squared of 7.80 between the baseline model, which constrains all parameters to be equal for the two groups of girls, and model M_1 which allows β_{31} to vary between groups. With 1 degree of freedom, the ρ value for this change in chi-squared is .005, indicating that the difference in the relationship between economic pressure and psychological well-being for girls high and low on adult support is statistically significant.

Table 11.1 indicates that for girls the association between harsh parenting and psychological well-being (β_{31}) varies little by adult support.

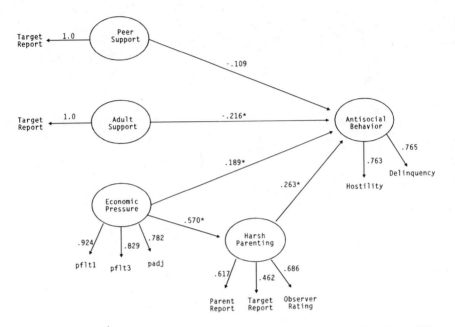

Figure 11.2. Main-effects model for boys. χ^2_{30} = 42.13, P = .07, *GFI* = .959.

The coefficient is −.274 for girls high on adult support and −.298 for those low on such support. A multigroup test showed that permitting the path between harsh parenting and psychological well-being to vary between groups produces an improvement in chi-squared of only .03. Thus, there is no indication that the relationship between harsh parenting and psychological well-being varies by level of adult support.

Turning to the results for boys, Table 11.1 shows that the association between economic pressure and antisocial behavior is very similar for boys high versus low on adult support (.157 and .118, respectively). The same is true regarding the relationship between harsh parenting and antisocial behavior, where the coefficient is .232 for those high and .224 for those low on adult support. Multigroup tests showed that these differences are not statistically significant. Thus, for boys, adult support does not buffer the adverse effect of either economic pressure or harsh parenting.

Table 11.2 presents LISREL VII estimates of the impact of economic strain (β_{31}) and harsh parenting (β_{32}) upon adjustment for girls and boys high and low on peer support. For both girls and boys, the distribution of scores on peer support was highly skewed, with over half receiving the maximum score possible on the scale. Thus both girls and boys were divided into two groups: those receiving the maximum score were de-

Table 11.1. Standardized Maximum Likelihood Estimates for Youth High (Top One-Third) Versus Low (Bottom One-Third) on Adult Support From Outside the Nuclear Family

	Boys		Girls	
	Antisocial behavior		Psychological well-being	
Predictor variables	High[a]	Low[b]	High[a]	Low[b]
Economic pressure (β_{31})	.157*	.118*	.060	−.402*
Harsh parenting (β_{32})	.232*	.224	−.274*	−.298*
χ^2	9.80	10.81	13.11	21.44
df	15	15	15	15
GFI	.977	.976	.963	.942
p-value	.832	.766	.594	.123

[a] High adult support groups (boys: $N = 69$; girls: $N = 79$).
[b] Low adult support groups (boys: $N = 86$; girls: $N = 84$).
* Significant at the .05 level.

fined as high on peer support ($N = 143$ for girls and $N = 122$ for boys) while those with less than the maximum score ($N = 83$ for both girls and boys) were classified as low on peer support.

Consonant with a moderator effect, Table 11.2 shows that the association between economic pressure and psychological well- being (β_{32}) is −.069 for girls high and −.572 for those low on peer support. A multi-group test produced a change in chi-squared of 4.87 with 1 degree of freedom ($p < .027$) achieved by freeing β_{31} to differ between groups. Thus the association between economic pressure and girls' psychological well-being varies by level of peer support in a manner consistent with the buffering hypothesis, and the difference is statistically significant.

In contrast, there is no evidence that peer support moderates the impact of harsh parenting upon girls' psychological well-being. The findings are in the wrong direction, with the coefficient being stronger for girls high (−.272) than for those low (−.079) on peer support. A multi-group test found that allowing the association between harsh parenting and self-esteem to differ between the groups failed to produce an improvement in chi-squared ($p = .354$). Hence, it appears that for girls, the association between harsh parenting and psychological well-being does not differ significantly by level of peer support.

As was the case for girls, Table 11.2 indicates that peer support serves to moderate the impact of economic pressure on the adjustment of boys. The association between economic pressure and antisocial behavior is .030 for boys high and .206 for those low on peer support. The multi-group test produced a significant change in chi-squared ($p < .02$) by permitting the relationship between economic pressure and antisocial

Table 11.2.   Standardized Maximum Likelihood Estimates for Youth
High Versus Low on Peer Support

| | Boys | | Girls | |
| | Antisocial behavior | | Psychological well-being | |
Predictor variables	High[a]	Low[b]	High[a]	Low[b]
Economic pressure (β_{31})	.030	.206*	−.069	−.572*
Harsh parenting (β_{32})	.033	.154	−.272	−.079
χ^2	12.29	16.61	13.56	19.55
df	15	15	15	15
GFI	.976	.957	.978	.945
p-value	.657	.343	.559	.190

[a] High peer support groups (boys: $N = 122$; girls: $N = 143$).
[b] Low peer support groups (boys: $N = 83$; girls: $N = 83$).
* Significant at the .05 level.

behavior to vary by level of peer support. The findings regarding the relationship between harsh parenting and antisocial behavior are also consistent with a moderator effect. The associations for boys high and low on peer support are .033 and .154, respectively. The difference in these path coefficients, however, does not approach statistical significance. Thus the results suggest that peer support serves to buffer boys against the stress of economic hardship but not the deleterious consequences of harsh parenting.

Summarizing the findings, for both boys and girls, economic pressure showed both a direct association with adolescent adjustment and an indirect relation through harsh parenting. Peer support had a main effect on the psychological well-being of girls, and both adult and peer support served to moderate the negative influence of economic pressure upon their psychological well-being. For boys, adult support had a main effect on antisocial behavior, while peer support moderated the relationship between economic pressure and antisocial behavior. Neither adult support nor peer support moderated the detrimental effect of harsh parenting upon the adjustment of either boys or girls.

DISCUSSION

Past research has shown that girls tend to respond to stress with psychological distress (i.e., internalizing disorders) whereas boys tend to react with conduct problems (i.e., externalizing disorders). Based upon this gender difference, psychological well-being was utilized as a developmental outcome for females, while involvement in antisocial behavior was used for males. Economic pressure was directly related to these indicators of adjustment, as well as indirectly through its association with harsh parenting practices. These results suggest that the model proposed in Chapter 1 may need modification. Our theoretical framework suggested that family economic stress will have only an indirect effect on early adolescents through the changing moods and behaviors of parents. These findings support the mediational aspect of the model, but add a direct path from economic pressure to adolescent adjustment.

During the past decade, behavioral scientists have gone beyond investigating the influence of risk factors on child adjustment to searching for protective factors that reduce the deleterious effects of potentially hazardous events and circumstances (Garmezy, 1983; Rutter, 1985, 1990). Consonant with this research strategy, we examined the extent to which the adverse direct and indirect effects of economic hardship are altered by support from either peers or adult friends and relatives.

The results showed peer support to be related to girls' psychological well-being and adult support to be associated with boys' antisocial behavior. While these findings suggest that the two types of support have main effects that may operate to counter the negative impact of family economic strain, our major concern was with the potential buffering influence of social support.

The results indicated that support from outside the nuclear family did not moderate the indirect effect of economic pressure through harsh parenting. The relationship between harsh parenting and adolescent adjustment was unaffected by the level of either peer or adult support. Presumably harsh parenting is related to the adjustment of adolescent females because it undermines perceptions of mastery and self-esteem, and such parenting has an association with the adjustment of males because it is an ineffective approach to discipline and control. Findings from the present chapter suggest that extrafamilial social support does not serve to buffer adolescents against these negative consequences of such parental behavior.

In contrast to this finding, analysis showed that extrafamilial support did serve to moderate the direct effect of family economic strain. For both boys and girls, support from peers reduced the association between economic pressure and adjustment. We assume that the direct effect of economic pressure on adolescent adjustment represents the consequences of frustration and negative social comparisons attendant to living in a financially stressed family. Findings from the present study suggest that supportive peers are able to temper this effect. This buffering effect is probably produced because friends communicate through their supportive actions that these factors do not matter, that the adolescent is accepted and valued regardless of the economic circumstances of his or her family.

For girls, support from adults outside the nuclear family also moderated the direct effect of economic pressure. Adult support did not serve this function for boys. This gender difference may be a product of differences between boys and girls in the quality of social relationships. Past research indicates that girls tend to establish more intimate and self-disclosing relationships than those formed by boys (Belle & Longfellow, 1984; Bryant, 1985; Lever, 1976; Tietjen, 1982; Waldrop & Halverson, 1975; Youniss & Smollar, 1985), and that girls are more inclined than boys to seek help and emotional comfort from others (Nelson-LeGall, Gumerman, & Scott-Jones, 1983; Wolchik, Sandler, & Braver, 1984). These studies suggest that whereas girls may be favorably disposed to discussing their problems with adult friends and relatives, boys are likely to be uncomfortable doing so. Consequently, access to relationships with caring adults may have little impact upon boys' ability to cope with the difficulties and concerns attendant to economic hardship.

Overall, the results suggest that extrafamilial support may operate as an important coping resource for adolescents. The findings also indicate, however, that the such support is able to moderate the impact of some stressors (viz., economic hardship) but not others (viz., harsh parenting). Further, there appear to be gender differences in the types of support that buffer against stress. The present study considered a limited number of stressors and developmental outcomes. Future studies need to consider other types of risk factors and additional dimensions of adjustment.

Also the present study did not investigate the mechanisms whereby extrafamilial support produces its effect. There may be important gender differences in the mechanisms involved. Past research indicates that boys tend to participate in peer groups of three or more persons in which the focus is upon shared activities, whereas girls prefer dyadic interaction with an emphasis upon intimate conversation and self-disclosure (Belle & Longfellow, 1984; Bryant, 1985; Lever, 1976; Tietjen, 1982; Waldrop & Halverson, 1975; Youniss & Smollar, 1985). Thus for boys, support from peers may involve shared activities that communicate acceptance and offer distraction from problems, whereas for girls, peer support may consist of emotional sharing, catharsis, and expressions of concern. There is a need for studies that go beyond mere documentation of moderator effects to investigation of the processes whereby buffering effects are produced.

In the next chapter we move from consideration of social systems outside the family to an examination of sibling influences in the economic stress process. Will siblings play a role similar to peers and other adults in adolescent adjustment to economic pressures and parental behavior?

Chapter 12

Sibling Relations During Hard Times

Katherine J. Conger, Rand D. Conger, and Glen H. Elder, Jr.

Brothers and sisters can make life easy or difficult for one another. . . . Brothers and sisters can act as buffers for each other, interposing themselves between their siblings and the outside world.
—S. P. Bank and M. D. Kahn (1975) in J. D. Schvaneveldt and
M. Ihinger, "Sibling Relationships in the Family"

Previous chapters have shown how conditions of economic hardship can have a pervasive influence on family members and their relationships. Parents are influenced by stagnant or declining income, unstable employment, and mounting debt. Economic pressure increases parents' risk for depressed mood (Chapter 8), marital conflict (Chapter 9), and parenting behaviors that are both harsh and inconsistent (Chapter 10). Disruptions in parenting in turn adversely affect adolescent adjustment (Chapter 11). This chapter extends these earlier findings by considering the role that brothers and sisters play in these processes.

ECONOMIC PRESSURE, SIBLING RELATIONS, AND ADOLESCENT ADJUSTMENT

The importance of siblings in studies of family stress is illustrated by Christensen and Margolin's research (1988) on conflict and alliance within families as well as by Patterson's (1984, 1986a) studies of antisocial boys and their families. Their work indicates that the sibling relationship may help to explain the spread or containment of conflict within the family. Although, as reviewed in Chapter 1, many studies have examined the effects of economic hardship on marriage, parent-child interactions, and individual development, none has specifically included the third family subsystem, the sibling relationship.

235

Research on relationships within families suggests that hostility that occurs within one family subsystem, such as marital conflict, may spill over into other family subsystems, such as the sibling dyad (e.g., Brody, Stoneman, McCoy, & Forehand, 1992). In addition, hostile patterns of behavior within the family may diminish prosocial behaviors between siblings. This chapter extends previous models of family relationships and the economic stress process by examining the interactional quality of the sibling relationship and its role as a mediator and moderator of the association between parenting behaviors and adolescent adjustment.

As shown in Chapters 9 through 11, economically stressed parents are at increased risk for being hostile and irritable toward one another and toward their children. We postulated in Chapter 1 that these behaviors in parents would place children at increased risk for experiencing developmental problems. Now we ask, Will these behaviors by parents affect the quality of the sibling relationship and, if so, how will that process affect adolescent adjustment?

Discovering Siblings

Research on family relationships has traditionally focused on marriage (Berado, 1980, 1990; Glenn, 1990), parent-child interactions (Dunn, 1983; Maccoby & Martin, 1983; Rollins & Thomas, 1979), or some combination of these two family subsystems (Bowerman & Dobash, 1974; Sussman & Steinmetz, 1987). Little systematic research on sibling relationships was carried out until recently (e.g., Dunn & Kendrick, 1979, 1982; Lamb, 1978). After decades of neglect, this lifelong relationship is being investigated by sociologists, psychologists, and anthropologists (e.g., Bedford & Gold, 1989; Lamb & Sutton-Smith, 1982; Zukow, 1989). This contemporary work, however, already has shown that siblings play important roles in one another's lives during early (Dunn & Kendrick, 1982; Dunn & Munn, 1986; Lamb, 1978) and middle childhood (Bryant, 1982; Bryant & Crockenberg, 1980; Patterson, 1984, 1986b), and also in later life (Bedford & Gold, 1989; Cicirelli, 1982; Ross & Milgram, 1982). Despite these advances, a large gap exists in the available knowledge concerning sibling relationships during the transition from early to late adolescence and on into young adulthood.

Few studies, for example, have closely examined the nature and functions of sibling relationships during adolescence. Two studies that have focused on this age group find that a relationship with an older sibling may have important consequences for younger children. Daniels, Dunn, Furstenberg, and Plomin (1985) reported that an older sibling who acts as teacher and caregiver may provide important support to a younger sibling. Werner and Smith (1982, 1992), in their longitudinal studies of children at risk in Hawaii, found that an older sibling may act as an important source of support for a younger child and also may serve as a buffer against stressors affecting the family. Older siblings who are successful themselves in coping with stressful circumstances can serve as positive role models for children who are at risk for developing adjustment problems.

Passing on a Hostile Legacy

Because, as we have hypothesized and demonstrated, economic stress leads to greater aversive behavior by spouses and parents, an especially important finding is that parents who create a hostile family environment during early adolescence increase the risk of adjustment problems for their children (Patterson, 1982; Rohner, 1986; Rutter, 1980, 1990; Simons, Conger, & Whitbeck, 1988). Siblings who emulate their parents' hostile behaviors may put the young adolescent at even greater risk for developing and maintaining a hostile, interactional style (Patterson, 1984, 1986b). On the other hand, sibling relations that are warm and supportive may be able to withstand or buffer the negative effect of parents' hostility (Bank and Kahn, 1982; Bryant, 1982; Werner & Smith, 1982).

While many researchers and laypersons alike view conflict between siblings as "normal" behavior, for some sibling pairs hostile, aggressive behaviors may escalate into abusive exchanges. Straus, Gelles, & Steinmetz (1980) reported that sibling abuse occurred in over half of the families studied in their nationally representative sample. These results suggest that conflict among siblings is an important factor to consider and that parents' behavior toward their children may have a great deal to do with the frequency and magnitude of the conflict (e.g., Felson & Russo, 1988; Patterson, 1984, 1986b).

Siblings as a Source of Support

Although parental behavior disrupted by economic stress may foster a negative family environment (Patterson, 1975, 1982; Simons et al., 1991), a highly satisfactory, supportive sibling relationship may buffer the adolescent from the negative influence of marital conflict and explosive discipline. Bank and Kahn suggest that siblings may turn to each other as a source of "support and solace" (1982b, p. 217) when marital conflict is present. Other researchers also suggest that siblings may form important supportive alliances during stressful times (Brody, Pellegrini, & Seigel, 1986; Christensen & Margolin, 1988).

In particular, an older sibling may be especially likely to have the experience and personal resources necessary to shield a younger sibling from the full impact of parents' stress-related emotional or behavioral problems. Older siblings may also provide needed emotional support when parents are too preoccupied with financial worries to provide such nurturance.

A MODEL FOR SIBLING INFLUENCE

Drawing on our theoretical framework (Chapter 1) and empirical evidence reviewed here and in previous chapters, we expected that economic pressure would be positively related to parents' hostility toward their children. As have other investigators (e.g., Patterson, 1984), we proposed that hostile behaviors by parents play a key role in intensifying similar actions by siblings. Since earlier chapters that discussed parenting behaviors involved more than the hostility concept, the first step in this analysis examined the direct relationship between economic pressure and parents' hostility toward children.

Our thesis that hostility displayed by mother and father will be positively associated with hostile, conflictual interactions between siblings is consistent with findings reported by Hetherington (1988). The critical outcome of hostility between siblings is the development of hostile, antisocial interaction patterns with others (Patterson, 1984, 1986b). For example, Patterson finds that antisocial boys train other siblings in the family to engage in coercive interaction chains. Consequently, we propose that hostile behavior in the sibling dyad will be positively associated with antisocial, hostile feelings and behaviors by the seventh-grader.

We also expect that hostile exchanges with a sibling will be associated with symptoms of internalized distress. Angry, derogating behaviors by a sibling suggest to the recipient that he or she is of little value (Whitbeck et al., 1991a). In addition, hostility in the sibling dyad may moderate (i.e., high sibling hostility may amplify) the negative consequences of hostile behavior by parents for both the seventh-grader's externalizing and internalizing distress.

Next, we proposed that a high level of warmth and support in a relationship with an older sibling may act as a buffer (i.e., moderator) of the relationship between hostile parents and adolescent distress. Finally, we predicted that most of the effect of hostile parenting on adolescent externalizing and internalizing behaviors will be mediated by sibling interactions, which are psychologically central to young adolescents and which serve as a training ground for other social relations (Patterson, 1986).

MEASUREMENT

The results reported in this chapter are based on a subsample (N = 221) that includes all seventh-graders with older siblings who had complete information on the variables of interest. Basic demographic information on these families was about the same on average as the full sample. There were 125 girls and 96 boys. Siblings ranged in age from 12 years (including 3 twins) to 17 years, with a mean of 15 years. There were 128 female and 93 male older siblings.

Family economic pressure. This construct is represented by three indicators: (1) can't make ends meet, (2) not enough money to meet material needs, and (3) economic adjustments (which were described in detail in Chapters 4 and 8).

Parental hostility. Three sources—seventh-grader report, older sibling report, and observer report—were used to assess both mother's and father's hostile behaviors directed toward both children. Each adolescent answered five items, which assessed how often in the past month first mother and then father had gotten angry, shouted or yelled, gotten into a fight or argument, and hit, pushed, grabbed, or shoved the respondent. Each item was answered on a 7-point scale, from *parents never* (1) to *always* (7) *behaved that way*. Internal consistency (alpha) for reports of mother's hostility were .81 and .86 (father's was .82 and .87) for seventh-grader and older sibling, respectively.

Four observer ratings of father and mother behavior directed toward the seventh-grader and his or her older sibling were combined to create a subscale for each parent's hostility. The items included hostile, antisocial, and angry coercive behaviors directed toward the children. The fourth item, transactional conflict, rated the tendency of the parent to reciprocate or escalate hostile behaviors with the sibling and target seventh-grader. Ratings of parents' behavior by independent observers from Task 1 (family discussion) and Task 2 (problem-solving) were combined to create a global measure of father's (α = .87), and then mother's (α = .90) hostility toward both children in the study.

Hostility between siblings. Hostile adolescent exchanges were assessed by three different sources: seventh-grade target child report, sibling report, and observer report. The target child reported how often his or her sibling in the study behaved in an angry or hostile fashion during the previous month [1 (*never behaved that way*) to 7 (*always behaved that way*)]. The five items included behaviors like gets angry, shouts or yells, fights and argues, and hitting, pushing, or shoving. The sibling reported on the same items, which were summed to create an index of seventh-grader hostility. Internal consistency for the target child report and sibling report was .89 and .87, respectively.

Hostile behaviors between the siblings were rated on the same four dimensions as those used to create the observer report of parents' hostility. These four items were summed across Tasks 1, 2, and 3, each task rated by a different observer, to create a composite score of hostility between seventh-graders and their older siblings across all three family interaction settings ($\alpha = .88$).

Warmth and support between siblings. This concept was included to investigate possible buffering effects that a warm, supportive sibling relationship might provide for a young adolescent living in an otherwise hostile family environment (cf. Bank & Kahn, 1982a). As with the sibling hostility construct, this construct was estimated using three different sources of information: seventh-grader report, older sibling report, and observer report of sibling interactions. The first measure consisted of seven items reported by the seventh-grader about his or her older sibling's behavior during the previous month [1 (*never*) to 7 (*always behaved that way*)]. Items included behaviors such as listens carefully to your point of view, acts loving and affectionate, lets you know he or she appreciates you and your ideas ($\alpha = .92$). These same items were answered by the older sibling about the seventh-grader's behaviors ($\alpha = .90$).

Consistent with the hostility construct, the third indicator of warmth and support between siblings was based on observer ratings of five behavioral dimensions such as warmth, prosocial exchanges, and listener responsiveness. Ratings for each child were summed across Task 1 (family discussion), Task 2 (problem solving), and Task 3 (sibling discussion) to create a composite rating of warmth and support between the two siblings in the study ($\alpha = .75$).

Adolescent externalizing behavior. This construct is defined by three indicators based on self-report by the seventh-grader. Antisocial feelings and behaviors are measured with seven items, which asked how the seventh-grader would feel or act in certain situations (Buss & Durkee, 1957). Adolescents were asked how much each item matched their behavior. Responses ranged from 1 (*not at all*) to 5 (*exactly*) on items such as "When someone hits me first, I let them have it" and "When people yell at me, I yell back" ($\alpha = .76$). Hostile feelings and behaviors also were assessed using the hostility subscale of the SCL-90-R (Derogatis, 1983), which was split into two subscales, one representing feelings of hostility ($\alpha = .65$) and one representing hostile behaviors ($\alpha = .68$). For both subscales, the respondent indicated whether he or she was *not at all* (1) to *extremely* (5) *bothered or distressed* by each feeling or behavior.

Adolescent internalizing behavior. This construct is defined by three additional subscales from the SCL-90-R (Derogatis, 1983): depression, anxiety, and somatization. The depression subscale included 12 items such as feeling lonely, feeling blue, feeling no interest in things, and feeling everything is an effort ($\alpha = .87$). Anxiety was assessed with 10 items asking about problems such as nervousness, suddenly scared for no reason, feeling tense or keyed up, and spells of terror or panic ($\alpha = .85$). The 12 items for somatization included problems like faintness, pains in the chest, trouble getting one's breath, and feeling weak in parts of the body ($\alpha = .78$). The respondent indicated whether he or she was *not at all* (1) to *extremely* (5) *bothered or distressed* by each feeling or behavior during the previous week.

RESULTS

The results for this chapter are presented in three sections, starting with a brief summary of bivariate correlations among indicators. The second section presents the results of latent variable structural equation estimation of the conceptual model, and the third section presents additional analysis of sibling warmth and support as a moderator of parents' hostility.

Correlational Analyses

Indicators for economic pressure are modestly correlated (e.g., $r = .18$ between observer report of father hostility and economic adjustments) in the expected direction with child and observer reports of parents' hostility toward children, with all but one of the correlations slightly higher for father, as shown in Table 12.1.

Correlations between each parent's indicators of hostility were significantly and positively correlated with measures of siblings' hostility both within and across all three reporting agents. All but one of these correlations were statistically significant ($r = .08$, NS, between seventh-grader report of mother's hostility and observer report of hostile sibling interactions).

As expected, the correlations between seventh-grader report of father's and mother's hostility and seventh-grader report of own hostility, anxiety, depression, and somatization were quite robust (e.g., $r = .32$ and .37 for father's and mother's hostility respectively correlated with seventh-grader's report of own hostile feelings). These associations were supported by modest correlations in the same direction (ranging from $r = $

Table 12.1. Correlations, Means, and Standard Deviations for Mother and Father Hostility with Other Study Variables (N = 221)

Study variables	Father's hostility[a]			Mother's hostility[a]				
	Seventh-grader report	Older sibling report	Observer report, Tasks 1,2	Seventh-grader report	Older sibling report	Observer report, Tasks 1,2	Mean	SD
1. Can't make ends meet	11	12	12	10	13	09	−.08	4.84
2. Material needs	18	17	16	08	19	14	34.99	10.44
3. Economic adjustments	16	11	18	12	08	07	6.05	4.19
4. Older sibling's hostility, seventh-grader report	48	18	29	41	21	25	23.43	8.19
5. Seventh-grader's hostility, older sibling report	24	37	27	19	42	29	24.13	7.25
6. Hostility between siblings, observer report, Tasks 1,2,3	22	15	44	08	12	50	9.06	2.84
7. Emotional support from older sibling, seventh grader report	−19	−11	−14	−09	−10	−15	25.83	9.78
8. Emotional support from seventh-grader, older sibling report	−16	−22	−16	−06	−18	−13	31.29	9.13
9. Warmth and support between siblings, observer report, Tasks 1, 2, 3	−15	−13	−14	−11	−21	−05	11.68	2.11
10. Seventh-grader's antisocial attitudes and behaviors	25	06	17	31	08	17	18.42	5.33
11. Seventh-grader's hostile feelings	32	15	14	37	08	12	5.08	2.25
12. Seventh-grader's hostile behaviors	29	23	13	43	20	14	4.74	2.20
13. Seventh-grader's depression	37	15	06	36	05	13	19.92	7.38
14. Seventh-grader's anxiety	31	13	13	39	05	15	15.51	5.66
15. Seventh-grader's somatization	21	14	06	29	02	04	18.70	5.74
Mean	14.81	15.36	31.19	15.79	16.14	31.43		
SD	6.03	6.84	10.35	5.77	6.15	8.73		

[a] Decimal points omitted (for $r \geq .13$, $p < .05$; for $r \geq .175$, $p < .01$).

.06 to .23) by both sibling and observer report of parental hostility correlated with other variables of interest.

Table 12.2 provides the correlations among all of the seventh-grader and older sibling variables used in these analyses. Correlations among indicators within each latent construct were all quite good. There were moderate to high correlations between all three sources reporting on hostility between siblings (e.g., $r = .55$ between sibling and seventh-grader reports of one another's hostility). Correlations ranged from $r = .25$ to .43 among the three reporters of warmth and support between siblings. As in earlier research, reports of internalizing and externalizing symptoms were significantly correlated (see Cicchetti & Toth, 1991).

Economic Pressure and Parental Hostility

Standardized path coefficients for all models were estimated using maximum likelihood procedures (LISREL 7; Joreskog & Sorbom 1989). Figure 12.1 shows the results for the first proposed path linking economic pressure to mother's and father's hostility toward their children. As expected, family economic pressure was positively and significantly related to mother's hostility (.26) and father's hostility (.34). These positive relationships are quite good, especially considering that there is no overlap in source of information between the two constructs. All factor loadings on the constructs were statistically significant and the summary statistics indicated a good fit between the model and the data (e.g., GFI = .991 for the mother model).

Parental Hostility and Adolescent Adjustment

Figure 12.2 provides the results of the analyses for the mediational models linking mother's and father's hostility to seventh-grader's antisocial feelings and behaviors. The two models presented in this figure introduce hostility between siblings as a mediator that helps explain the relationship between parental hostility and adolescent externalization. Using the nested models evaluation technique described in Chapter 2, we compared each mediational model to the corresponding recursive model (i.e., adding the direct path from parent hostility to adolescent externalization). Although we do not suggest that parents have no direct influence on their adolescent children's adjustment, the recursive model showed no significant improvement in the chi-square; hence, there is support for selecting the more parsimonious models shown in Figure 12.2.

Turning to the specific results shown in Figure 12.2A, the structural coefficients from mother's hostility to hostility between siblings (.58) and from

Table 12.2. Intercorrelations Among Sibling Relationship Indicators and Adolescent Outcome Indicators[a]

Study variables	1	2	3	4	5	6	7	8	9	10	11	12
1. Older sibling hostility, seventh-grader report	—											
2. Seventh-grader hostility, older sibling report	*55*	—										
3. Hostility between siblings, observer report, Tasks 1,2,3	*40*	*33*	—									
4. Emotional support from older sibling, seventh-grader report	-44	-28	-28	—								
5. Emotional support from seventh-grader, older sibling report	-41	-40	-13	*43*	—							
6. Support between siblings, observer report, Tasks 1,2,3	-27	-16	-13	28	25	—						
7. Seventh-grader's antisocial attitudes and behaviors	23	15	22	-18	-03	-07	—					
8. Seventh-grader's hostile feelings	36	23	15	-14	-05	01	*46*	—				
9. Seventh-grader's hostile behaviors	37	20	12	-11	-09	-08	*40*	*67*	—			
10. Seventh-grader's depression	30	07	07	-17	-05	-09	20	54	58	—		
11. Seventh-grader's anxiety	32	11	12	-14	-05	-06	30	62	67	*79*	—	
12. Seventh-grader's somatization	29	07	15	-17	-07	-12	19	51	47	*69*	*67*	—

[a] Decimal points are omitted (for $r \geq .13$, $p < .05$; for $r \geq .175$, $p < .01$). Correlations within latent constructs are italicized.

sibling hostility to the adolescent's hostile, antisocial feelings and behaviors (.38) were both statistically significant and in the expected direction. Mother's hostility accounted for 34% of the variance in hostility between seventh-graders and their older siblings. Fifteen percent of the variance in seventh-graders' hostile, antisocial feelings and behavior was explained.

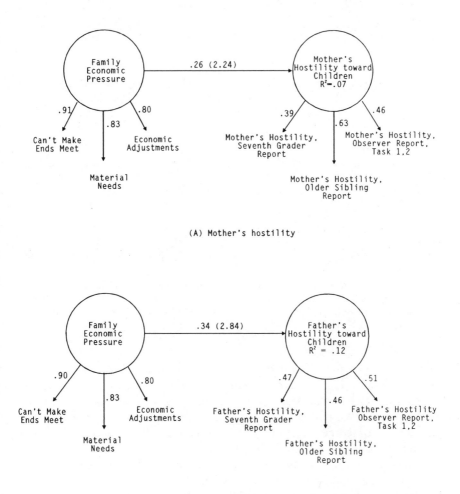

(A) Mother's hostility

(B) Father's hostility

Figure 12.1. Standardized path coefficients for economic pressure predicting parents' hostility toward children, *t*-values in parentheses. (A) Family economic pressure predicting mother's hostility toward children. $\chi^2_8 = 5.86$, $P = .662$, $GFI = .991$, $HCN = 575$. (B) Family economic pressure predicting father's hostility toward children. $\chi^2_8 = 6.14$, $P = .601$, $GFI = .991$, $HCN = 525$.

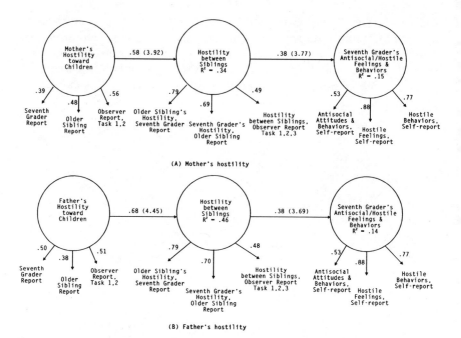

Figure 12.2. Standardized coefficients for parental hostility and hostility between siblings predicting adolescent externalization ($N = 221$). (A) Predicting adolescent externalization with mother's hostility and hostility between
siblings. $\chi^2_{16} = 22.09$, $P = .140$, $GFI = .979$, $HCN = 261$. (B) Predicting
adolescent externalization with father's hostility and hostility between siblings. $\chi^2_{16} = 19.38$, $P = .250$, $GFI = .981$, $HCN = 296$.

The pattern of relationships between constructs was similar in the
father's model (Figure 12.2B), where the coefficient from father's hostility to hostility between siblings was slightly higher than mother's, .68 as
opposed to .58. The relationship between dyadic sibling hostility and
adolescent outcome remained the same as found in the mother's model.
Father's hostility accounted for 46% of the variance in hostility between
siblings. For both models in Figure 12.2, the fit indices suggest the proposed mediational model fits the data fairly well.

Figure 12.3 provides the results for adolescent internalization. The
coefficients linking parent's hostility to hostility between siblings are essentially the same as shown previously: mother's (.59) and father's (.69).
This is expected since the same indicators were used to measure the
latent constructs in both models. The structural coefficient between sibling dyadic hostility and internalization (.18 in Figure 12.3A, .15 in Fig-

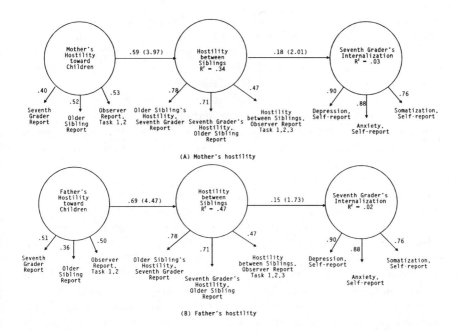

Figure 12.3. Standardized coefficients for parental hostility and hostility between siblings predicting adolescent internalization ($N = 221$). (A) Predicting adolescent internalization with mother's hostility and hostility between siblings. $\chi^2_{16} = 17.22$, $P = .371$, $GFI = .983$, $HCN = 334$. (B) Predicting adolescent externalization with father's hostility and hostility between siblings. $\chi^2_{16} = 17.04$, $P = .383$, $GFI = .983$, $HCN = 338$.

ure 12.3B) is much lower than the relationship between siblings' hostility and seventh-graders' external distress. The amount of explained variance is quite small, about 3% in each case.

The proposed models with sibling warmth and support mediating the relationship between parents' hostility and adolescent outcomes were not supported by the data analyses. Using the same analysis strategy described for Figures 12.2 and 12.3, we tested the same four mediational models with warmth and support between siblings as the mediator. Although the simplex (fully mediated) models initially looked promising, when the direct path from parental hostility to adolescent outcome was added, the path between the sibling relationship and adolescent internalization and externalization became nonsignificant.

The moderator models. The third stage of the analyses involved the assessment of the sibling relationship as a moderator of the relationship between parental hostility and adolescent adjustment problems. The proposed moderator models were not supported by the data analysis. The hypothesized model proposed that the strength of the relationship between parental hostility and adolescent outcome was contingent on the level of either hostility or warmth between siblings. Since each proposed moderator variable was a latent construct in these models, the reports from the three different sources were standardized and summed before the variable was dichotomized by dividing at the median. The low group and high group then were compared following the guidelines for stacked models listed in Chapter 2.

Alternative moderator models. Although not originally proposed in the theoretical model, we added an alternative model that used adolescent perception of older sibling's warmth and support as the moderator variable. Perhaps as Rohner (1975, 1986) suggests, it is the child's perception of the warmth and support (or lack thereof) from the sibling that is important in determining the impact of parenting on their development.

The proposed moderator variable, seventh-grader report of older sibling's warmth and support during the previous month, was dichotomized by splitting it at the median and comparing the two groups simultaneously as described earlier. Some support for a moderator effect is shown in Figure 12.4 for mother's hostility.

When the seventh-grader reported a low level of support from an older sibling (Panel A), mother's hostility was significantly related to adolescent antisocial, hostile feelings and behaviors (.33, Figure 12.4). However, for seventh-graders reporting high warmth and support from the older sibling, the relationship between mother's hostility and adolescent externalization becomes fairly small (.14) and nonsignificant. The findings for father hostility and seventh-grader antisocial behavior, moderated by sibling warmth and support, are quite comparable with the findings for mothers (see Figure 12.5).

Results were quite surprising when these high and low support models were compared. Despite the fact that mother hostility and father hostility predicted adolescent antisocial development only when sibling warmth and support was low, the differences between the path coefficients for the high and low support models were not statistically significant. Moreover, similar models predicting adolescent internalizing symptoms also showed no differences between adolescents reporting high versus low sibling warmth and support. Based on these data, we can infer some tentative support for the thesis that high sibling supportiveness may reduce the adverse impact of parent hostility on externalizing problems.

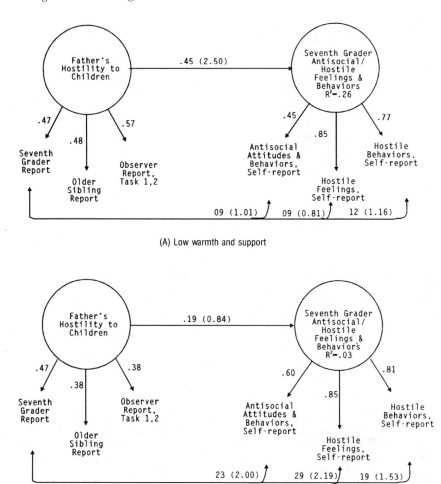

(A) Low warmth and support

(B) High warmth and support

Figure 12.4. Standardized coefficients for mother's hostility and seventh-grader's antisocial hostile feelings and behavior moderated by older sibling's warmth and support. Residuals correlated across constructs for same source; *t*-values are in parentheses. (A) Predicting adolescent externalization with mother's hostility under conditions of low warmth and support from older sibling. (B) Predicting adolescent externalization with mother's hostility under conditions of high warmth and support from older sibling.

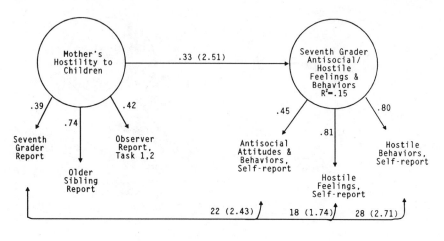

(A) Low warmth and support

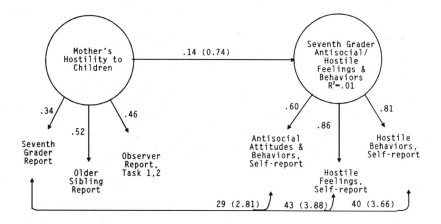

(B) High warmth and support

Figure 12.5. Standardized coefficients for father's hostility and seventh-grader's antisocial hostile feelings and behavior moderated by older sibling's warmth and support. Residuals correlated across constructs for same source; *t*-values are in parentheses. (A) Predicting adolescent externalization with father's hostility under conditions of low warmth and support from older sibling. (B) Predicting adolescent externalization with mother's hostility under conditions of high warmth and support from older sibling.

DISCUSSION

The current analyses were designed to elaborate previous research on economic distress by including sibling relationships as an important factor in explaining family processes and adolescent adjustment. The primary question focused on the interactional quality of the sibling relationship, hostile or supportive, and its role as a mediator and moderator of the association between parental hostility and adolescent adjustment.

Although the results should be interpreted with caution due to the cross-sectional nature of the data, in general, the results presented here support our hypotheses regarding the importance of including the sibling subsystem in studies of family stress and relationships.

There was a strong positive association between feelings of economic pressure and both mothers' and fathers' hostility toward their children. The pattern of findings was quite similar for both parents. These results suggest that both parents suffer when they cannot keep up with their bills, cannot afford adequate housing, clothing, health care, etc., and are forced to cut back on insurance coverage, family activities, and everyday expenses. One consequence of these ongoing economic pressures is an irritable, hostile interactional style with their children. These results are consistent with those reported in earlier chapters.

Both mother's and father's hostility had negative consequences for both the sibling relationship and for adolescent adjustment. These results suggest that siblings may emulate their parents' hostile interactional style in their own interactions. These hostile interactions in turn appear to put the young adolescent at increased risk for developing an antisocial, hostile interpersonal style. These results are consistent with those reported by Patterson (1984, 1986b) that indicate that parents and siblings play important roles in establishing and maintaining hostile interpersonal behavior patterns within the family system.

Of particular interest was the strong negative effect parents' hostility had on warm and supportive feelings between siblings. If hostile behaviors by parents act both to increase hostile behaviors between siblings and to diminish feelings of warmth and support, a young adolescent may be most at risk for developing a hostile interactional style (cf. Patterson, 1986b) or feelings of depression and worthlessness (e.g., Rohner, 1986; Whitbeck et al., 1991a). It may be that feelings and behaviors of hostility and warmth must be considered simultaneously to gain a better understanding of the emotional nature of the sibling relationship.

Consistent with this perspective, in a study of sibling relations in families with divorced parents, Hetherington found about 22% of the siblings in the sample had a hostile, alienated relationship, which was "characterized by low involvement, communication, warmth, empathy, and high coercion and aggression" (1988, p. 327). Siblings who are in a relationship devoid of any warmth or caring during times of stress may be at especially high risk for becoming hostile and aggressive or withdrawn and depressed (Hetherington, 1988; Kahn & Lewis, 1988). In any case, the findings reported here demonstrate that hostile behaviors by parents and siblings work together to increase both internalizing and, especially, externalizing symptoms of early adolescents.

The modest evidence reported here for a possible "buffering" effect of warmth and support from an older sibling raises more questions than it answers at this point. Although there is evidence of sibling support among children of divorced parents (Hetherington, 1988), children in high-risk family environments (Werner & Smith, 1982), and siblings in therapy (Kahn & Lewis, 1988), it is not yet clear what factors predict the development and maintenance of sibling support. Perhaps siblings who have a history of involvement, concern, and communication may be especially well-equipped to maintain that type of relationship even when parents' behavior promotes a hostile, nonsupportive family environment. This question is one that deserves further careful research.

Despite their apparent limitations, the present findings are consistent with an accumulating body of evidence that siblings play important roles in children's lives. Behavior in the sibling relationship may contribute to the spread or containment of hostility within the family system and in turn help explain the consequences of those behaviors for adolescent psychological adjustment. In our study of families' lives in changing economic times, the addition of a sibling provides another perspective on family interactions and individual development. It is increasingly apparent that we need to include the different pictures painted by each family member in order to gain a complete portrait of individuals and their families, particularly as families struggle to adapt to stressful pressures in their lives.

PART V

Reviewing the Evidence

Chapter 13

Family Stress and Adaptation: Reviewing the Evidence

Rand D. Conger and Glen H. Elder, Jr.

Conditions in America's rural communities are far worse than is generally recognized. Contrary to national assumptions of rural tranquility, many small towns . . . today warrant the label "ghetto."
—O. G. Davidson, *Broken Heartland*

As shown in previous chapters in this report, the inability to meet one's basic material needs creates enormous personal concern as well as increased demands for day-to-day coping with economic pressures. Hardship within families multiplies the impact of economic stress in that individual responsibilities become social obligations for maintaining not only one's own welfare but also the economic health of the family unit. Adults in the family must direct their attention to their own, one another's, and their children's material well-being. In many cases, children also assume a significant portion of the burden for maintaining the family's financial solvency.

In extreme cases, such as in the plight of homeless families, daily existence can become a continuing nightmare of uncertainty, worry, and herculean efforts to secure sustenance and shelter. For the Iowa families who participated in the Iowa Youth and Families Project, resources are sufficient to maintain a household, but for many of them any diminution in the collective effort to balance income with expenditures will be a prescription for economic disaster and despair. As illustrated by Davidson's (1990) quote that begins this chapter, rural families in general must cope with an environment increasingly characterized by economic uncertainty, stagnation, and disadvantage.

We began this book, however, by noting that the experiences of these families not only reflect the changing economic fortunes of rural people,

255

but also tell an important story regarding the lives of both rural and urban families in an era of economic restructuring and change. The findings reported here have important implications for contemporary and future families who must be increasingly capable of adapting to a volatile and uncertain financial environment. The globalization of economic life brings with it new demands for individual effort and creativity.

In the following discussion we review the evidence for our thesis that economic stress has a dramatic influence on family well-being and that the experience of these Iowa families provides more general lessons for families of today and tomorrow. This chapter considers the empirical, theoretical, methodological, and practical implications of our results.

We begin with an overview of the findings in relation to our model of family stress and in relation to earlier research on families and economic hardship. The next section considers the methodological significance of the results. Finally, we evaluate the role that these families' experiences might play in the development of social services and policies designed to reduce the adverse impact of economic stress on children and adults.

STUDY FINDINGS IN THEORETICAL CONTEXT

In Chapter 1 we developed a general model of family stress according to which stressful events or conditions, such as economic hardship, influence family members through the chronic strains or pressures they create in daily living. In the case of parents and early adolescents, the theory suggests that economic pressures will first affect the emotional lives and marital interactions of adults, and through this process the caretaking environment and developmental course of children. Drawing on depression-era findings, the conceptual model also suggests that children may play an important role in family adaptation to economic hardship.

The Family Economy in Rural Iowa

After reviewing the theory (Chapter 1) and methods (Chapter 2) that guided the study, in Chapters 3 through 6 we considered the economic circumstances in the communities and families that participated in the research. An important question is whether the research site provided the economic variability necessary to examine the impact of financial conditions on individuals and families. The evidence indicates that it does.

For example, the data presented in Chapter 3 showed that, on average, the study counties suffered serious reductions in economic activity and population during the 1980s. Net retail sales, personal earnings, and school enrollments declined. Approximately one out of every five farms was lost and this disruption in the agricultural economy led to bankruptcies in other business sectors in these rural areas and small towns in central Iowa. Moreover, official statistics showed that social problems often associated with hardship, such as child abuse, increased during this period of economic reversals.

At the community level, then, evidence regarding economic and social circumstances suggests that the study area provided an appropriate site for the research. Chapters 4 through 6 document the extension of these community changes to family life and also provide initial evidence in support of the theoretical model.

The findings reported in Chapter 4 demonstrated that nonfarm families and families that were displaced from farming suffered the greatest economic stress of all of the participants in the study. These results corroborate at the individual family level the impact of the general decline in the farm economy and its ripple effect in rural communities across the region. In sociological terms, our families represent the social-psychological results emanating from macrolevel social and economic changes.

Many of the farm families in our study, however, were doing quite well financially. They represent that segment of the agricultural sector that survived and rebounded from the farm crisis. Many of these families likely have profited from reduced land prices, which allowed them to expand their operations. These farmers likely entered the crisis years with relatively low debt loads and thus were able to survive the financial chaos of the 1980s (Friedberger, 1989). Their survival in farming was not without costs, however. Lengthy episodes of depressed mood during the 1980s were reported by farm and nonfarm adults as well as by couples who lost farms. Moreover, both farm and nonfarm families reflect the urban trend toward an increase in the number of working mothers. Many of them commented on their distress in response to this necessary economic adaptation.

The most economically distressed families in the sample, and in particular the displaced farm families, demonstrated greater risk for emotional problems and disruptions in family relationships. Especially important, the results in Chapter 4 showed that economic conditions such as unstable work and low income increased daily strains and pressures in economic life. According to our theoretical perspective, economic pressure should provide the primary conduit through which economic disadvantage impacts the psychological and interpersonal well-being of family members. The results from this chapter established the predicted associations among the initial constructs in the model.

The farm crisis years had a major impact on both farm and nonfarm families. For many farm families this period represents an important turning point in the nature of the occupation and in possibilities for the future, as discussed in Chapter 5. We found that men were far more distressed by the loss of farming as a way of life than their wives, although women often mourned the loss of family time together as they pursued outside employment to combat growing financial difficulties.

Some farm families followed a conservative pattern of adaptation to the farm crisis by increasing family effort in the operation and reducing the costs of outside inputs. Others increased the hours of work off the farm as an adjustment strategy. In either case, men seemed to suffer most when their lives in farming were threatened while women were most distressed by the loss of economic resources. Men who had lost farms generally longed to return to that life; their wives and children more often expressed a desire to move on to less stressful and demanding work and living situations.

For most farm families, the 1980s produced difficult choices that led many out of farming and others to a new life-style that involved both agricultural and other forms of employment. For the majority of farmers in our study, their occupation will not, by itself, provide sufficient financial support to maintain the family economy. These difficult adjustments during the 1980s for both farm and nonfarm participants in the study suggested an affirmative response to our question regarding the suitability of this sample for evaluating our family stress model.

The data also showed, as expected, that children played an important role in family response to hardship. Both boys and girls in the study were more likely to contribute their efforts to household work and paid employment when their families experienced significant economic pressure and when mothers pursued employment outside the home. These early adolescents also tended to make more substantial contributions to necessary family purchases when family finances were strained. The results also showed important gender differences in these processes.

Girls more often contributed to household work than boys, a pattern observed during the Great Depression (Elder, 1974). Farm boys in particular pursued paid employment and they were the only youth in the study who were more positively perceived by parents as a function of their employment. Thus, farm culture appears to motivate and appreciate paid work by young males. This finding suggests an important contextual difference between boys living in the countryside and their urban or small-town counterparts who were not more positively evaluated by parents as a function of their employment status.

In summary, the early chapters established important economic changes and adjustments in the rural families and communities that were the focus for the study. The decade of the 1980s created changes for these families that will have a continuing impact on their lives for the foreseeable future. They clearly represent the range of economic experience necessary to evaluate our model of family stress. In the following section, we consider the results of those analyses.

Adult Response to Economic Stress

According to our theoretical model (Chapter 1), economic pressure will first affect the emotions and behaviors of parents. We also predicted that adults would be more or less prepared to cope with financial distress depending on their childhood experiences. The findings reported in Chapter 7 provided support for this thesis in that parents who experienced an atmosphere of rejection and emotional distress in their families of origin were as adults less self-confident and less capable of eliciting social support from others. Thus, the life histories of these parents played an important role in tempering their current response, either positively or negatively, to family economic stress.

The significance of social support as a coping resource was clearly illustrated in Chapter 8. Here we were interested in evaluating the postulated link in the theoretical model between economic pressure and parent emotional distress. The findings were consistent with the hypothesis that difficulties in meeting financial needs (economic pressure) would mediate the relationship between hardship conditions (low income, unstable work, high debts, income loss) and psychological impairment (depressive symptoms). These results, then, provided additional support for the postulated theoretical processes.

Moreover, the findings showed that social support from family and friends diminished the harmful influence of economic pressure on emotional status. Thus, those parents with a child-rearing history that promoted interpersonal skills were in a better position to withstand the psychological onslaught of economic disadvantage than those who were less socially competent. Consistent with much of the earlier research (e.g., Kessler et al., 1985), we did not find a moderating influence for social support; rather, support had a direct or main effect on parents' depressive symptoms.

Interestingly, however, higher income women who were more likely to have extensive social networks outside the home benefited most from extrafamilial social supports. Lower income women, on the other hand, were less likely to be depressed if they received a high level of support within the nuclear family. Apparently these women derive their most important social satisfactions from their network of family relationships, perhaps because they are less likely to be employed or involved in a broad array of other community activities. These findings suggest interesting social class differences in social support influences that merit additional attention in future research.

The next step in the theoretical model hypothesized that economic stress and emotional difficulties should affect the quality of the marriage. More specifically, we postulated that financial problems and depressed mood would exacerbate hostile behaviors toward one's spouse. This process, in turn, was expected to reduce the quality of the marriage for both parents. The results reported in Chapter 9 supported most aspects of the model.

As predicted, depressive symptoms for either mothers or fathers were strongly related to their own hostile behaviors toward their partner. However, with depressed mood in the regression equation, economic pressure had no direct impact on adult hostility, contrary to the original model proposed in Chapter 1. Rather, the influence of financial strain was indirect through the dysphoric feelings it intensified in parents. The combination of a depressed and hostile spouse, in turn, markedly reduced perceived marital quality for both husbands and wives.

To summarize, the findings reported through Chapter 9 were mostly consistent with the postulated stress process. Hardship conditions increased daily pressures and difficult adjustments in family economic life. This economic pressure, in turn, increased risk for depressed mood in parents, although enmeshment in supportive social networks helped to diminish the negative impact of financial troubles. Contrary to predictions, only emotional distress had a direct effect on hostility toward spouse. Economic pressure indirectly influenced hostility in marriage through parents' depressed mood. For adults, the economic stress process produced increased risk for hostility and dissatisfaction in marital relations.

These findings for adults experiencing economic hardship are similar to those for depression-era families, but there are also noteworthy differences. First, we proposed and found an intervening mechanism, economic pressure, between hardship conditions such as low income and disruptions in parents' psychological health and marital functioning. Although this process is implied in many of the Great Depression studies (e.g., Angell, 1965; Komarovsky, 1940; Elder, 1974), it was never specifically hypothesized or tested.

The identification of economic pressure or strain as a mediating mechanism in the economic stress process clearly places the experience of financial difficulties within the broader conceptual framework provided by our proposed Family Stress Model. Consistent with current perspectives on the social epidemiology of psychological distress (Mirowsky & Ross, 1989; Pearlin, 1989), our model suggests that acute or chronic stressors have an impact on individual functioning through the disruptions they create in daily living. The indicators for the economic pressure construct represent important dimensions of such disruptions in relation to economic hardship. Thus, the present findings extend earlier research by adding this important mediating mechanism to our understanding of the economic stress process.

A second significant extension in the present study, compared to earlier research on family response to economic stress, involves the addition of parents' demoralization or depressed mood as an explanatory variable. Elder's research with depression-era families made a significant breakthrough by identifying father's emotional instability as an important mediating mechanism between income loss and disruptions in marriage and parenting (Elder & Caspi, 1988; Liker & Elder, 1983). The only available measure of emotional instability, however, involved irritable and explosive behaviors that may be a more typical stress response of men than of women. Moreover, only men high on instability prior to economic decline seemed to become even more psychologically distressed as economic problems increased (Liker & Elder, 1983).

The present findings suggest that an even more basic response to economic stress involves dysphoric mood and feelings of hopelessness. By introducing this new measure of emotional instability into the analyses, we were able (1) to bring women directly into the economic stress process and (2) find a direct relation between economic stress and men's emotional instability. That is, when economic stress led to high levels of depressive symptoms for women, they were just as likely to become angry, hostile, and irritable toward their husbands as their spouses were toward them. Moreover, men in general, not just those who were previously unstable, were vulnerable to increasing depressive symptoms as a result of high levels of economic pressure.

The findings tell us, then, that both men and women in contemporary families are likely to be adversely affected by economic disadvantage through its impact on disruptions in daily living. These day-to-day pressures intensify feelings of hopelessness and anger, which in turn engender hostile interactions and dissatisfactions in marriage. We hypothesized in Chapter 1 that these disruptions in the lives of adults should have adverse consequences for children. The following discussion considers the evidence for that hypothesis.

From Parents' Distress to Adolescent Adjustment

The next step in the set of postulated associations among study constructs linked parents' stress-related emotional and marital problems to disruptions in parenting practices. Less competent child-rearing was expected to place adolescents at risk for adjustment problems. In general, the results were consistent with theoretical predictions.

The analyses reported in Chapter 10 produced the expected path from parents' hostility toward one another to their explosive disciplinary practices with their children. These results replicate depression-era findings for fathers and extend them to mothers as well (Elder & Caspi, 1988). Especially important, continued support from a spouse under conditions of high economic pressure served to reduce the adverse impact of economic stress on marital hostility and conflict. As proposed in Chapter 1 then, social support either from within or outside the family tended to mitigate the negative influence of financial difficulties on family functioning.

The results suggest that spouses who maintain a supportive relationship with one another when times are hard will be less likely to engage in chronic cycles of interpersonal hostility. In turn, marital support will reduce the risk that marital conflict will spill over into interactions with children in the form of angry, explosive disciplinary practices. How do these disruptions in appropriate discipline affect adolescent adjustment?

The results discussed in Chapters 11 and 12 demonstrated that hostile, explosive behaviors by parents directly affected adjustment problems of adolescents and also had adverse consequences for the quality of sibling relationships. The findings reported in Chapter 11, for example, showed that economic pressure indirectly diminished girls' self-confidence and psychological well-being through harsh parenting practices. For boys, the same mediating process predicted antisocial and hostile behaviors.

Contrary to our original hypotheses, however, economic pressure also had a direct influence on adjustment problems for these boys and girls. We expect this direct path resulted from the fact that we had to simplify the model and examine fewer variables in any single analysis. This simplifying strategy maintained a sufficient number of cases to subdivide the sample and examine predicted moderating effects involving social support. The end result of this process was that the adolescent adjustment analyses were limited to a single mediator, harsh parenting practices.

We suspect that if the number of available cases had allowed us to include the full set of postulated mediators in a single analysis (e.g., parent mood, marital conflict, and positive as well as negative parenting practices), the direct path from economic pressure to adolescent adjustment quite likely would have been reduced to a nonsignificant coefficient, consistent with the theoretical model (see Conger et al., 1992; Conger, Conger, et al., 1993, for an elaborated analysis of the model).

In any case, the hypothesized model was largely supported by the predicted mediated effect through harsh parenting. In addition, social support for both boys and girls from outside the nuclear family reduced the risk of antisocial behavior for boys and poor self-confidence in girls. And, although supportive behaviors from others diminished the negative impact of economic pressure on adolescent maladjustment, such support did not reduce the detrimental consequences of harsh parenting, an even more dramatic life stress in the lives of these early adolescents.

Just as the theoretical model predicted disruptions in marital and parent-child relations, in Chapter 12 we postulated that stress-related parent hostility toward children should exacerbate conflict in the sibling dyad. In addition, we proposed that high levels of hostility between a target adolescent and older sibling would increase risk for adjustment problems for the seventh-graders in the study. Finally, drawing on the social support paradigm investigated in earlier chapters, we proposed that emotional support from an older brother or sister should reduce the negative impact of parent hostility on the target adolescent's adjustment problems.

The analyses added important new information to understanding of (1) the impact of one family subsystem on another (Hinde & Hinde, 1988) and (2) the critical role of hostile family relations in the social epidemiology of personal distress (Coyne & Downey, 1991; Mirowsky & Ross, 1989). The results showed that disruptions in the parent-child subsystem (hostile parent behaviors) predicted conflict in sibling interactions, which served as the primary conduit through which parent irritability led to externalizing symptoms for the target adolescents. To a lesser degree, the same mediating process applied to internalizing problems. Finally, the analyses also provided preliminary evidence for the thesis that social support from an older sibling attenuates the negative influence of parent hostility on early adolescent adjustment.

SUMMARY

Taken together, the results reported throughout the prior chapters suggest that the economic decline experienced by Iowa families during the 1980s had a significant and lasting impact on their emotional well-being and interpersonal relations. Today, many of these families have become chronically stressed by their economic circumstances.

As proposed by our Family Stress Model, financial difficulties directly increase risk for emotional problems, especially among parents. Personal unhappiness and irritability translate into hostile and angry behaviors with other family members, including children. The data show that these disrupted patterns of behavior threaten the perceived quality of family relationships for all family members. Ultimately, family conflict and turmoil increases the risk of adjustment problems in the developmental trajectories of children and adolescents.

Fortunately, even within this unhappy process there are strengths of family members and their relationships that serve to attenuate these difficulties. Support from within and outside the nuclear family helps to reduce the adverse impact of economic pressures on both parents and adolescents. Perhaps the most important source of this support comes from family members themselves, an important finding when one considers interventions that might help families successfully negotiate difficult economic transitions. We return to this issue in later discussion. For the moment, we turn to questions regarding the methodological implications and limitations of the present study.

METHODOLOGICAL CONSIDERATIONS

In Chapter 2 we began our discussion by noting Kish's (1987) admonition that any single study represents a compromise between competing research priorities. Typically, scarce resources dictate that no single study can address equally well all of the possible goals that direct social and behavioral research. Kish suggests three major research priorities: internal validity, external validity, and realism in measurement. Because the present research was not an experiment, the major goals were to generate a sample that fairly represented the phenomena of interest (external validity) and measures that most closely approximated the realities experienced by these families.

As discussed throughout Chapter 2, the sample used for these analyses included families representing a wide range of economic well-being. Thus, the economic variation among these families allowed a fair test of the theoretical model; that is, the findings are generalizable at the level of theory. Moreover, their consistency with results from urban research (Voydanoff, 1990) and with research from different historical eras (Elder & Caspi, 1988) increases confidence that these findings do not apply only to contemporary rural families living in central Iowa.

Nevertheless, it remains to be seen whether the findings reported here will actually replicate when the same measurement procedures are used with single-parent, urban, or ethnically diverse families attempting to cope with the economic vicissitudes of modern America. As always, the real test of external validity for the results from a single study involves replication with new samples that represent the theoretical issues of interest. The research team conducting the IYFP is currently pursuing this type of replicative work.

As indicated in Chapter 2, we pursued the present study with a relatively homogeneous sample of two-parent families to assure that a sufficient number of cases would be available for the necessary analyses. That is, subdividing along too many parameters such as family type and child age would quickly lead to too few cases within the various subgroups to pursue a causal modeling analytic strategy.

In addition to this necessary limitation in sample characteristics, the analyses reported here are also limited by the cross-sectional nature of the data. Ultimately, the Family Stress Model will be most adequately tested with longitudinal data that allow stronger inferences regarding causal priorities in relationships among constructs. We are pursuing additional years of data collection with these Iowa families to determine if the present findings will replicate across time. The present results do indicate, however, that the findings do not contradict the postulated family stress processes, a reasonable first step in establishing the existence of hypothesized causal relationships (Mulaik, 1987).

Following Kish (1987), the second major research priority for the present study concerned realism in measurement. We were especially interested in avoiding a too common practice in family research: reliance on a single source of information regarding family process and individual adjustment. Too frequently, earlier research has depended on a single reporter, e.g., a mother, to provide data regarding all aspects of family life. As is now well known, relationships among study variables measured in this fashion are as likely to reflect the individual dispositions and biases of the reporter as they are the daily phenomena of family interactions and individual psychological functioning (Bank et al., 1990; Lorenz et al., 1991).

A real strength and advance in the present research is the use of multiple informants, including trained observers, to assess the phenomena of interest. Throughout, we have greater confidence in the validity of study findings in that they are based on the shared perspective, or common variance, from multiple reporters. In addition, the utilization of a structural equation analytic approach allowed us to compensate for the errors in measurement, both random and systematic, common to social and behavioral science data. That is, the estimates of regression coefficients in the analyses more closely approximate relationships among "true scores" than is possible with more traditional approaches such as ordinary least squares regression (Bollen, 1989).

Thus, although the findings reported here have noteworthy limitations, as is true for the results from any single study, we also believe they significantly advance our understanding of family response to economic stress. Moreover, they suggest new standards for conducting family research with community populations. It is our view that studies based on single informants cannot be relied upon to provide valid estimates of the interrelationships among environmental conditions, family process, and individual well-being. The present study provides one example of how we can move beyond earlier, more limited family research methodologies.

In addition to theoretical and methodological insights, the current study also provided new data on possible strategies for assisting families faced with stressful economic times. We next turn to these practical implications of the research.

HELPING ECONOMICALLY STRESSED FAMILIES

In addition to fostering intellectual enlightenment, theoretical understanding brings with it the possibility of reducing the trauma produced by stressful life events and conditions. As we build and empirically test models of how economic stress influences individual well-being and family relationships, we are also identifying potential points of intervention or prevention that can be used to develop programs designed to mitigate the negative impact of financial difficulties.

In a perfect world, we might imagine an economic system that meets each person's and each family's material needs without interruption. Until that day arrives, it is painfully clear that a significant portion of the American population will, at any given point in time, experience dramatic declines in economic prosperity. For many others economic hardship involves chronic disadvantage with no clear means of resolution (Voydanoff, 1990).

Yet society does very little to provide information or assistance that forewarns individuals of the personal difficulties that economic hardship may exacerbate. Moreover, assistance programs that respond after economic problems already exist are usually not capable of dealing with the sequences of relationships we have demonstrated in the economic stress process. As we have seen in previous chapters, the hardship experience involves a complex scenario of disruptions and difficulties, all of which require attention to prevent lasting problems in family life.

The findings reported here suggest several points of intervention that may help families more successfully cope with or recover from a period of financial stress. Central to any effort, of course, is the alleviation of economic disadvantage. Our model of family stress begins with a set of conditions (income level, job disruptions, income loss, debt-to-asset ratio) that are amenable to intervention. Job skills training, assistance in the location of new employment opportunities, and government assistance programs can all help to improve family income and reduce the continuing loss of material resources. These intervention strategies should also curtail job disruptions that intensify economic pressure. In addition, financial counseling programs can help families restructure their debts and thus improve their situation in terms of debts relative to assets.

All of these steps can be helpful, but all of them take time and involve continuing family stress while the resolution of financial difficulties is pursued. Indeed, the period of adaptation to hardship—and hopefully its reversal—brings with it the potential for emotional and relationship problems that may last well beyond the period of economic hardship (Liker & Elder, 1983). Drawing on our model of family economic stress, for example, the emotional distress intensified by economic pressures may be long lasting and, as we have seen, may also lead to chronic difficulties in family relationships.

Thus, effective intervention for family economic problems must also deal with the adverse impact that financial pressures have on emotional distress and disruptions in family relationships. An important first step in the intervention process should seek to alleviate the feelings of depression and anger fostered by economic strain. Our process model also suggests that marital counseling can be an important dimension in programs designed to assist couples with their financial difficulties. A holistic approach to family financial problems should attempt to provide spouses with effective means for reducing conflicts that may result from the frustrations produced by these negative life conditions. Fortunately, innovative and comprehensive programs that concurrently target psychological dysfunction, acute and chronic family stress, and marital difficulties are available and show promise of success (Beach, Sandeen, & O'Leary, 1990).

Interventions aimed at improving the family's economic situation, reducing parents' emotional distress, and promoting the couple's capacity to deal constructively with marital conflict should decrease the probability that a period of economic turmoil will have long-term negative consequences for individual and family functioning. Especially important, our results show that successful intervention at these earlier points in the family economic stress process should reduce risk for child and adolescent adjustment problems. Consistent with the Family Stress Model, we found that stress-related disruptions in the lives of parents are associated with less competent parenting and with greater hostility toward children.

For that reason, a truly comprehensive intervention for economic stress should also work with parents to help them maintain effective child-rearing practices during difficult times. This approach should reduce the risk for child and adolescent adjustment problems that, over time, will simply add to parental stress. Family stress intervention should also build on a continuing theme that permeates the findings reported here.

For all phases of the economic stress process, from the exacerbation of parent depressed mood to the development of adolescent antisocial behavior, we found that nurturance and support from both within and outside the family reduced the adverse impact of these life conditions. The evidence clearly suggests that programs designed to assist economically stressed families should help family members learn the skills needed to provide and elicit support from others as they attempt to cope with difficult financial events.

As noted earlier, these findings must be replicated with other families in other places and over time to gain our complete confidence. They must also be used to develop and evaluate specific intervention strategies designed to reduce the adverse impact of family stress on individual well-being and family functioning. We are currently engaged in that next step in this program of research at the Center for Family Research in Rural Mental Health at Iowa State University.

However, the consistency of the findings reported here with a family stress theory derived from social epidemiological studies involving multiple urban and rural populations from varying historical eras suggests that the results do provide important information for families of the future. The results from this research can be used in the development of social policies and interventions that can help reduce the oftentimes tragic impact of economic hardship on families. That, of course, is their ultimate value.

Appendix

Brief Observer Rating Definitions

IOWA FAMILY INTERACTION RATING SCALES: ABBREVIATED SCALE DEFINITIONS

I. General Interaction Rating Scales
   A. Individual Characteristic Scales
   1. Physically Attractive (PA): the observer's subjective assessment of the focal's physical appearance (excluding personality).
   2. Humor/Laugh (HU): display of funny, good natured, nonsarcastic, light-hearted behaviors.
   3. Physical Movement (PH): amount of motion or physical activity.
   4. Facial Movement (FM): variety of facial expression and amount of change.
   5. Internalized Negative (IN): emotional distress expressed as dysphoria (unhappiness, sadness) or anxiety (worry, fear).
   6. Externalized Negative (EX): negative emotions expressed in an angry or hostile manner regarding people, events, or things outside the immediate setting.
   7. Positive Mood (PM): feelings of contentment, happiness, and optimism toward self, others, or things in general.
   8. Escalate Negative (EN): building onto one's own negative (hostile) behaviors toward other interactors.
   9. Escalate Positive (EP): building onto one's own positive (warmth/supportive) behaviors toward other interactors.
   10. Intellectual Skills (IS): extent of mental ability displayed during the interaction task; includes knowledge, creativity, and reasoning skills.
   11. Rater Response (RR): the coder's subjective reaction to or emotional feelings, positive or negative, regarding the focal.
   12. Seating Order (SO): the seating position of the focal, relative to the place of the other interactors.

B. Dyadic Interaction Scales

1. Hostility (HS): the extent to which hostile, angry, critical, disapproving, or rejecting behavior is directed toward another interactor's behavior (actions), appearance, or personal characteristics.

2. Verbal Attack (VA): personalized and unqualified disapproval of another interactor's personal characteristics; criticism of a global and enduring nature.

3. Physical Attack (AT): aversive physical contact, including hitting, pinching, grabbing.

4. Angry Coercion (AC): control attempts that include hostile, threatening, or blaming behavior.

5. Guilty Coercion (GC): control attempts that use crying, whining, guilt-inducing, or manipulative behavior.

6. Dominance (DO): demonstrated control or influence (either positive or negative) of other interactors and/or the situation.

7. Lecture/Moralize (LM): behavior that is overwhelming, intrusive, unrelenting, moralizing, and/or does not give others a chance to respond, initiate, or think independently.

8. Interrogation (IT): insistent, systematic questioning designed to solicit specific information or to make a point.

9. Denial (DE): active rejection of the existence of or personal responsibility for a past or present situation for which one actually is responsible or shares responsibility.

10. Warmth/Support (WM): expressions of interest, care, concern, support, encouragement, or responsiveness toward another interactor.

11. Endearment (ED): personalized and unqualified approval of another interactor's personal characteristics; approval or affection of a global and enduring nature.

12. Physical Affection (AF): affectionate physical contact, including hugs, and pats.

13. Assertiveness (AR): the speaker's ability to express him/herself through clear, appropriate neutral and/or positive avenues using an open, straightforward, self-confident, nonthreatening and nondefensive style.

14. Listener Responsiveness (LR): nonverbal and verbal responsiveness to the verbalizations of the other interactor that indicate attentiveness by the listener.

15. Communication (CO): the speaker's ability to neutrally or positively express his/her own point of view, needs, wants, etc., in a clear, appropriate, and reasonable manner, and

        to demonstrate consideration of the other interactor's point of view; the good communicator promotes rather than inhibits exchange of information.

16. Prosocial (PR): demonstrations of helpfulness, sensitivity toward others, cooperation, sympathy, and respectfulness toward others in an age-appropriate manner; reflects a level of maturity appropriate to one's age.

17. Antisocial (AN): demonstrations of self-centered, egocentric, acting out, and out-of-control behavior that show defiance, active resistance, insensitivity toward others, and lack of constraint; immaturity, age-inappropriate behaviors.

18. Verbally Involved (VI): amount of verbalization; how active or verbally engaged focal is with another interactor.

19. Body Toward (BT): the extent to which the front of the focal's body is oriented toward the other interactor.

20. Body Away (BA): the extent to which the front of the focal's body is oriented away from the other interactor.

C. Dyadic Relationship Scales

1. Transactional Conflict (TC): extent to which the dyad is involved in initiating and/or reciprocating hostility, coercion, or verbal/physical attacks.

2. Transactional Positive (TP): extent to which the dyad is involved in initiating and/or reciprocating warmth, endearments, or physical affection.

3. Silence/Pause (SP): the presence in the dyad of tense or uncomfortable gaps in the flow of conversation.

4. Relationship Quality (RQ): the observer's evaluation of the quality of the dyad's relationship from *poor* (1) to *good* (5).

D. Group Interaction Scales

1. Group Enjoyment (GE): evidence of enjoyment, pleasure, fun, and/or satisfaction evident in the family's interaction.

2. Group Disorganization (GD): evidence of confused, chaotic, and/or fragmented family interaction; the interaction lacks unity and cohesiveness.

3. Environmental Organization (EO): the coder's subjective assessment of the orderliness of the interaction setting, from *disorganized* to *organized.*

4. Environmental Attractiveness (EA): the coder's subjective assessment of the aesthetic quality of the interaction setting, from *unattractive* to *attractive.*

5. Picture Quality (PQ): the coder's subjective assessment of the clarity, color, focus, etc., of the video image.

II. PARENTING AND PROBLEM-SOLVING SCALES
     A.   Parenting Scales[1]
          1. Neglecting/Distancing (ND): the degree to which the parent minimizes the amount of time, contact, or effort he/she expends on the child; ignoring or psychological/physical distancing in the interaction situation.
          2. Indulgent/Permissive (IP): the degree to which the parent is excessively lenient and tolerant of the child's misbehavior or has given up attempts to control the child; a *laissez faire* or a *defeated* attitude by the parent regarding the child's behavior.
          3. Quality Time (QT): the extent of the parent's regular involvement with the child in settings that promote opportunities for conversation, companionship, and mutual enjoyment.
          4. Parental Influence (PI): the parent's direct and indirect attempts to influence, regulate, or control the child's life according to commonly accepted, age-appropriate standards.
          5. Child Monitoring (CM): the extent of the parent's specific knowledge and information concerning the child's life and daily activities. Indicates the extent to which the parent accurately tracks the behaviors, activities, and social involvements of the child.
          6. Consistent Discipline (CD): the degree of consistency and persistence with which the parent maintains and adheres to rules and standards of conduct for the child's behavior.
          7. Inconsistent Discipline (ID): the degree of parental inconsistency and lack of follow-through in maintaining and adhering to rules and standards of conduct for the child's behavior.
          8. Harsh Discipline (HD): the extent to which the parent responds to the child's misbehavior or violation of specific parental standards through the use of punitive or severe disciplinary techniques, either verbal (e.g., yelling and screaming) or physical (e.g., hitting or punching).
          9. Positive Reinforcement (PO): the extent to which the parent responds positively to the child's appropriate behavior or behavior that meets specific parental standards.
         10. Encourages Independence (EI): parental demonstrations of trust in and encouragement of the child's independence in thought and actions.

11. Inductive Reasoning (IR): the extent to which the parent encourages the child, in a neutral or positive manner, to understand possible consequences of the child's behavior, seeks voluntary compliance, avoids the use of power assertion, and uses reasoning to encourage the child to consider the feelings of others.

12. Easily Coerced (EC): the extent to which the parent is overwhelmed or intimidated by the child; the child's demonstrated ability to manipulate or control the parent through angry or guilty coercion.

B. Individual Problem-Solving Scales

1. Solution Quantity (SN): the number of specific proposals/ideas suggested that present an action or change in behavior as a means for reaching a goal or solving a problem.

2. Solution Quality (SQ): the degree to which proposed solutions are reasonable, realistic, potentially beneficial, specific, feasible, contingent, nonexploitive, seriously offered, or achievable.

3. Effective Process (EF): behavior that actively assists the general problem-solving process.

4. Disruptive Process (DS): behavior that actively hinders or obstructs the problem-solving process.

5. Negotiation/Compromise (NC): willingness to settle differences, or to help others settle differences, by arbitration or consent reached by mutual concessions.

C. Family Problem-Solving Scales

1. Family Enjoyment (FE): the degree of pleasure, fun, and/or satisfaction the whole family displays during the problem-solving process.

2. Agreement on Problem Description (AP): the extent to which the family reached mutual agreement/consensus on the description of the problem to be scored during the problem-solving interaction task.

3. Agreement on Solution (AS): the extent to which the family resolved and/or reached agreement on a solution to a problem.

4. Implementation Commitment (IC): the extent of the family's commitment to a plan to accomplish or carry out an agreed-upon solution.

5. Problem Difficulty (PD): the difficulty (magnitude, persistence and/or intensity) of the problem the family attempted to solve during the problem-solving task.

NOTE

1. The Parenting Scales are the only scales that allow inferences outside the interaction task. For example, type of discipline is coded from parental behavior during the task as well as from statements by family members about what kind of discipline normally occurs in the home.

Bibliography

Achenbach, T., McConaughy, S., & Howell, C. (1987). Child/adolescent behavioral and emotional problems: Implications of cross-informant correlations for situational specificity. *Psychological Bulletin, 101,* 213–232.

Alwin, D., & Hauser, R. (1975). The decomposition of effects in path analysis. *American Sociological Review, 40,* 37–47.

Anderson, J., & Gerbing, D. (1988). Structural equation modeling in practice: A review and recommended two-step approach. *Psychological Bulletin, 103,* 411–423.

Anderson, J., & Gerbing, D. (1992). Assumptions and comparative strengths of the two-step approach: Comments on Fornell and Yi. *Sociological Methods and Research, 20,* 321–333.

Aneshensel, C. S., Rutter, C. M., & Lachenbruch, P. A. (1991). Social structure, stress, and mental health: Competing conceptual and analytic models. *American Sociological Review, 56,* 166–178.

Angell, R. C. (1965). *The family encounters the depression.* Gloucester, MA: Peter Smith.

Armstrong, P. S., & Schulman, M. D. (1990). Financial strain and depression among farm operators: The role of perceived economic hardship and personal control. *Rural Sociology, 55,* 475–493.

Atkinson, T., Liem, R., & Liem, J. (1986). The social costs of unemployment: Implications for social support. *Journal of Health and Social Behavior, 27,* 317–331.

Bakeman, R., & Gottman, J. (1986). *Observing interaction: An introduction to sequential analysis.* Cambridge, England: Cambridge University Press.

Bakke, E. Wright. (1940). *Citizens without work: A study of the effects of unemployment upon the worker's social relations and practices.* New Haven, CT: Yale University Press for the Institute of Human Relations; London: H. Milford, Oxford University Press.

Bank, L., Dishion, T., Skinner, M., & Patterson, G. R. (1990). Method variance in structural equation modeling: Living with "glop." In G. R. Patterson (Ed.), *Depression and aggression in family interaction* (pp. 247–279). Hillsdale, NJ: Erlbaum.

Bank, L., & Patterson, G. (1991). *The use of structural equation modeling in combining data from different types of assessment.* Unpublished manuscript, Oregon Social Learning Center, Eugene.

Bank, S. P., & Kahn, M. D. (1982). *The sibling bond.* N.Y.: Basic Books.

Barlett, P. F. (1993). *American dreams, real realities: Family farms in crisis.* Chapel Hill: University of North Carolina Press.

Baron, R., & Kenny, D. (1986). The moderator-mediator variable distinction in social psychological research: Conceptual, strategic, and statistical considerations. *Journal of Personality and Social Psychology, 51,* 1173–1182.

Baucom, D. H., Sayers, S., & Duhe, A. (1989). Attributional style and attributional patterns among married couples. *Journal of Personality and Social Psychology, 56,* 596–607.

Beach, S. R. H., Sandeen, E. E., & O'Leary, K. D. (1990). *Depression in marriage.* New York: Guilford.

Beardslee, W., Bemporad, J., Keller, M., & Klerman, G. (1983). Children of parents with major affective disorder: A review. *American Journal of Psychiatry, 140,* 825–832.

Bedford, V. H., Gold, D. T. (Eds.). (1989). Siblings in later life: A neglected family relationship [special issue]. *American Behavioral Scientist, 33(1).*

Belle, D., & Longfellow, C. (1984). *Turning to others: Children's use of confidants.* Paper presented at the annual meeting of the American Psychological Association, Toronto.

Belsky, J. (1990). Parental and nonparental child care and children's socioemotional development: A decade in review. *Journal of Marriage and the Family, 52,* 885–903.

Belsky, J., Gilstrap, B., & Rovine, M. (1984). The Pennsylvania Infant and Family Development Project I: Stability and change in mother-infant and father-infant interaction in a family setting at one, three and nine months. *Child Development, 55,* 692–705.

Belsky, J., & Vondra, J. (1989). Lessons from child abuse: The determinants of parenting. In D. Cicchetti, V. Carlson (Eds.), *Child maltreatment: Theory and research on the causes and consequences of child abuse and neglect* (pp. 153–202). New York: Cambridge University Press.

Belyea, M. J., & Lobao, L. M. (1990). Psychosocial consequences of agricultural transformation: The farm crisis and depression. *Rural Sociology, 55,* 58–75.

Bender, L., Green, B., & Campbell, R. (1971). *The process of rural poverty ghettoization: Population and poverty growth in rural regions.* Paper presented to the American Association for the Advancement of Science. Philadelphia, PA.

Bender, L., Green, B., Hady, T., Kuehn, J., Nelson, M., Perkinson, L., & Ross, P. (1985). *The diverse social and economic structure of nonmetropolitan America* (Rural Development Research Report Number 49). Washington, DC: Economic Research Service, U.S. Department of Agriculture.

Bentler, P. M. (1989). *EQS: Structural Equations Program Manual.* Los Angeles: BMDP Statistical Software.

Bentler, P. M. (1990). Comparative fit indexes in structural models. *Psychological Bulletin, 107,* 238–246.

Bentler, P. M., & Bonett, D. G. (1980). Significance tests and goodness-of-fit in the analysis of covariance structures. *Psychological Bulletin, 88,* 588–606.

Berado, F. M. (1980). Decade preview: Some trends and directions for family research and theory in the 1980s. *Journal of Marriage and the Family, 42,* 723–728.

Berado, F. M. (1990). Trends and directions in family research in the 1980s. *Journal of Marriage and the Family, 52,* 809–817.

Berk, R. A. (1979). Generalizability of behavioral observations: A clarification of interobserver agreement and interobserver reliability. *American Journal of Mental Deficiencies, 8,* 460–472.

Berkowitz, L. (1989). Frustration-aggression hypothesis: Examination and reformulation. *Psychological Bulletin, 106,* 59–73.

Biemer, P. P., Groves, R. M., Lyberg, L. E., Mathiowetz, N. A., & Sudman, S. (Eds.). (1991). *Measurement errors in surveys.* New York: Wiley.

Billings, A., & Moos, R. (1983). Comparisons of children of depressed and non-depressed parents: A social-environmental perspective. *Journal of Abnormal Child Psychology, 11,* 463–486.

Blalock, H. M., Jr. (1968). The measurement problem: A gap between the languages of theory and research. In H. M. Blalock, Jr., & A. B. Blalock (Eds.), *Methodology in social research* (pp. 5–27). New York: McGraw-Hill.

Block, J., & Gjerde, P. (1990). Depressive symptoms in late adolescence: A longitudinal perspective on personality antecedents. In J. Rolf, A. S. Masten, D. Cicchetti, K. H. Nuechterlein, & S. Weintraub (Eds.), *Risk and protective factors in the development of psychopathology* (pp. 334–360). New York: Cambridge University Press.

Blundall, J. (1990). *Report to the National Rural Mental Health Hearing.* Minnesota Hearings. April 12. Marshall, MN.

Bollen, K. A. (1989). *Structural equations with latent variables.* New York: Wiley.

Bollen, K. A. (1990). Overall fit in covariance structure models: Two types of sample size effects. *Psychological Bulletin, 107,* 256–259.

Bowerman, C., & Dobash, R. (1974). Structural variations in inter-sibling affect. *Journal of Marriage and the Family, 36,* 48–54.

Bowlby, J. (1973). *Attachment and loss.* Vol. 2. Separation: Anxiety and anger. New York: Basic Books.

Bowlby, J. (1980). *Attachment and loss.* Vol 3. Loss: Sadness and depression. New York: Basic Books.

Bowlby, J. (1982). *Attachment and loss.* Vol 1. Attachment, (2nd ed.). New York: Basic Books.

Brody, G. H., Pellegrini, A. D., & Seigel, I. E. (1986). Marital quality and mother-child and father-child interactions with school-aged children. *Devlopmental Psychology, 22,* 291–296.

Brody, G. H., Stoneman, Z., McCoy, J. K., & Forehand, R. (1992). Contemporaneous and longitudinal associations of sibling conflict with family relationship assessments and family discussions about sibling problems. *Child Development, 63,* 391–400.

Brown, B. (1989). *Lone tree: A true story of murder in America's heartland.* New York: Crown.

Bryant, B. K. (1982). Sibling relationships in middle childhood. In M. E. Lamb, B. Sutton-Smith (Eds.), *Sibling relationships: their nature and significance across the lifespan* (pp. 87–121). Hillsdale, NJ: Erlbaum.

Bryant, B. K. (1985). The neighborhood walk: Sources of support in middle childhood. *Monographs of the Society for Research in Child Development, 50(3).*

Bryant, B. K., Crockenberg, S. (1980). Correlates and dimensions of prosocial behavior: A study of female siblings with their mothers. *Child Development, 51*, 529–544.

Bultena, G., Lasley, P., Geller, J. (1986). The farm crisis: Patterns and impacts of financial distress among Iowa farm families. *Rural Sociology, 51*, 436–448.

Burenstam Linder, S. (1970). *The harried leisure class.* New York: Columbia University Press.

Buss, A., & Durkee, A. *(1957). An inventory for assessing different kinds of hostility. Journal of Consulting Psychology, 21*, 343–349.

Cairns, R. B., & Green, J. A. (1979). Appendix A. How to assess personality and social patterns: Observations or ratings. In R. B. Carins (Ed.), *The Analysis of Social Interactions: Methods, Issues and Illustrations* (pp. 209–226). Hillsdale, NJ: Erlbaum.

Campbell, A., Converse, P. E., & Rogers, W. (1976). *The quality of American life: Perceptions, evaluations, and satisfactions.* New York: Russell Sage Foundation.

Campbell, D. T., & Fiske, D. W. (1959). Convergent and discriminant validation by the multitrait-multimethod matrix. *Psychological Bulletin, 56*, 81–105.

Capaldi, D. M., & Patterson, G. R. (1989). *Psychometric properties of fourteen latent constructs from the Oregon Youth Study.* New York: Springer-Verlag.

Caplan, G. (1974). *Support systems and community mental health: Lectures on concept development.* New York: Behavioral Publications.

Caspi, A., & Elder, G. H., Jr. (1988). Emergent family patterns: The intergenerational construction of problem behavior and relationships. In R. A. Hinde, J. Stevenson-Hinde (Eds.), *Relationships within families: Mutual influences* (pp. 218–240). Oxford: Clarendon; New York: Oxford University Press.

Cassel, J. (1974). Behavioral factors associated with the etiology of physical disease: An epidemiological perspective of psychosocial factors in disease etiology. *American Journal of Public Health, 64*, 1040–1043.

Cattell, R. B. (1957). *Personality and motivation, structure and measurement.* Yonkers-on-Hudson, NY: World Book.

Cavan, R. S., & Ranck, K. H. (1938). *The family and the depression: A study of 100 Chicago families.* Chicago: University of Chicago Press.

Christensen, A., Margolin, G. (1988). Conflict and alliance in distressed and non-distressed families. In R. A. Hinde, J. Stevenson-Hinde (Eds.), *Relationships within families: Mutual influences* (pp. 263–282). Oxford: Clarendon; New York: Oxford University Press.

Cicchetti, D., & Rizley, R. (1981). Developmental perspectives on the etiology, intergenerational transmission and sequelae of child maltreatment. *New Directions for Child Development, 11*, 31–55.

Cicchetti, D., & Toth, S. L. (Eds.) (1991). *Internalizing and externalizing expressions of dysfunction.* Rochester Symposium on Developmental Psychopathology (Vol. 2). Hillsdale, NJ: Erlbaum.

Cicirelli, V. G. (1982). Sibling influences throughout the lifespan. In M. E. Lamb, B. Sutton-Smith (Eds.), *Sibling relationships: Their nature and significance across the lifespan* (pp. 267–284). Hillsdale, NJ: Erlbaum.

Clarke-Stewart, K. A. (1980). The father's contribution to children's cognitive and social development in early childhood. In Frank Pedersen (Ed.), *The father-infant relationship: Observational studies in the family setting* (pp. 111–146). New York: Praeger.

Cobb, S. (1976). Social support as a moderator of life stress. *Psychosomatic Medicine, 38,* 300–314.

Cochrane, W. W. (1979). *The development of American agriculture: A historical analysis.* Minneapolis: University of Minnesota Press.

Cohen, S., & Hoberman, H. (1983). Positive events and social supports as buffers of life change stress. *Journal of Applied Social Psychology, 13,* 99–125.

Cohen, S., Mermelstein, R., Kamarck, T., & Hoberman, H. (1985). Measuring the functional components of social supports. In I. G. Sarason, B. R. Sarason (Eds.), *Social support: Theory, research and applications* (pp. 73–94). Dordrecht, Netherlands: Martinus Nijhoff.

Cohen, S., & Syme, S. L. (1985). *Social support and health.* Orlando, FL: Academic.

Cohen, S., & Wills, T. A. (1985). Stress, social support, and the buffering hypothesis. *Psychological Bulletin, 98,* 310–357.

Conger, R. D., Burgess, R. L., & Barrett, C. (1979). Child abuse related to life change and perceptions of illness: Some preliminary findings. *Family Coordinator, 28,* 73–78.

Conger, R. D., Conger, K. J., Elder, G. H., Jr., Lorenz, F. O., Simons, R. L., & Whitbeck, L. B. (1992). A family process model of economic hardship and adjustment of early adolescent boys. *Child Development, 63,* 526–541.

Conger, R. D., Conger, K. J., Elder, G. H., Jr., Lorenz, F. O., Simons, R. L., & Whitbeck, L. B. (1993). Family economic stress and adjustment of early adolescent girls. *Development Psychology, 29,* 206–219.

Conger, R. D., Elder, G. H., Jr., Lorenz, F. O., Conger, K. J., Simons, R. L., Whitbeck, L. B., Huck, S., & Melby, J. N. (1990). Linking economic hardship to marital quality and instability. *Journal of Marriage and the Family, 52,* 643–656.

Conger, R. D., Lorenz, F. O., Elder, G. H., Jr., Melby, J. N., Simons, R. L., & Conger, K. J. (1991). A process model of family economic pressure and early adolescent alcohol use. *Journal of Early Adolescence, 11,* 430–449.

Conger, R. D., Lorenz, F. O., Elder, G. H., Jr., Simons, R. L., & Ge, X. J. (1993). Husband and wife differences in response to undesirable life events. *Journal of Health and Social Behavior, 34,* 71–88.

Conger, R. D., McCarthy, J., Yang, R., Lahey, B., & Kropp, J. (1984). Perception of child, child-rearing values, and emotional distress as mediating links between environmental stressors and observed maternal behavior. *Child Development, 55,* 2234–2247.

Coopersmith, S. (1967). *The antecedents of self-esteem.* San Francisco: W. H. Freeman.

Copeland, A. P., & White, K. M. (1991). *Studying families.* Newbury Park, CA: Sage.

Costa, P. T., & McCrae, R. R. (1985). *The NEO Personality Inventory Manual.* Odessa, FL: Psychological Assessment Resources, Inc.

Cox, M., Owen, M. R., Lewis, J. M., & Henderson, V. K. (1989). Marriage, adult adjustment, and early parenting. *Child Development, 60,* 1015–1024.

Coyne, J. C., & Downey, G. (1991). Social factors and psychopathology: Stress, social support and coping processes. *Annual Review of Psychology, 42,* 401–425.

Cutrona, C. E. (1989). Ratings of social support by adolescents and adult informants: Degree of correspondence and prediction of depressive symptoms. *Journal of Personality and Social Psychology, 57,* 723–730.

Cutrona, C. E. (1990). Stress and social support-in search of optimal matching. *Journal of Social and Clinical Psychology, 9,* 3–14.

Cutrona, C. E., & Russell, D. W. (1990). Type of social support and specific stress: Toward a theory of optimal matching. In B. R. Sarason, I. G. Sarason, & G. R. Pierce (Eds.), *Social support: An interactional view* (pp. 319–366). New York: Wiley.

Cutrona, C. E., Suhr, J. A., & MacFarlane, R. (1990). Interpersonal transactions and the psychological sense of support. In S. Duck with R. C. Silver (Eds.), *Personal relationships and social support* (pp. 30–45). London: Sage.

Daniels, D., Dunn, J., Furstenberg, F. F., Jr., & Plomin, R. (1985). Environmental differences within the family and adjustment differences within pairs of adolescent siblings. *Child Development, 56,* 764–774.

Davidson, O. G. (1990). *Broken heartland: The rise of America's rural ghetto.* New York: Free Press.

Derogatis, L. R. (1983). *SCL-90-R: Administration, scoring and procedures manual II* (2nd ed.). Towson, MD: Clinical Psychometric Research.

Dooley, D., & Catalano, R. (Eds.). (1988). Psychological effects of unemployment. *Journal of Social Issues, 44(4),* 1–191.

Dowdney, L., Mrazek, D., Quinton, D., & Rutter, M. (1984). Observation of parent-child interaction with two- to three-year-olds. *Journal of Child Psychology and Psychiatry, 25,* 379–407.

Downey, G., & Coyne, J. C. (1990). Children of depressed parents: An integrative review. *Psychological Bulletin, 108,* 50–76.

Dubow, E. F., & Tisak, J. (1989). The relationship between stressful life events and adjustment in elementary school children: The role of social support and social problem-solving skills. *Child Development, 60,* 1412–1423.

Duncan, G. J. (1984). *Years of poverty, years of plenty: The changing economic fortunes of American workers and families.* Ann Arbor: Survey Research Center, Institute for Social Research, University of Michigan.

Duncan, O. D. (1975). *Introduction to structural equation models.* New York: Academic.

Dunn, J. (1983). Sibling relationships in early childhood. *Child Development, 54,* 787–811.

Dunn, J., & Kendrick, C. (1979). Interaction between young siblings in the context of family relationships. In M. Lewis, & L. A. Rosenblum (Eds.), *The child and its family* (pp. 143–168). New York: Plenum.

Dunn, J., & Kendrick, C. (1982). *Siblings: Love, envy, and understanding.* Cambridge, MA: Harvard University Press.

Dunn, J., & Munn, P. (1986). Siblings and the development of prosocial behavior. *International Journal of Behavioral Development, 9,* 265–284.

Easterbrooks, M. A., & Emde, R. N. (1988). Marital and parent-child relationships: The role of affect in the family system. In R. A. Hinde, & J. Stevenson-Hinde (Eds.), *Relationships within families: Mutual influences* (pp. 83–103). Oxford: Clarendon; New York: Oxford University Press.

Ebata, A. T., Petersen, A. C., & Conger, J. J. (1990). The development of psychopathology in adolescence. In J. Rolf, A. S. Masten, D. Cicchetti, K. H. Nuechterlein, & S. Weintraub (Eds.), *Risk and protective factors in the development of psychopathology* (pp. 308–333). New York: Cambridge University Press.

Eckenrode, J., & Wethington, E. (1990). The process and outcome of mobilizing social support. In S. Duck with R. C. Silver (Eds.), *Personal relationships and social support* (pp. 83–103). London: Sage.

Ehrensaft, D. (1983). When women and men mother. In J. Trebilcot (Eds.), *Mothering: Essays in feminist theory* (pp. 41–61). Totowa, NJ: Rowan & Allanfeld.

Elder, G. H., Jr. (1974). *Children of the Great Depression: Social change in life experience.* Chicago: University of Chicago Press.

Elder, G. H., Jr. (1980). Adolescence in historical perspective. In J. Adelson (Ed.), *Handbook of adolescent psychology* (pp. 3–46). New York: Wiley.

Elder, G. H., Jr. (1985). *Life course dynamics: Transitions and trajectories.* Ithaca, NY: Cornell University Press.

Elder, G. H., Jr. (1992). Life course. In E. Borgatta, & M. Borgatta (Eds.), *Encyclopedia of Sociology* (pp. 1120–1130). New York: MacMillan.

Elder, G. H., Jr. (1994). Time, human agency, and social change; Perspectives in the life course. *Social Psychology Quarterly.*

Elder, G. H., Jr., & Caspi, A. (1988). Economic stress in lives: Developmental perspectives. *Journal of Social Issues, 44(4),* 25–45.

Elder, G. H. Jr., Caspi, A., & Downey, G. (1986). Problem behavior and family relationships: Life course and intergenerational themes. In A. B. Sorensen, F. Weinert, & L. R. Sherrod (Eds.), *Human development and the life course: Multidisciplinary perspectives* (pp. 293–340). Hillsdale, NJ: Erlbaum.

Elder, G. H., Jr., Conger, R. D., Foster, E. M., & Ardelt, M. (1992). Families under economic pressure. *Journal of Family Issues, 13,* 5–37.

Elder, G. H., Jr., Liker, J. K., & Cross, C. E. (1984). Parent-child behavior in the Great Depression: Life course and intergenerational influences. In P. B. Baltes, & O. G. Brim (Eds.), *Life span development and behavior* (Vol. 6, pp. 109–158). New York: Academic.

Elder, G. H., Jr., Robertson, E. B., & Conger, R. D. (1993). Fathers and sons in rural America: Occupational choice and intergenerational ties across the life course. In Tamara K. Hareven (Ed.), *Aging and intergenerational relations.* Berlin: Aldine de Gruyter.

Elder, G. H., Jr., Van Nguyen, T., & Caspi, A. (1985). Linking family hardship to children's lives. *Child Development, 56,* 361–375.

Elliott, D. S., Huizinga, D., & Ageton, S. (1985). *Explaining delinquency and drug use.* Beverly Hills, CA: Sage.

Elliott, D. S., Huizinga, D., & Menard, S. (1989). *Multiple problem youth: Delinquency, substance use, and mental health problems.* New York: Springer-Verlag.

Engfer, A. (1988). The interrelatedness of marriage and the mother-child relationship. In R. A. Hinde, & J. Stevenson-Hinde (Eds.), *Relationships within families: Mutual influences* (pp. 104–118). Oxford: Clarendon; New York: Oxford University Press.

Ensel, W. M. (1986). Sex differences in the epidemiology of depression and physical illness: A sociological perspective. In A. Dean (Ed.), *Depression in a multidisciplinary perspective* (pp. 83–102). New York: Brunner-Mazell.

Estrada, P., Arsenio, W. R., Hess, R. D., & Holloway, S. D. (1987). Affective quality of the mother-child relationship: Longitudinal consequences for children's school-relevant cognitive functioning. *Developmental Psychology, 23,* 210–215.

Fauber, R., Forehand, R., Thomas, A. M., & Wierson, M. (1990). A mediational model of the impact of marital conflict on adolescent adjustment in intact and divorced families: The role of disrupted parenting. *Child Development, 61,* 1112–1123.

Feldman, S. S., Nash, S. C., & Aschenbrenner, B. (1983). Antecedents of fathering. *Child Development, 54,* 1628–1636.

Felson, R. B., & Russo, N. (1988). Parental punishment and sibling aggression. *Social Psychology Quarterly, 51,* 11–18.

Fincham, F. D., & Bradbury, T. N. (1987). The assessment of marital quality: A reevaluation. *Journal of Marriage and the Family, 49,* 797–809.

Fincham, F. D., & Bradbury, T. N. (1990). Social support in marriage: The role of social cognition. *Journal of Social and Clinical Psychology, 9,* 31–42.

Fink, D. (1986). *Open Country, Iowa: Rural women traditions and change.* Albany: State University of New York Press.

Finney, J. W., Mitchell, R. E., Cronkite, R., & Moos, R. H. (1984). Methodological issues in estimating main and interactive effects: Examples from the coping/social support and stress field. *Journal of Health and Social Behavior, 25,* 85–98.

Fitchen, J.. (1981). *Poverty in Rural America: A case study.* Boulder, CO: Westview.

Fornell, C., & Yi, Y. (1992). Assumptions of the two-step approach to latent variable modeling. *Sociological Methods and Research, 20,* 291–320.

Fox, J. (1980). Effect analysis in structural equation models: Extensions and simplified methods of computation. *Sociological Methods and Research, 9,* 3–28.

Fox, J. (1985). Effect analysis in structural equation models II: Calculation of specific indirect effects. *Sociological Methods and Research, 14,* 81–95.

Fried, M. (1963). Grieving for a lost home. In L. Duhl (Ed.), *The urban condition: People and policy in the metropolis* (pp. 151–171). New York: Basic Books.

Friedberger, M. (1988). *Farm families and change in 20th century America.* Lexington: University Press of Kentucky.

Friedberger, M. (1989). *Shake-out: Iowa farm families in the 1980s.* Lexington: University Press of Kentucky.

Furman, W., Jones, L., Buhrmester, D., & Adler, T. (1989). Children's, parents', and observer' perspectives on sibling relationships. In P. G. Sukow (Ed.), *Sibling interaction across cultures: Theoretical and methodological issues.* New York: Springer-Verlag.

Galambos, N., & Silbereisen, R. (1987). Income change, parental life outlook, and adolescent expectation for job success. *Journal of Marriage and the Family, 49,* 141–149.

Garmezy, N. (1983). Stressors of childhood: In N. Garmezy, & M. Rutter (Eds.), *Stress, coping and development in children* (pp. 43–84). New York: McGraw-Hill.

Garmezy, N., & Rutter, M. (1985). Acute reactions to stress. In M. Rutter and L. Hersov (Eds.), *Child and adolescent psychiatry: Modern approaches* (2nd ed.) (pp. 152–176). Oxford, England: Blackwell Scientific.

Gecas, V., & Schwalbe, M. L. (1986). Parental behavior and adolescent self-esteem. *Journal of Marriage and the Family, 48,* 37–46.

George, L. K. (1993). Sociological perspectives on life transitions. *Annual Review of Sociology, 19,* 353–373.

Glenn, N. D. (1990). Quantitative research on marital quality in the 1980s: A critical review. *Journal of Marriage and the Family, 52,* 818–831.

Glenn, N. D., & Weaver, C. N. (1981). The contribution of marital happiness to global happiness. *Social Forces, 43,* 161–168.

Goodnow, J. J. (1988). Children's household work: Its nature and functions. *Psychological Bulletin, 103,* 5–26.

Gore, S., & Colten, M. E. (1991). Adolescent stress, social relationships, and mental health. In M. E. Colten, & S. Gore (Eds.), *Adolescent stress: Causes and consequences.* Hawthorne, NY: Aldine de Gruyter.

Gotlib, I. H., & McCabe, S. B. (1990). Marriage and psychopathology. In F. E. Fincham, & T. N. Bradbury (Eds.) *The psychology of marriage: Basic issues, & applications* (pp. 226–257). New York: Guilford.

Gottlieb, B. H. (1985). Social support and the study of personal relationships. *Journal of Social and Personal Relationships, 2,* 351–375.

Gottman, J. M. (1979). *Marital interaction: Experimental investigations.* New York: Academic.

Graham, P. (1979). Epidemiological studies. In H. C. Quay, & J. S. Werry (Eds.), *Psychopathological disorders of childhood* (2nd ed., pp. 185–209). New York: Wiley.

Greenberger, E., & Steinberg, L. D. (1986). *When teenagers work: The psychological and social costs of adolescent employment.* New York: Basic Books.

Haines, M. R. (1979). Industrial work and the family life cycle, 1889–1890. *Research in Economic History: A Research Annual, 4,* 289–356.

Hall, R. H. (1986). *Dimensions of work.* Beverly Hills, CA: Sage.

Hareven, T. K. (1982). *Family time and industrial time: The relationship between the family and work in a New England industrial community.* New York: Cambridge University Press.

Harl, N. (1987). The financial crisis in the United States. In G. Comstock (Ed.), *Is there a moral obligation to save the family farm?* (pp. 112–128). Ames: Iowa State University Press.

Harl, N. (1990). *The farm debt crisis of the 1980s.* Ames: Iowa State University Press.

Harris, L. (1975). *The myth and reality of aging in America.* Washington, DC: National Council on Aging.

Harter, S. (1983). Developmental perspectives on the self-esteem. In P. M. Mussen (Ed.), *Handbook of Child Psychology.* Vol. 4, E. M. Hetherington (Ed.), *Socialization, personality, and social development* (pp. 275–385). New York: Wiley.

Heffernan, W. D., & Heffernan, J. B. (1986). Impact of the farm crisis on rural families and communities. *Rural Sociologist, 6,* 160–170.

Hetherington, E. M., & Clingempeel, G. (1986). *Global coding manual.* Charlottesville: Department of Psychology, University of Virginia.

Hetherington, M. (1988). Parents, children, and siblings: Six years after divorce. In R. A. Hinde, & J. Stevenson-Hinde (Eds.), *Relationships within families:*

Mutual influences (pp. 311–331). Oxford: Clarendon; New York: Oxford University Press.

Hinde, R. A., & Stevenson-Hinde, J. (Eds.) (1988). *Relationships within families: Mutual influences.* Oxford: Clarendon; New York: Oxford University Press.

Hobfoll, S. E., & Stokes, J. P. (1988). The process and mechanics of social support. In S. W. Duck, D. F. Hay, S. E. Hobfoll, W. A. Ickes, & B. M. Montgomery (Eds.), *Handbook of personal relationships* (pp. 497–517). New York: Wiley.

Hoelter, Jon W. (1983). The analysis of covariance structures: Goodness-of-fit indices. *Sociological Methods and Research, 11,* 325–344.

Hops, H., Biglan, A., Arthur, J., Warner, P., Holomb, C., Sheman, L., Oostennick, N., Osteen, V., & Tolman, A. (1988). *Living in Family Environments (LIFE) Coding System.* Unpublished manuscript, Oregon Research Institute, Eugene.

Horwitz, A. V. (1984). The economy and social pathology. *Annual Review of Sociology, 10,* 95–119.

House, J. S., Umberson, D., & Landis, K. R. (1988). Structures and processes of social support. *Annual Review of Sociology, 14,* 293–318.

Joreskog, K. G., & Sorbom, D. (1989). *LISREL 7: User's Reference Guide* (1st ed.). Mooresville, IN: Scientific Software.

Judge, G. G., Griffiths, W. E., Hill, R. C., & Lee, T. (1988). *The theory and practice of econometrics (2nd ed.).* New York: Wiley.

Kaduschin, A., & Martin, J. A. (1981). *Child abuse: An interactional event.* New York: Columbia University Press.

Kahn, M. D., & Lewis, K. G. (1988). *Siblings in therapy: Life span and clinical issues.* New York: Norton.

Katz, M. B., & Davey, I. F. (1978). Youth and early industrialization in a Canadian city. *American Journal of Sociology, 84,* s81–s119.

Kellam, S. G. (1990). Developmental epidemiological framework for family research on depression and aggression. In G. E. Patterson (Ed.), *Depression and aggression in family interaction* (pp. 11–48). Hillsdale, NJ: Erlbaum.

Kessler, R. C., Price, R. H., & Wortman, C. B. (1985). Social factors in psychopathology: Stress, social support and coping processes. *Annual Review of Psychology, 36,* 531–572.

Kessler, R. C., Turner, J. B., & House, J. S. (1988). Effects of unemployment on health in a community survey: Main, modifying and mediating effects. *Journal of Social Issues, 44,* 69–85.

Kish, L. (1987). *Statistical design for research.* New York: Wiley.

Kohn, H. (1988). *The last farmer: An American memoir.* New York: Harper and Row.

Komarovsky, M. (1940). *The unemployed man and his family.* New York: Octagon Books.

Lakely, B., & Cassidy, P. B. (1990). Cognitive processes in perceived social support. *Journal of Personality and Social Psychology, 59,* 337–343.

Lamb, M. E. (1977). *The role of the father in child development.* New York: Wiley.

Lamb, M. E. (1978). Interactions between eighteen-month-olds and their preschool-aged siblings. *Child Development, 49,* 51–59.

Lamb, M. E., & Sutton-Smith, B. (Eds.). (1982). *Sibling relationships: Their nature and significance across the lifespan.* Hillsdale, NJ: Erlbaum.

LaRossa, R. (1986). *Becoming a parent.* Beverly Hills, CA: Sage.

Larson, J. H. (1984). The effect of husband's unemployment on marital and family relations in blue-collar families. *Family Relations, 33,* 503–512.

Larzelere, R. E., & Patterson, G. R. (1990). Parental management: Mediator of the effect of socioeconomic status on early delinquency. *Criminology, 28,* 301–323.

Lasley, P. (1990). *An overview of the changing structure of Iowa agriculture.* Staff paper. Ames: Department of Sociology, Iowa State University.

Lasley, P., & Conger, R. D. (Eds.). (1986). *Farm crisis response: Extension and research activities in the north central region.* Ames: North Central Regional Center for Rural Development, Iowa State University.

Lasley, P., & Fellows, J. (1990). *Farm families adaptations to severe economic distress: Regional summary.* RRD 154. Ames: North Central Regional Center for Rural Development.

Lasley, P., & Goudy, W. (1982). *Changes in Iowa's agriculture: 1969–1978.* Cooperative Extension Service, Iowa State University, Ames.

Lasley, P., & Goudy, W. (1989). *Changes in Iowa agriculture: 1978–1987.* Cooperative Extension Service, Iowa State University, Ames.

Lasley, P., & Kettner, K. (1991). *Iowa farm and rural life poll: 1991 Summary report.* PM-1435. Ames: Cooperative Extension Service, Iowa State University.

Laub, J. H., & Sampson, R. J. (1988). Unraveling families and delinquency: A reanalysis of the Clueks' data. *Criminology, 26,* 355–380.

Lavee, Y., McCubbin, H., & Olson, D. H. (1987). The effect of stressful life events and transitions on family functioning and well-being. *Journal of Marriage and the Family, 49,* 857–843.

Lee, G. R. (1978). Marriage and morale in later life. *Journal of Marriage and the Family, 40,* 131–139.

Lempers, J. D., Clark-Lempers, D., & Simons, R. L. (1989). Economic hardship, parenting, and distress. *Child Development, 60,* 25–39.

Lever, J. (1976). Sex differences in the games children play. *Social Problems, 23,* 478–487.

Liker, J. K., & Elder, G. H., Jr. (1983). Economic hardship and marital relations in the 1930s. *American Sociological Review, 48,* 343–359.

Lorenz, F. O., Conger, R. D., Simons, R. L., Whitbeck, L. B., & Elder, G. H., Jr. (1991). Economic pressure and marital quality: An illustration of the method variance problem in the causal modeling of family processes. *Journal of Marriage and the Family, 53,* 375–388.

Lyson, T. A. (1984). Pathways into production agriculture: The structure of farm recruitment in the United States. In H. K. Shwarzweller (Ed.), *Research in rural sociology and development. Vol. 1, Focus on agriculture* (pp. 79–103). Greenwich, CT: JAI.

Maccoby, E. E., & Martin, J. A. (1983). Socialization in the context of the family: Parent-child interaction. In P. M. Mussen (Ed.), *Handbook of Child Psychology. Vol. 4,* E. M. Hetherington (Ed.), *Socialization, personality, and social development* (pp. 1–101). New York: Wiley.

Margolin, G., & Wampold, B. E. (1981). Sequential analysis of conflict and accord in distressed and nondistressed marital partners. *Journal of Consulting and Clinical Psychology, 49,* 554–567.

Markman, H. J., & Notarius, C. I. (1987). Marital and family interaction: Current status. In T. Jacob (Ed.), *Family interaction and psychopathology* (pp. 329–390). New York: Plenum.

Masten, A. S., & Garmezy, N. (1985). Risk, vulnerability, and protective factors in developmental psychopathology. *Advances in Clinical Child Psychology, 8,* 1–52.

McGillicuddy-DeLisi, A. V. (1985). The relationship between parental beliefs and children's cognitive level. In I. E. Sigel (Ed.), *Parental belief systems: The psychological consequences for children* (pp. 7–24). Hillsdale, NJ: Erlbaum.

McGowan, R. J., & Johnson, D. L. (1984). The mother-child relationship and other antecedents of childhood intelligence: A casual analysis. *Child Development, 55,* 810–820.

McHale, S. M., Bartko, W. T., & Crouter, A. C. (1991). *Children's housework in context.* University Park: Pennsylvania State University Press.

McLeod, J. D., & Kessler, R. C. (1990). Socioeconomic status differences in vulnerability to undesirable life events. *Journal of Health and Social Behavior, 31,* 162–172.

McLoyd, V. C. (1989). Socialization and development in a changing economy: The effects of paternal job and income loss on children. *American Psychologist, 44,* 293–302.

McLoyd, V. C. (1990). The impact of economic hardship on black families and children: Psychological distress, parenting, and socioemotional development. *Child Development, 61,* 311–346.

Melby, J., Conger, R. D., Book, R., Rueter, M., Lucy, L., Repinski, D., Ahrens, K., Black, D., Brown, D., Huck, S., Mutchler, L., Rogers, S., Ross, J., & Stavros, T. (1990). *The Iowa Family Interaction Rating Scales.* Unpublished manuscript, Center for Family Research in Rural Mental Health, Iowa State University, Ames.

Meyer, H. J. (1988). Marital and mother-child relationships: Developmental history, parent personality, and child difficultness. In R. A. Hinde, & J. Stevenson-Hinde (Eds.), *Relationships within families: Mutual influences* (pp. 181–192). Oxford: Clarendon; New York: Oxford University Press.

Mirowsky, J., & Ross, C. E. (1989). *Social causes of psychological distress.* Hawthorne, NY: Aldine de Gruyter.

Moen, P., Kain, E., & Elder, G. H., Jr. (1983). Economic conditions and family life: contemporary and historical perspectives. In R. R. Nelson, & Felicity Skidmore (Eds.), *American families and the economy: The high costs of living* (pp. 213–254). Washington, DC: National Academy Press.

Mooney, P. H. (1988). *My own boss? Class, rationality, and the family farm.* Boulder, CO: Westview.

Mortimer, J. T., Finch, M., Shanahan, M., & Ryu, S. (1991). Work experience, mental health, and behavioral adjustment in adolescence. *Journal of Research on Adolescence, 1.*

Mrazek, D. A., Dowdney, L., Rutter, M. L., & Quinton, D. L. (1982). Mother and preschool child interaction: A sequential approach. *Journal of the American Academy of Child Psychiatry, 21,* 453–464.

Mulaik, S. A. (1987). Toward a conception of causality applicable to experimentation and causal modeling. *Child Development, 58,* 18–32.

Murdock, S. H., & Leistritz, F. L. (1988). *The farm financial crisis: Socioeconomic dimensions and implications for producers and rural areas.* Boulder, CO: Westview.

Naples, N. A. (1992, June). *Women's experiences of economic restructuring in rural Iowa: Changing dynamics of class, race-ethnicity, and gender.* Paper presented at Symposium on Rural/Farm Women in Historical Perspective, University of California, Davis.

Nelson-LeGall, S., Gumerman, R. A., & Scott-Jones, D. (1983). Instrumental help-seeking and everyday problem-solving: A developmental perspective. In B. DePaulo, A. Nadler, & J. Fisher (Eds.), *New directions in helping. Vol. 2, Help-seeking* (pp. 265–283). New York: Academic.

Newcomb, M. D. (1990). What structural equation modeling can tell us about social support. In B. R. Sarason, K. G. Sarason, & G. R. Pierce (Eds.), *Social support: An interactional view* (pp. 26–63). New York: Wiley.

Newcomb, M. D., & Bentler, P. M. (1986). Loneliness and social support: A confirmatory factor analysis. *Personality and Social Psychology Bulletin, 12,* 520–535.

Noller, P., & Fitzpatrick, M. A. (1990). Marital communication in the eighties. *Journal of Marriage and the Family, 52,* 832–843.

Nunnally, J. C. (1978). *Psychometric theory* (2nd ed.). New York: McGraw-Hill.

Oates, R. K., & Peacock, D. (1985). Self-esteem and early background of abusive mothers. *Child Abuse and Neglect, 9,* 89–93.

Orvaschel, H. (1983). Maternal depression and child dysfunction. *Advances of clinical child psychology, 6,* 169–197.

Parke, R. D. (1981). *Fathers.* Cambridge, MA: Harvard University Press.

Patterson, G. R. (1975). *Families.* Champaign, IL: Research Press.

Patterson, G. R. (1982). *Coercive family process.* Eugene OR: Castilia.

Patterson, G. R. (1984). Siblings: Fellow travelers in coercive family processes. In R. J. Blanchard (Ed.), *Advances in the study of aggression* (pp. 173–214). New York: Academic.

Patterson, G. R. (1986a). Performance models for antisocial boys. *American Psychologist, 41,* 432–444.

Patterson, G. R. (1986b). The contribution of siblings to training for fighting: A microsocial analysis. In D. Olweus, J. Block, & M. Radke-Yarrow (Eds.), *Development of antisocial and prosocial behavior: Research, theories, and issues* (pp. 235–261). Orlando, FL: Academic.

Patterson, G. R. (1991, April). *Interaction of stress and family structure, and their relation to child adjustment: An example of across-site collaboration.* Paper presented at the biennial meeting of the Society for Research in Child Development, Seattle.

Patterson, G. R., & Bank, L. (1987). *Some amplifying mechanisms for pathological processes in families.* Paper presented at the Minnesota Symposium on Child Psychology.

Patterson, G. R., DeBaryshe, B. D., & Ramsey, E. (1989). A developmental perspective on antisocial behavior. *American Psychologist, 44,* 329–335.

Pearlin, L. I. (1983). Role strains and personal stress. In H. B. Kaplan (Ed.), *Psychosocial stress: Trends in theory and research* (pp. 3–32). New York: Academic.

Pearlin, L. I. (1989). The sociological study of stress. *Journal of Health and Social Behavior, 30,* 241–256.

Pearlin, L. I., Lieberman, M. A., Menaghan, E. G., & Mullan, J. T. (1981). The stress process. *Journal of Health and Social Behavior, 22,* 337–356.

Pearson, J., Cowan, P., & Cohn, D. (1991). *Working models of adult attachment and adult child-older parent relations.* Paper presented at the Society for Research on Child Development Meetings, Seattle, WA.

Pederson, F. (1982). Mother, father and infant as an interactive system. In J. Belsky (Ed.), *In the beginning: Readings on infancy.* New York: Columbia University Press.

Pellegrini, A. D., Brody, G. H., & Sigel, I. E. (1985). Parents' teaching strategies with their children: The effect of parental and child status variables. *Journal of Psycholinguistic Research 14, 509–521.*

Perrucci, C. C., & Targ, D. B. (1988). Effects of a plant closing on marriage and family life. In P. Voydanoff, & L. C. Majka (Eds.), *Families and economic distress: Coping strategies and social policy* (pp. 55–71). Newbury Park, CA: Sage.

Perrucci, C., Targ, D., Perrucci, R., & Targ, H. (1987). Plant closing: A comparison of effects on women and men workers. In R. Lee (Ed.), *Redundancy, layoffs, and plan closures: Their character, causes and consequences* (pp. 181–207). London: Croom Helm.

Pfeffer, Max J., & Gilbert, J. (1991). Gender and off-farm employment in two farming systems: Responses to farm crisis in the cornbelt and the Mississippi delta. *Sociological Quarterly, 32,* 593–610.

Piotrkowski, C. S., Rapoport, R. N., & Rapoport, R. (1987). Families and work. In M. B. Sussman, & S. K. Steinmetz (Eds.), *Handbook of marriage and the family* (pp. 251–283). New York: Plenum.

Prairiefire Rural Action. (1991). *Shattered Promises. A report by Prairiefire Rural Action.* Des Moines, IA: Author.

Quinton, D., & Rutter, M. (1988). *Parenting breakdown: The making and breaking of intergenerational links.* Aldershot, England; Brookfield, VT: Avebury.

Rachman, S. (1979). Life events, stress, and illness. *Science, 194,* 1013–1020.

Reis, H. T. (1990). The role of intimacy in interpersonal relations. *Journal of Social and Clinical Psychology, 9,* 15–30.

Rhodes, R. (1989). *Farm: A year in the life of an American farmer.* New York: Simon and Schuster.

Rindskopf, David. (1984). Structural equation models: Empirical identification, Heywood cases, and related problems. *Sociological Methods and Research, 13,* 109–120.

Ritter, C. (1988). Social supports, social networks, and health behaviors. In D. S. Gochman (Ed.), *Health behavior: Emerging research perspectives* (pp. 149–161). New York: Plenum.

Robertson, E. L., Elder, G. H., Jr., Skinner, M. L., & Conger, R. D. (1991). The costs and benefits of social support in families. *Journal of Marriage and the Family, 53,* 403–416.

Rohner, R. P. (1975). *They love me, they love me not: A worldwide study of the effects of parental acceptance and rejection.* New Haven, CT: Human Relations Area Files.

Rohner, R. P. (1986). *The warmth dimension: Foundations of parental acceptance-rejection theory.* Beverly Hills, CA: Sage.

Rollins, B. C., & Thomas, D. L. (1979). Parental support, power, and control techniques in the socialization of children. In W. R. Burr, R. Hill, F. I. Nye, & I. L. Reiss (Eds.), *Contemporary theories about the family. Vol. 1, Research-based theories* (pp. 317–364). New York: Free Press.

Rosenberg, M. (1965). *Society and the adolescent self-image.* Princeton, NJ: Princeton University Press.

Rosenberg, M. (1968). *The logic of survey analysis.* New York: Basic Books.

Rosenblatt, P. (1990). *Farming is in our blood: Farm families in economic crisis.* Ames: Iowa State University Press.

Rosenfeld, R. A. (1985). *Farm women: Work, farm, and family in the United States.* Chapel Hill: University of North Carolina Press.

Ross, H. G., & Milgram, J. I. (1982). Important variables in adult sibling relationships: A qualitative study. In M. E. Lamb, & B. Sutton-Smith (Eds.). *Sibling relationships: Their nature and significance across the lifespan* (pp. 225–250). Hillsdale, NJ: Lawrence Erlbaum.

Rutter, M. (1980). *Changing youth in a changing society: Patterns of adolescent development and disorder.* Cambridge, MA: Harvard University Press.

Rutter, M. (1985). Resilience in the face of adversity: Protective factors and resistance to psychiatric disorder. *British Journal of Psychiatry, 147,* 598–611.

Rutter, M. (1990). Psychosocial resilience and protective mechanisms. In J. Rolf, A. S. Masten, D. Cicchetti, K. H. Nuechterlein, & S. Weintraub (Eds.), *Risk and protective factors in the development of psychopathology* (pp. 181–214). Cambridge, NY: Cambridge University Press.

Ryan, V. (1991, February). *Farm and community trends in a decade of transition.* Paper presented at the Rural Planning and Development: Visions of the 21st Century Conference, Orlando, Florida.

Sachs, C. E. (1983). *The invisible farmers: Women in agricultural production.* Totowa, NJ: Rowan & Allenfeld.

Salamon, S. (1992). *Prairie patrimony: Family, farming, and community in the Midwest.* Chapel Hill: University of North Carolina Press.

Schvaneveldt, J. D., & Ihinger, M. (1979). Sibling relationships in the family. In W. R. Burr, R. Hill, F. I. Nye, & I. L. Reiss (Eds.), *Contemporary theories about the family. Vol. 1, Research-based theories* (pp. 453–467). New York: Free Press.

Shanas, E. (1977). *National survey of the aged: 1975.* Chicago: University of Illinois Chicago Circle.

Silbereisen, R., & Sabinewalter, S. (1988). A person-process-context approach. In M. Rutter (Ed.), *Studies of psycho-socio risks: The power of longitudinal data* (pp. 96–113). New York: Cambridge University Press.

Sillars, A. (1985). Interpersonal perception in relationships. In W. Inkes (Ed.), *Compatible and incompatible relationships* (pp. 277–305). New York: Springer-Verlag.

Simons, R. L., Beaman, J., Conger, R. D., & Wu, C. (1992). Gender differences in the intergenerational transmission of parenting beliefs. *Journal of Marriage and the Family, 54,* 823–836.

Simons, R. L., Conger, R. D., & Whitbeck, L. B. (1988). A multistage social learning model of the influences of family and peers upon adolescent substance abuse. *Journal of Drug Issues, 18,* 293–315.

Simons, R. L., Lorenz, F. O., Conger, R. D., & Wu, C. (1992). Support from spouse as mediator and moderator of the disruptive influence of economic strain on parenting. *Child Development, 63,* 1282–1301.

Simons, R. L., Whitbeck, L. B., Conger, R. D., & Melby, J. N. (1990). Husband and wife differences in determinants of parenting: A social learning/ exchange model of parental behavior. *Journal of Marriage and the Family, 52,* 375–392.

Simons, R. L., Whitbeck, L. B., Conger, R. D., & Wu, C. (1991). Inter-generational transmission of harsh parenting. *Developmental Psychology, 27,* 159–171.

Smiley, J. (1992). *A thousand acres.* New York: Alfred A. Knopf.

Sobel, M. E. (1982). Asymptotic confidence intervals for indirect effects in structural equation models. In S. Leinhardt (Ed.), *Sociological methodology, 1982* (pp. 290–313). San Francisco: Jossey-Bass.

Sobel, M. E. (1986). Some new results on indirect effects and their standard errors in covariance structure analysis. In N. B. Tuma (Ed.), *Sociological methodology, 1986* (pp. 159–186). San Francisco: Jossey-Bass.

Sobel, M. E. (1987). Direct and indirect effects in linear structural equations. *Sociological Methods and Research, 16,* 155–176.

Sobel, M. E., & Bohrnstedt, G. W. (1985). Use of null models in evaluating the fit of covariance structure models. In N. B. Tuma (Ed.), *Sociological methodology, 1985* (pp. 152–178). San Francisco: Jossey-Bass.

Sroufe, L. A., & Fleeson, J. (1988). The coherence of family relationships. In R. A. Hinde, & J. Stevenson-Hinde (Eds.), *Relationships within families.* Oxford: Clarendon; New York: Oxford University Press.

Stone, K. (1985). *Effect of the agricultural recession on communities and business firms.* Paper presented at the National Planning Association, Food and Agriculture Committee, San Francisco.

Stover, R. G., & Clark, V. L. (1991). Successful family farming: The intersection of economics and family life. In *Research in rural sociology and development. Vol. 5, Household strategies* (pp. 113–129). Greenwich, CT: JAI.

Straus, M. A., Gelles, R. J., & Steinmetz, S. K. (1980). *Behind closed doors: Violence in the American family.* New York: Anchor Books.

Suen, Hoi K., & Ary, D. (1989). *Analyzing quantitative behavioral observational data.* Hillsdale, NJ: Erlbaum.

Sussman, M. (1985). The family life of old people. In R. Binstock, & E. Shanas (Eds.), *Handbook of Aging and the Social Sciences* (pp. 415–499). New York: Van Nostrand Reinhold.

Sussman, M. B., & Steinmetz, S. K. (Eds.). (1987). *Handbook of marriage and the family.* New York: Plenum.

Teachman, J. D., Polonko, K. A., & Scanzoni, J. (1987). Demography of the family. In M. B. Sussman, & S. K. Steinmetz (Eds.), *Handbook of marriage and the family* (pp. 3–36). New York: Plenum.

Thoits, P. A. (1983). Dimensions of life events that influence psychological distress: An evaluation and synthesis of the literature. In H. B. Kaplan (Ed.),

Psychosocial stress: trends in theory and research (pp. 33–103). New York: Academic.

Thoits, P. A. (1987). Gender and marital status differences in control and distress: Common stress versus unique stress explanations. *Journal of Health and Social Behavior, 28,* 7–22.

Thomas, L. E., McCabe, E., & Berry, J. (1980). Unemployment and family stress: A reassessment. *Family Relations, 29,* 517–524.

Thomson, E., & Williams, R. (1984). A note on correlated measurement error in wife-husband data. *Journal of Marriage and the Family, 46,* 643–649.

Tietjen, A. M. (1982). The social networks of preadolescent children in Sweden. *International Journal of Behavioral Development, 5,* 111–130.

Tilly, C. (1991). Understanding income inequality. *Sociological Forum, 6,* 739–756.

Tucker, L. R., & Lewis, C. (1973). A reliability coefficient for maximum likelihood factor analysis. *Psychometrika, 38,* 1–10.

U.S. Bureau of the Census. (1989). *Money income and poverty status in the United States: 1988.* Current Population Reports. Consumer Income (Series P-60, No. 166). Washington, DC: U.S. Department of Commerce.

U.S. Bureau of the Census. (1991). *Statistical abstract of the United States.* Washington, DC: U.S. Department of Commerce.

Vaux, A. (1988). *Social Support: Theory, research, and intervention.* New York: Praeger.

Voydanoff, P. (1990). Economic distress and family relations: A review of the eighties. *Journal of Marriage and the Family, 52,* 1099–1115.

Voydanoff, P., & Donnelly, B. W. (1988). Economic distress, family coping, and quality of family life. In P. Voydanoff, & L. C. Majka (Eds.), *Families and economic distress: Coping strategies and social policy* (pp. 97–117). Newbury Park, CA: Sage.

Waldrop, M., & Halverson, C. (1975). Intensive and extensive peer behavior: Longitudinal and cross-sectional analysis. *Child Development, 46,* 19–26.

Warren, R. D., White, J. K., & Fuller, A. (1974). An errors in variables analysis of managerial role performance. *Journal of the American Statistical Association, 69,* 886–893.

Watson, D., & Clark, L. A. (1984). Negative affectivity: The disposition to experience aversive emotional states. *Psychological Bulletin, 96,* 465–490.

Weissman, M., Paykel, E., & Klerman, G. (1972). The depressed woman as a mother. *Social Psychiatry, 7,* 98–108

Werner, E. E., & Smith, R. S. (1982). *Vulnerable but not invincible: A longitudinal study of resilient children and youth.* New York: McGraw-Hill.

Werner, E. E., & Smith, R. S. (1992). *Overcoming the odds: High risk children from birth to adulthood.* Ithaca, NY: Cornell University Press.

Wethington, E., & Kessler, R. (1986). Perceived support, received support, and adjustment to stressful life events. *Journal of Health and Social Behavior, 27,* 78–89.

Wheaton, B. (1985). Models for the stress-buffering functions of coping resources. *Journal of Health and Social Behavior, 26,* 352–364.

Whitbeck, L. B., Hoyt, D. R., Simons, R. L., Conger, R. D., Elder, G. H., Jr., Lorenz, F. O., & Huck, S. M. (1992). Intergenerational continuity of paren-

tal rejection and depressed affect. *Journal of Personality and Social Psychology,*
63, 1036–1045.

Whitbeck, L. B., Simons, R. L., Conger, R. D., Lorenz, F. O., Huck, S., & Elder,
G. H. Jr. (1991a). Family economic hardship, parental support, and adolescent self-esteem. *Social Psychology Quarterly, 54,* 353–363.

Whitbeck, L. B., Simons, R. L., & Conger, R. D. (1991b). The effects of early
family relationships on contemporary relationships and assistance patterns
between adult children and their parents. *Journal of Gerontology, 46,* S330–
337.

Wills, T. A. (1990). Social support and the family. In E. A. Blechman (Ed.),
Emotions and the family: For better or for worse (pp. 75–98). Hillsdale, NJ:
Erlbaum.

Wilson, W. J. (1987). *The truly disadvantaged.* Chicago: University of Chicago
Press.

Wolchik, S. A., Sandler, I., & Braver, S. L. (1984, August). *The social support
networks of children of divorce.* Paper presented at the American Psychological
Association meeting, Toronto.

Wolchik, S. A., Sandler, I., & Braver, S. L. (1987). Social support: Its assessment
and relation to children's adjustment. In N. Eisenberg (Ed.), *Contemporary
topics in developmental psychology* (pp. 319–349). New York: Wiley.

Youniss, J., & Smollar, J. (1985). *Adolescent relations with mothers, fathers, and friends.*
Chicago: University of Chicago Press.

Zelkowitz, P. (1981, August). *Children's support networks: Their role in families under
stress.* Paper presented at the biennial meeting of the Society for Research in
Child Development, Boston.

Zeller, Richard A., & Carmines, E. G. (1980). *Measurement in the social sciences.*
Cambridge: Cambridge University Press.

Zukow, P. G. (Ed.). (1989). *Sibling interaction across cultures: theoretical and methodological issues.* New York: Springer-Verlag.

Author Index

Achenbach, T., 38
Adler, T., 38, 40
Ageton, S., 227
Alwin, D., 31
Anderson, J., 46, 180
Aneshensel, C. S., 226
Angell, R. C., 7, 260
Ardelt, M., 9, 16, 184
Armstrong, P. S., 184
Arsenio, W. R., 27
Ary, D., 29, 30
Aschenbrenner, B., 209, 220
Atkinson, T., 189

Bakeman, R., 27
Bakke, E. Wright, 168, 188
Bank, L., 38, 44–45, 150, 193, 200, 265
Bank, S. P., 11, 23, 235, 237, 240
Barlett, P. F., 86, 99, 100, 105, 114, 119
Baron, R., 31, 32
Barrett, C., 6
Bartko, W. T., 134
Baucon, D. H., 23
Beach, S. R. H., 267
Beaman, J., 210, 221
Beardslee, W., 151
Bedford, V. H., 236
Belle, D., 234
Belsky, J., 208, 210, 220, 221
Belyea, M. J., 184
Bemporad, J., 151
Bender, L., 57, 59–60, 72–73
Bentler, P. M., 36, 46, 49, 52
Berado, F. M., 236
Berkowitz, L., 13, 189, 192, 208, 219
Berk, R. A., 46
Berry, J., 208
Biemer, P. P., 33
Billings, A., 151
Blalock, H. M., Jr., 33

Block, J., 226
Blundall, J., 77–78
Bohrnstedt, G. W., 49, 52
Bollen, K. A., 34, 36, 44, 52, 100, 181, 198, 219, 265
Bonnett, D. G., 46, 49, 52
Bowerman, C., 236
Bowlby, J., 150
Bradbury, T. N., 171
Braver, S. L., 226, 234
Brody, G. H., 26, 236, 237
Brown, B., 75
Bryant, B. K., 234, 236, 237
Buhrmester, D., 38, 40
Bultena, G., 64, 77, 99
Burgess, R. L., 6

Cairns, R. B., 27
Campbell, A., 221
Campbell, D. T., 40
Campbell, R., 72–73
Capaldi, D. M., 37
Caplan, G., 169
Carmines, E. G., 33, 39
Caspi, A., 7, 149, 164, 189, 207, 224, 261, 262, 264
Cassel, J., 169, 184
Cassidy, P. B., 46, 171
Catalano, R., 188, 189
Cattell, R. B., 23, 40
Cavan, R. S., 7
Christensen, A., 235, 237
Cicchetti, D., 210, 243
Circelli, V. G., 236
Clarke-Stewart, K. A., 221
Clark, L. A., 171
Clark-Lempers, D., 207
Clark, V. L., 108
Clingempell, G., 27
Cobb, S., 169, 170
Cochrane, W. W., 59, 63

293

Subject Index

Adaptations
  of marital relations to economic
    hardship, 187–188
  off-farm employment, 107–108,
    110, 112–114
  quitting the farm, 118–124
  social trends and, 106–107
  variations of, 105, 258
Adjusted goodness-of-fit index
    (AGFI), 46
Adolescents (*See also* Labor of adoles-
    cents; Resilient adolescents)
  economic hardship and, 13–14,
    223–224
  economic pressure and, 18
  externalizing behavior of, 240
  Family Stress Model and, 13–14
  farm crisis and, 125–126
  internalizing behavior of, 241
  parental hostility and, 243, 245–
    247, 251
  self-confidence of, 151
  "semi-autonomous adolescence"
    and, 135
  social competence of, 151
Adult support, 228
AGFI (adjusted goodness-of-fit in-
    dex), 46
Agriculture (*See also* Farm crisis)
  "culture" of, 57
  in future, 72–73
  historical patterns of, 58–59, 61–
    62
  in Iowa, 57–58
  losses in, 105
  structure of, 74
  survival in, 105
Antisocial behavior, 227

Baseline model, 49, 52–53

CFA (confirmatory factor analysis),
    40–41, 157, 177–178

Child abuse, 77
Child-rearing (*See* Adolescents;
    Parent-child relationship)
Chi-squared statistics, 51–52, 181
Confirmatory factor analysis (CFA),
    40–41, 157, 177–178
Continuity model, 151–152, 158–159
Coping scale, 47–48
Correlational analyses, 241, 243

Data collection procedures, 25–30
Debt-to-asset ratio, 99–100, 173, 198
Delinquency checklist, 227
Depression
  gender differences and, 172
  grandparent generation and, 150
  hostility and, 11
  measurement of, 175
  as mediator between stressful
    events and familial conflict, 12
  observer rating of, 175
  parent-child relationship and, 151
  quitting the farm and, 120
  self-reported, 175
  spouse report of, 175
Design of study
  advances in measurement and, 24–
    26
  challenges of, 22
  Iowa family interaction rating sys-
    tem and, 27–30
  observing family interaction and,
    26–27
  realism in measurement and, 23–
    24
Developmental processes, 14–15
Dyadic Adjustment Scale, 189
Dynamic in control cycles, 8–9

Economic crisis, 5
Economic cycles, 3
Economic decline, 4–6, 144

299